P9-BJV-519

A Look At Wyoming Government

by

Marguerite A. Herman

for

League of Women Voters of Wyoming

LWV Publications
P.O. Box 3887
Gillette, WY 82717

First Edition 1958
Second Edition 1970 (Revised)
Third Edition 1975 (Revised)
Fourth Edition 1979 (Revised)
Fifth Edition 1990 (Centennial)
Sixth Edition 1998 (Revised)
Seventh Edition 2006 (Revised)

ISBN 0-9776526-0-2

Copyright © League of Women Voters
of Wyoming 2006

Vision Graphics
Loveland, Colorado, Printer

Contents

Appendices, continued

Introduction

A *Look at Wyoming Government* gives students of Wyoming state government an introduction to its institutions, its Constitution, its laws, and the diverse forces that shape those elements: history, geography, economics, politics, and personalities.

The League of Women Voters of Wyoming first published this book in 1958 and has tried to keep up with changes in government with five editions since then.

This seventh edition includes a number of updates, including government reorganization in the 1990s, greater citizen access to the Legislature through technology, judicial reorganization, the new revenue picture for Wyoming, and political history from territorial days to the current administration of Gov. Dave Freudenthal. A major addition is a separate chapter devoted to government on the Wind River Indian Reservation.

This edition includes extensive information in appendices about the politics, people, and economy of Wyoming. It also includes two important historical documents: the constitution approved by Wyoming voters in November 1889 and the Act of Admission approved by Congress and signed by President Benjamin Harrison on July 10, 1890, which made Wyoming the 44th state in the Union.

We hope the result is a comprehensive "look" at Wyoming government that will be useful to students of government, in the halls of government and in the classroom. The book is written to be useful for those who will read whole chapters and those who are looking for just a narrow slice of information. The index is detailed to aid in locating information, and the text provides background and context in a way that allows the reader to extract information by the chapter or by the paragraph.

The book can be read in seven sections:

• Chapters 1-3 set the stage with the history of how Wyoming was settled, the organization of an official Wyoming Territory and its admission to the union as the 44th state.

• Chapters 4-7 describe the executive, legislative and judicial branches of state government , as well as local government (cities, towns and counties).

• Chapters 8-10 are devoted to "good government" issues of citizen participation and means of assuring the integrity of government: Good Government, Initiative & Referendum, Voting & Running for Office.

• Chapter 11 tells of the origins and structure of tribal government on the Wind River Indian Reservation.

• Chapters 12-14 deal with political issues: the History of Wyoming Politics, Women's Suffrage and Political Parties

• Chapters 15 and 16 deal with revenue and the economy, which can both pay for government and drive its politics.

• A final chapter, 17, traces the development of Wyoming's school finance reform efforts in the courts, in the Legislature and in the classroom.

Wyoming and U.S. Governments

The United states is organized on the federal system, which divides power between the federal government and the states. In the American federal system, the U.S. Constitution grants certain autonomous powers to the central government, while states have limited powers.

The U.S. Constitution states that all powers not specifically given to the federal government are retained by the individual states "or by the people." (See Ninth Amendment, United States Constitution). The powers given by the states to the federal government, for instance building and maintaining a federal highway system, are delegated powers. States keep some powers known as reserved powers, for instance setting their own taxes, calling their own elections and creating and maintaining public schools. Implied powers are those granted to the federal government which are, by implication, denied to the states. For example, states cannot mint money nor tax the U.S. Postal Service, because, as Supreme Court Chief Justice John Marshall said in 1819, "The power to tax involves the power to destroy." Therefore, if the federal government has the power to operate a postal system, the states cannot burden or negate that power by taxing it out of existence. Likewise, the U.S. government cannot tax state agencies.

The voters of each state elect citizens to represent them in Congress. Once elected, these members of the U.S. House and Senate make laws that govern all the states in the Union.

Many federal government powers have a direct impact on Wyoming and its economy. The federal government regulates commerce and industry within U.S. borders and regulates commerce with other nations. The U.S. government can impose embargoes on commodities, such as corn or wheat, which are sold to other nations. For example the United States might put an embargo on the sale of grain to another nation for violating human rights. The embargo creates an economic hardship on commodity producers, and thus the U.S. government might buy the commodity in order to save its citizens from economic hardship. Decisions such as these impact Wyoming's agricultural industry, demonstrating that not only the actions of the federal government, but the actions of all nations may affect Wyoming's economy.

Federal government powers are the supreme law of the land, which states cannot violate or ignore. However, states may direct laws in subdivisions of local governments.

In 1889, the people of Wyoming adopted a constitution that mandates a separation of powers among the three branches of state government. At the beginning of Article 2, the Wyoming Constitution lays down the basic framework of state government as being divided into three distinct departments: the legislative, executive and judicial (Wyoming Constitution, Art. 2, Sec.1, 1890). The separateness of these departments is ensured in that same section with the provision, "no person or collection of persons charged with the exercise of powers properly belonging to one of these departments shall exercise any powers properly belonging to either of the others, except as in this constitution expressly directed or permitted."

The Constitution describes powers of the three branches, but conflicts continue to arise over the exact demarcation of lines separating powers. Usually, complaints arise from disputes between the executive and legislative branches over budget-setting, appointment powers, vetoes and other issues. However, legislators have bristled in recent years over decisions by the Wyoming Supreme Court. Many lawmakers publicly questioned the presumption of the Wyoming Supreme Court in its 1995 opinion in *Campbell County School District vs. State*, 907 P.2d 1238 (Wyo. 1995). In that opinion, the court ordered the Legislature to rewrite school finance laws to comply with the Wyoming Constitution.

Disputes also can arise over the authority of the governor's office over the other top four elected officials. In 2004-2005, the state treasurer, auditor and superintendent of public instruction sought greater authority to make appointments, contract for services, set budgets and hire in-house attorneys for legal advice. During the 2006 session, the Wyoming Legislature invoked "separation of powers" in rallying votes to override a veto concerning the confidentiality of the bill drafting process.

Learning about government is central to the purpose of American education and essential to the well-being of American democracy. President Abraham Lincoln talked about "government of the people, by the people and for the people." In our country, people have the right to control their government, but that right is meaningless unless they have the knowledge to exercise that control, that is, to understand how their government operates and how they may participate.

"Government" can be understood several ways:
- It is the exercise of control over a political unit.
- It is the system of control or political administration -- the laws, rules, regulations and procedures.
- It is all the agencies and people who administer the affairs of a state or other unit.
- It is the policy used to govern a political unit.

A Look at Wyoming Government describes the framework of our state's governmental structure prescribed in the Wyoming Constitution and Wyoming Statutes, as well as the ways our state raises money to finance government activities. But the study of government is not complete without a look at the history and mechanics of politics, which is the human element of government.

Politics is the process by which people with differing opinions and interests come together to reach collective decisions. Politics is where these interests exercise influence on institutions and lawmaking, and the result is decisions by the government that affect all of us. Politics is one way Wyoming residents can affect their government. Of course, the direct way to affect government is to be elected to office or be named to an important decision-making role in state or local government. For most of us, however, the political process of making our voice heard by government officials – as individuals or as an interest group – is a powerful way to participate in our government.

This seventh edition of *A Look at Wyoming Government* significantly expands previous versions to include material on Wind River Indian Reservation tribal government, on state government revenue, and on the personalities and politics that have driven significant government decisions in the past. These all provide an important context for understanding how government works and specifically how Wyoming government works.

We hope this revised and expanded seventh edition also sparks an interest to learn more about the history of Wyoming. *A Look at Wyoming Government* is available on compact disc, with the additional historical documents of memorials written to Congress seeking statehood and proclamations calling for elections and then convening the newly-elected Legislature November 12, 1890.

In continuing to publish *A Look at Wyoming Government*, the League of Women Voters of Wyoming hopes the citizens of our state – young and old – gain an understanding of Wyoming government and are able to exercise their rights to get involved in the political process.

The League recognizes the generosity of the Wyoming State Archives and the State Office of Historic Preservation in providing nearly 100 images from its photograph collection for this book, without charge. Their staff was immensely helpful in locating and copying the images. The League also thanks Dave McGary for his generosity in allowing the League to use images of his Chief Washakie sculpture.

Steven Thulin, associate professor of history at Northwest College, provided valuable insights into Wyoming government and contributed his keen copyediting skills to this book. John Washakie, descendant of Eastern Shoshone Chief Washakie, assured the accurate rendering of his tribe's history in Wyoming and treaties that shaped the Wind River Indian Reservation.

The author also wants to express gratitude to the board of directors of the League of Women Voters of Wyoming for their support in completion of this revision.

A Look at Wyoming Government

Chapter 1

Settling Wyoming

"You can fight armies or disease or trespass, but the settler never. He advances slowly, surely, silently, like a great motor truck, pushing everything before him. He is cringing in distress, autocratic in prosperity and yet he is a builder, a great Western asset, peopling the childless land, planting schools by the side of cattle corrals, preaching in a practical way the salvation that is coming to the arid West. The old timers thought their work was a flash in the pan, but it remained a luminous light over valleys and divide."

John Clay, Wyoming historian, quoted in *Footprints on the Frontier*, Virginia Trenholm, 1945, p.123.

Wyoming's government and politics grow out of its land and its people. This chapter begins with the original inhabitants, settlers of the Eighteenth and Nineteenth centuries, geography and mineral wealth, and early economic influences.

The land that eventually became the State of Wyoming was first inhabited by Native American tribes of the Plains: Eastern Shoshones and Crows. Anthropologists have found traces of their living and hunting in the 1700s. Some studies near Bairoil and Jackson Lake indicate that Native Americans followed bison trails into Wyoming and also wintered in Wyoming .

Explorers, trappers. adventurers, conquering armies, and settlers came in succession to Wyoming. Here was a land of animals, including bison, beaver, elk, and deer. Fur trappers sold or traded their pelts for goods at the summer rendezvous held on the Green River from 1824 to 1840, except when in the summers of 1830 and 1838 the rendezvous was held on the Wind River at the confluence of the Popo Agie and the Little Wind (Brink 1986, p. 89). Rendezvous attracted trappers, Indian tribes, fur company merchants, and occasionally artists, missionaries, and others.

Early in Wyoming's history the game that was abundant enough to feed the Indians and trappers, and later on to supply the forts and wagon trains of the emigrants, became so scarce that finally both trappers and hunters were forced to turn to other ways of life. Many scouted for the Army or managed trading posts.

By the mid-1800s a system of forts was established throughout the West to control the "Indian Problem" and protect pioneer settlers, travelers, and gold miners on the Oregon, Bozeman, and Overland Trails, which passed through Wyoming. Gold was discovered in California in 1849. The California Trail, passing through Fort Laramie and crossing southern Wyoming, was the trail of choice during the gold rush. More than 300,000 people passed through Fort Laramie on the way west between 1825 and 1869. (Larson 1978, 44)

The Plains Indian tribes were profoundly affected by the invasion of settlers and travelers. Their way of life was destroyed when bison herds were deci-

"Chief," painted by muralist Allen Tupper True in Wyoming State Senate chamber, recognizes Native Americans in the history of early Wyoming. See front cover for "Homesteaders," a True mural in the House.

mated by hunters and when settlers interrupted traditional hunting areas, nomadic patterns, and territorial agreements among tribes. Native Americans, who once were estimated to number between 40,000 and 50,000 in eastern Wyoming and western Nebraska, were forced farther and farther west. The Wind River Indian Reservation was established in central Wyoming in 1868 for the Eastern Shoshones. Ten years later the Northern Arapaho tribe was ushered onto the same reservation by the United States government as a temporary home. Today both tribes remain on the combined reservation in Fremont County. They have separate tribal identities, governments, and schools, but a joint council handles reservation issues. (See Chapter 11 Tribal Government.)

Parts of Wyoming were at various times claimed by France, Great Britain, Mexico, Spain, and Texas. A part of Wyoming was included in the Louisiana Purchase. Later, Wyoming was part of the territories of Louisiana, Missouri, Nebraska, Utah, Idaho, Dakota, Oregon, and Washington.

The time of mountain men and trapping was relatively short, the 20 or so years between the early 1820s and early 1840s. As they left the state, settlers of European ancestry came through, usually headed to the greener pastures of Oregon, California, and Utah.

"The travelers spent less than 30 days in Wyoming and left little besides ruts, names and dates on trailside cliffs, a few place names and some graves," Wyoming historian T.A. Larson wrote in his *History of Wyoming* (1977, p. 10-11)

Railroads

All that changed with the construction of the transcontinental railroad. Congress passed the Pacific Railway Act of 1862, which offered the Union Pacific and Central Pacific railroad companies land along the proposed line, loans, and the promise of future government contracts to build the railroad. Union Pacific built from Council Bluffs, Iowa, in the east. Central Pacific built from Sacramento, California, in the west. The line joined at Promontory Summit, Utah, on May 10, 1869.

The new line had a tremendous impact on the transportation of goods and people, linking East and West in new ways. The impact on the settlement of Wyoming was just as dramatic. The Union Pacific built its section of the line across southern Wyoming, a route that provided a natural break in the Rocky Mountains. Construction of the line opened up Wyoming to development, as it did the rest of the region. Just as important, it also brought thousands of workers who stayed. At the same time, U.S. Army troops were sent to the area – what was then part of the Dakota Territory – to protect non-Indian construction crews and settlers. Some of the communities that sprang up along the UP line lasted just long enough for the construction to come through. Others became permanent cities and towns: Cheyenne, Laramie, Green River.

An Army doctor who had visited Cheyenne a year earlier wrote in October 1867, "When I left here last July all the land was bare, and the only habitations were tents. Cheyenne has now a population of fifteen hundred, two papers, stores, warehouses, restaurants, gambling halls, etc." (Gould 1968, p. 1)

In the summer of 1867, Union Pacific surveyors laid out the town site of Cheyenne. It was just a tent town. By August, Cheyenne was organized and elected a mayor. On September 19, Colorado newspaper man N.A. Baker started publication of *The Leader*. Two months later, the first school was established. On November 13, the railroad was completed to Cheyenne. Within six months of construction of the first house, 3,000 dwellings and business houses populated the new frontier town. (Trenholm 1945, 294)

Wyoming Government

Right away, early residents started thinking about creation of their own territory. UP created Laramie County, which covered everything in Wyoming east of the Continental Divide. Residents in Yankton, the seat of Dakota Territory, were just as eager to see the western part of the territory cut loose. (Larson 1978, p. 65) Communication between Yankton and Cheyenne, 800 miles apart, was difficult, and the territory was so large, division was inevitable. Also, folks in Yankton feared that the growing population in the western region might control the territory.

The Dakota Territorial Legislature sent a memorial (a statement of facts in petition form) to the United States Congress asking that a new

"Wyoming" Territory be recognized. UP physician Hiram Latham went to Washington, D.C, on behalf of Cheyenne's business and professional community and assured Congress there were 35,000 residents in the region, with another 25,000 expected to arrive in the next year. A census taken in July 1869 counted 8,000 people. (Miller 1981, pp. 6-7)

U.S. President Andrew Johnson signed the bill that created the Wyoming Territory on July 25, 1868.

The name for the new territory stirred quite a debate in Congress. Members considered names of Native American tribes and rivers and the recently assassinated president ("Lincoln"). They chose "Wyoming," inspired by a popular poem, "Gertrude of Wyoming," which was written in 1809 to describe the destruction of a colonial settlement in Pennsylvania in 1778, during the Revolutionary War. The name comes from Delaware Indian words *maugh-wau-wa-ma,* meaning "large plains" or "upon the great plain."

Cattle, Sheep and Open Range

At the same time, cattlemen realized the ability of Wyoming's open prairies to support large herds. Cattle driven from Texas could be fattened on Wyoming grass and shipped to market without substantial weight loss. The cattle "kings" lasted a few short years, from 1870 to 1887. Ranchers were displaced by homesteaders who discovered free land, made available under the various federal Homestead Acts.

The earliest date of cattle industry on the plains is December 1864, when a government trader with a wagon train of supplies drawn by oxen on the way to Utah was caught by a snow storm on the Laramie plains. He was forced into winter quarters and turned the cattle loose. He was amazed when spring came, and he found his herd had thrived on the nutritious high plains grass that had been blown clear of snow. In fact, they were in better condition than when he turned them out. (Trenholm 1945, p. 303)

Word spread about the nutritive value of Wyoming's gama grass, buffalo grass, and bluestem in the southeastern part of the state. The first permanent range herd to come into Wyoming arrived four years later, in October 1868. Space and lush grasses made the Wyoming plains a paradise for cattlemen, whether they stayed or were passing through on the trails to Montana or Kansas. Cattle barons came from the East and from Europe. The cattle industry boomed and populated Wyoming's plains until, as Natrona County historian Alfred J. Mokler described it, "every square mile of pasturage was utilized." (Trenholm 1945, p. 130) At the time, more than 80 percent of the state was public domain, providing cattle barons free forage for their herds.

Wyoming Territorial Gov. William Hale (1882-1885) reported to the federal secretary of the Interior that cattle raising was the chief industry for Wyoming. (Larson 1977, p. 167)   Scots and Englishmen came as individuals and as investors in heavily capitalized corporations. British investors put an estimated $45 million into the American cattle business in the 1880s. In 1885, the Scottish owned Swan Land and Cattle Company listed 123,460 head of cattle in Wyoming. The *Laramie Sentinel* warned of concentrating the cattle industry in the hands of a few large corporations. The newspaper editorialized in October 1883, "It is men – not steers—which make a state." (Larson 1977, pp. 167-168)

Prices for beef spiked in 1882 and then plummeted. The hot, dry summer of 1886 left feed and water very short. Then came the awful winter of 1886-87, which decimated some of the herds and led many to believe they had seen the end of the cattle industry in Wyoming. Poorly nourished cattle flooded the market, and prices dropped further.

English investors in the range cattle industry lost an estimated $10 million and Scots between $7 million and $8 million.

Gov. Francis E. Warren reported to the secretary of the Interior in 1889 the cattle business was less than half the territory's wealth, compared to more than three-fourths only five years earlier. (Larson 1977, p.193)

Natrona County historian Alfred J. Mokler quoted an observer as saying, "The fact that we now have to face is that the range of the past is gone; that of the present is of little worth and cannot be relied upon in the future. Range husbandry is ruined destroyed; it may have been caused by the insatiable greed of its followers." (Trenholm 1977, p. 131)

Of course, cattle ranching survived and thrived, with more reasonable demands put on the land for grazing and the feeding of cattle during the winter, and the cattle industry continued to have influence among Wyoming lawmakers. In 1873, the Wyoming Territorial Assem-

Sheep wagon and herd at the Pitchfork Ranch in northern Wyoming, undated. (Courtesy of Wyoming State Archives)

bly passed a law forbidding anyone to adopt the brand of another, and county clerks could not record the same brand to more than one person. The 1875 Legislature bowed to cattle interests and made railroad companies liable to cattle owners for killing or injuring stock, despite the power enjoyed by the Union Pacific and other railroads in the 1870s. The law had effect: cattle killed by trains numbered 976 in the 12 months ending March 31, 1883. Cattle mortality dropped to just 205 in the 12 months ending March 31, 1887. The Wyoming Stockgrowers Association formed in 1879, consolidating groups in Wyoming and in areas of Nebraska, Montana, and Dakota Territory.

Meanwhile, the sheep industry also prospered.

The first to bring sheep to the plains was Bostonian Robert H. Homer to Flagranch, on the Laramie Plains eight miles south of Laramie, in 1871. After the disastrous winter of 1886-87, many cattle companies started to raise sheep or ran sheep and cattle. (Larson 1977, p. 305)

Sheep, which were better able to thrive in difficult grazing conditions, crowded the public lands in Wyoming in 1900. Conflicts developed over limited range previously used only by cattlemen, whose claim was based partly on the fact they were in Wyoming first. The newcomers said public grazing lands were open to all. Sheepherders and sheep were increasingly attacked by cattle interests. Flock masters, who had become leading citizens of the state, formed the Woolgrowers Association in 1905.

A turning point in the range war came in April 1909. About 15 masked men attacked a sheep camp on Spring Creek near Ten Sleep. They killed wealthy wool growers Joe Allemand and Joe Emge and herder Joe Lazier. The Woolgrowers Association offered rewards and pressed for prosecution. One witness implicated prominent cattlemen and committed suicide. Five men pleaded guilty and were sent to the penitentiary for 3-5 years. (Larson 1977, p. 371)

Ranchers and farmers in Wyoming opposed the idea of leasing federal land. Meanwhile, conservation of timber, minerals, and big game on public lands became permanent policy in Washington, D.C., and the era of free access to public land was coming to an end. Stockgrowers used the Preemption Act of 1841, Homestead Act of 1862, Timber Culture Act of 1973, and Desert Land Act of 1877, and they bought land from the Union Pacific to put together large enough areas to support their herds.

In 1931, U.S. President Herbert Hoover proposed giving all vacant and non-appropriated lands to the states, which would have put an end to public lands and the idea of surface leasing. Wyoming

Wyoming cattle drive, undated. (Courtesy Wyoming State Archives)

ranchers rejected the prospects of having to buy grazing land and then pay taxes on it. The proposal died, and livestock grazing on public land continued unregulated until Congress passed the Taylor Grazing Act in 1934. The act requires a permit for access to some districts (Section 3 of the act), while access to other areas is leased (Section 15). The Bureau of Land Management, in the federal Department of the Interior, administers districts where operators hold permits.

The first non-experimental grazing district in the nation was established in Wyoming on March 20, 1935. The permit fee was 5 cents a month to graze either a cow and calf, one horse, one burro, or five sheep. (Jordan and DeBoer, p. 207)

The State of Nevada immediately sued, challenging the federal government's authority to require payment for use of public range land. Nevada lost.

Court rulings in the 1960s established the idea that grazing permits are a privilege that can be revoked or modified by the federal government. With the 1975 Federal Land Policy and Management Act, the federal government established the policy of retaining public land and managing it with the idea of "multiple use and sustained yield."

Land policy disputes between Wyoming and the federal government continue to the present.

Chapter 2

Territorial Wyoming

The history of Wyoming government began with the Ordinance of 1787, which was enacted by Congress under the Articles of Confederation, even before the writing of the United States Constitution. Congress passed the ordinance setting out how temporary, territorial governments might be set up in the area northwest of the Ohio River.

In 1867, Gov. A. J. Faulk of Dakota Territory recommended to the Dakota Legislative Assembly the southwestern district be "clothed with all the blessings and protection of a separate organization." An earlier attempt in Congress in 1865 to create a territory out of the southwestern district proposed it be named the "Territory of Lincoln."

Bills again were introduced in the U.S. House and Senate in 1868. A law creating the Territory of Wyoming passed as the Organic Act of Wyoming and was signed by the president on July 25, 1868. The new territory was defined as from 27 degrees to 34 degrees West longitude and from 41 degrees to 45 degrees North latitude. It included parts of the Dakota, Utah, and Idaho territories. The Organic Act of Wyoming established the three branches of territorial government – executive, judicial, and legislative. The Executive Department was composed of a governor and secretary of the Territory, each for a term of four years. (Those two offices became elected under the Wyoming Constitution.)

Congress was busy with the impeachment of President Andrew Johnson, which delayed confirmation of his executive and judicial appointments for the new territory. President Ulysses Grant was inaugurated

John Allen Campbell, first governor of the Wyoming Territory. (Courtesy Wyoming State Archives)

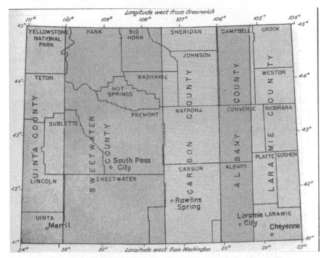

Map of Wyoming Territory in 1869. Five counties: Uinta, Sweetwater, Carbon, Albany and Laramie.

March 4, 1869. In less than a month, on April 7, 1869, he appointed the Wyoming Territory's first governor, secretary, chief justice, and two associate justices. They were confirmed by the U.S. Senate, and the last of the officers took the oath of office on May 19, 1869, which became the date when the Territory was officially inaugurated.

At that time, Wyoming had four counties created by the Dakota territorial government: Laramie, Albany, Carbon, and Carter counties. The new Territorial Assembly of Wyoming created a fifth county, Uinta, out of an unorganized strip of land in the west.

The first territorial governor was John Allen Campbell. He would have been considered a Westerner when he was born in Salem, Columbiana County, Ohio, on October 8, 1835. He was a Republican and former publicity officer with the Union Army. He took the oath of office on April 15, 1869, and served six years.

Other officials of the new territory were:
- Supreme Court: Chief Justice John H. Howe, born in Monroe County, New York; and Associate Justices John W. Kingman, born in Barrington, New Hampshire, and William T. Jones, born in Corydon, Harrison County, Indiana.
- Treasurer: John W. Donnellan, born in County Clare, Ireland.
- Territorial Auditor and Superintendent of Public Instruction: Benjamin Gallagher, born in Pleasant Grove, Iowa.
- Secretary: Edward Merwin Lee, born in Guildford, Connecticut.

Photo collages of the 11th and final House of Representatives (above) and Council (below) of the Wyoming Territorial Assembly in 1890. Wyoming became a state in December of that year.

The Wyoming State Capitol, shown in the Council photo had just been completed. Previously, Council and House members met in various locations around Cheyenne, changing locations every session.

Photo collages have been created for each session of the Legislative Assembly and State Legislature. They are displayed in the State House and Senate chambers and adjacent rooms of the second and third floors of the State Capitol.

(Courtesy Wyoming State Archives)

Duties of the territorial secretary were to record and preserve laws passed by the Legislative Assemblies and acts by the governor. If the governor died or otherwise left office, the secretary became acting governor.

The Organic Act fixed the governor's annual salary at $2,000, plus $1,000 as Superintendent of Indian Affairs. The act also gave the new governor the duties of Commander in Chief of the Militia.

The first official acts by Governor Campbell were to divide the Territory into three judicial districts and order the U.S. marshal to take a census. Both were necessary for elections to the Legislative Assembly. It was no small feat to cover such a large area to count everyone in every settlement, mining camp, and military outpost. The count was finalized on July 30, 1869 — 8,014. Congress reimbursed the Territory $1,500 for the census.

State Capitol Building in 1888, where the 10th Legislative Assembly met for its three-month session January 10-March 9, 1888. (Courtesy Wyoming State Archives)

With the census complete, Governor Campbell issued a proclamation on August 3, 1869, dividing the Territory into districts for the two chambers of the Territorial Assembly, the Council and House of Representatives. He set the election for September 2, 1869, to select the new territorial legislators and also a nonvoting delegate to Congress.

The First Legislative Assembly convened in Cheyenne on October 12, 1869, with twelve members in the House and nine in the Council, all of them Democrats. This Legislative Assembly passed an act apportioning the Territory into council and representative districts, according to population. However, Congress repealed the act on February 21, 1871, and ordered Campbell to apportion the Territory into districts by proclamation. The Territory was apportioned by proclamation in 1873, 1875, 1877, and 1879. (Erwin, p.137)

The first territorial government did not have a permanent home, and the Legislative Assemblies moved from one location to another for its sessions every other year. The First Legislative Assembly passed about 700 pages of laws, most modeled after other territories' laws. The legislators generally followed Governor Campbell's requests in adopting laws regulating mining, protecting game, setting judicial salaries, picking Laramie as the site of the prison, and Cheyenne as the capital.

The First Legislative Assembly gave Governor Campbell veto powers but overrode his vetoes of a gambling bill and "an act to prevent intermarriage between white persons and those of Negro or Mongolian blood" (Larson 1977, pp.76-78). Other action raised legislative pay from $4 a day to $10 a day, although it was nullified by the courts.

Governor Campbell selected Cheyenne as the temporary capital, provided housing for criminals, divided the Territory into council and representative districts, and ordered elections to the new Legislative Assembly to take place on September 2, 1869. The First Legislative Assembly convened on October 12, 1869, and created the other offices of the Executive Department, which Campbell filled by appointment. They were confirmed by the Council (which became the Senate when Wyoming became a state). They were: Auditor Benjamin Gallagher, born in 1840 in Pleasant Grove, Iowa; and Treasurer John W. Donnellan, born 1841 in County Clare, Ireland. The Assembly also created the offices of Superintendent of Public Instruction, which was filled by the state auditor.

In 1886, the Ninth Territorial Legislative Assembly authorized construction of the State Capitol – with the permission of Congress — in Cheyenne at a cost not to exceed $150,000. A five-member commission named by Gov. Francis E. Warren accepted plans by the firm David W. Gibbs and Company, Architects, and awarded the construction contract to Adam Feick & Brothers who had submitted the lowest bid, $131,275.13, on August 25, 1886.

Ground was broken September 9, 1886. Territorial lawmakers met in the new State Capitol for its Tenth Legislative Assembly, convening on January 10, 1888, and adjourning on March 9, 1888, although the building was still unfinished.

Campbell served until 1875, and his successors were appointed by United States presidents. Wyoming Territory had 10 governors in the 21 years before statehood.

The ninth governor was Thomas Moonlight, born of farmer parentage November 10, 1833, in Forfarshire, Scotland. He came to America at age 13 and joined the Army at age 19. He was placed in command of the Eleventh Kansas Cavalry at Fort Laramie in 1865. He was appointed governor of Wyoming Territory by President Grover Cleveland on January 5, 1887, and served two years. President Cleveland named him Minister to Bolivia in 1893.

Francis E. Warren was the seventh governor and the tenth governor. He served only six weeks of the second term before Wyoming became a state. As prescribed by the U.S. Constitution (before passage of the Seventeenth Amendment in 1913), the new Wyoming Legislature elected two U.S. senators, choosing Warren for one of the seats. Amos Barber, Secretary of State, became acting governor until 1893, to complete that term.

Official Seal of the Territory

Gov. John Campbell issued a proclamation May 19, 1869, ordering the adoption of a seal that would officially be adopted by the First Legislative Assembly later that year.

The seal is described in the Legislative Act:

"A Norman shield, on the upper half of which is emblazoned a mountain scene, with a railroad train, the sun appearing above the horizon, the figures '1868' below the middle point of the top of the shield. on the first quarter below, on a white ground, a plow, a pick, a shovel and a shepherd's crook; on the next quarter, namely: the lower point of the shield, on a red ground, an arm up-holding a drawn sword; the sheild to be surrounded by the inscription, 'Cedant Arma Toga,' and the entire design surrounded by the words, 'Territory of Wyoming, great seal.' "

Official Seal of the Wyoming Territory, approved by the First Territorial Legislative Assembly December 9, 1869.

"Cedant Arma Toga" is Latin for, "Let arms yield to the gown" or "Let military authority give way to civil power."

The Legislative Assembly changed the seal in 1882 to correct the spelling of "Togae" and the year to 1869.

(Courtesy Wyoming State Archives)

Chapter 3

Statehood

The admission of western territories to the Union was largely a matter of politics, and Wyoming was no exception.

In the early part of the 1880s, the Democrats were in control of the United States House of Representatives, while the Republicans controlled the United States Senate. Because the application for admission had to be approved by both houses, admission to the Union could be a matter of long discussion and compromise before a state was admitted. Each political party wanted admission for the territories in which it had the strongest representation.

Members of the Wyoming Constitutional Convention pose on the front steps of the recently completed Capitol Building in September 1889. Wyoming took the initiative to write a constitution before Congress approved its Act of Admission. (Photo courtesy of Wyoming State Archives)

In the election of 1888, Republicans gained control of both houses of Congress, and Republican Benjamin Harrison was elected President. Most of the territories that were awaiting admission to statehood were predominantly Republican, so it was likely they would be admitted in 1889, by the incoming Republicans. If Democrats wanted credit for admission of any Western state, however, they had to act quickly, while they still controlled the U.S. House during the "lame duck" session of the Fiftieth Congress. (A "lame duck" is a person who has lost an elected position, is term-limited, or who otherwise has a successor already elected but who continues to serve out the remainder of the current term of office.)

It was twelve years since a Western state (Colorado) had been admitted. In December 1888 the Democrats were prepared to offer compromises. They ceased to push statehood for New Mexico and allowed the Dakota Territory to be split into north and south. In 1889, an omnibus bill was passed allowing Washington, Montana, North Dakota, and South Dakota to become states. (Albright 1934, pp. 296-306)

At this time Wyoming was considered a conservative Republican territory. Joseph M. Carey, Territorial Delegate to the U.S. Congress from Wyoming, presented a petition to Congress for an enabling act that would allow the Wyoming Territory to begin making preparations for statehood. Nothing happened. Then, territorial Gov. Francis E. Warren took action. Other territories had waited for Congress to approve an act of admission before writing their constitutions. However, Governor Warren went ahead and called a Constitutional Convention in September 1889.

Fifty-five men were elected delegates to the constitutional convention. Forty-nine delegates attended and met for twenty-five days in September 1889.

The Constitution was unanimously approved by the delegates and was ratified by Wyoming voters on November 5, 1889. The vote was 6,272 for and 1,923 against, a meager turnout considering 18,008 votes had been cast in the election of election. One month later a bill was introduced in the U.S. Congress requesting statehood for Wyoming.

Wyoming took the initiative by adopting a constitution before Congress passed the Act of Admission granting statehood. The Terri-

torial Assembly and a committee of the Constitutional Convention
sent memorials to Congress seeking statehood, and they mentioned the
already-approved constitution as evidence of their readiness to join the
union. (The 1889 Constitution and 1890 Act of Admission are printed
at the end of this book.)

As the state waited for Congress to act on statehood, the last
Legislative Assembly of the territory met in 1890, with one notable
accomplishment – adoption of the so-called "Australian" secret ballot.
The Australian ballot was uncommon at the time and was considered a
radical idea.

Some members of the U.S. House objected to Wyoming's statehood. They complained that proceedings leading to the constitutional
convention were irregular, that the population was too small, that
women were granted suffrage, and that Wyoming had made literacy a
requirement to vote. (Recall that women's suffrage had been established by the Territorial Assembly in 1869.) Members of Congress
were skeptical about the population estimate of between 110,000 and
125,000 provided by Territorial Delegate Carey. In fact, the federal
census a few months later was half that amount. Historian T.A. Larson
writes that some of the protests over women's suffrage probably were a

Telegram from Congressional Delegate Joseph M.
Carey telling Territorial Gov. John Meldrum that
Wyoming had become the 44th member of the
"Indestructible union of American States." (Photo
courtesy of Wyoming State Archives)

cover for the real problem for Democrats – adding a Republican state to the union.

The Act of Admission cleared the U.S. House of Representatives on March 26, 1890, and the Senate on June 27, 1890. President Benjamin Harrison signed the statehood bill on July 10, 1890.

The unusual order of events -- Constitution before Act of Admission -- led the Wyoming Supreme Court to a controversial opinion in 2003 concerning the trust status of lands the federal government granted to Wyoming at statehood to hold in trust for support of schools. Wyoming and most other states in the West were granted two

Residents of Cheyenne re-enact original statehood celebration on the State Capitol steps during Wyoming's centennial celebration July 10, 1990. (State Historic Preservation Office photo)

sections per township, sections 16 and 36. The purpose of these grants and their trust status was stated in the states' acts of admissions and subsequently their constitutions. The Supreme Court said Wyoming's Constitution stated explicitly that the proceeds from sale of the school land (that is, the Permanent School Fund) was to be held in trust. However, the Constitution failed to be explicit about the school lands themselves, and Congress failed to correct the oversight in the subsequent Act of Admission. The Supreme Court concluded the school lands were not a constitutionally-established trust, although the Legislature made them so in statutes passed in 1997. (Wyoming Act of Admission 26 Stat. 222, Ch. 664, secs. 4 and 5) (Wyoming Constitution art.7 secs.2 and 7, art. 18 secs. 1-5) (Wyoming Statutes 36-5-105) (*Riedel v. Anderson,* 2003 WY 70, 70 P.3d 223 Wyo. 2003)

Wyoming's constitution borrowed heavily from other Western states. Unique elements included women's suffrage and Article 8, Irrigation and Water Rights. In that article, Wyoming adopted a complete system for state control of water.

Women were featured prominently at a statehood celebration on the Capitol Building steps on July 23, 1890. Theresa A. Jenkins spoke about the struggle for women's suffrage. Her daughter recalled 50 years later for the *Wyoming State Tribune* newspaper that her mother had been heard by even the most distant in the audience four blocks away, because she had practiced on the open prairie. Esther Hobart Morris presented Gov. Francis Warren a forty-four-star silk flag. Then, after a forty-four-gun salute, Mrs. I.S. Bartlett read an original poem, "The True Republic." Melvin C. Brown, president of the constitutional convention, presented a copy of the Wyoming Constitution to Amalia B. Post, as a "representative woman of Wyoming." (Larson 1977, pp. 259-260)

Article 6, section 20 of the Wyoming Constitution contains the oath of office for newly elected or appointed legislators and all judicial, state and county officers. The wording that describes prohibitions against selling votes or influence is cumbersome, and an attempt was made in the 2005 Wyoming Legislature to streamline the archaic language. The sponsor, Sen. Ken Decaria of Evanston, also proposed using the name "Wyoming," instead of merely referring to "this state." The proposed amendment was rejected by House members who liked things the old way and considered the proposal a frivolous use of legislative time.

A task for Wyoming voters in the first years of statehood was selection of a permanent site for their state capital. The Wyoming Constitution required that a permanent location be decided by popular vote. Cheyenne received 11,781 votes, which was more than any other proposed locations on the ballot but not a majority. Lander received 8,667 votes, Casper 3,610 votes, Rock Springs 429 votes, and Sheridan 122 votes. More than 100 years later, Cheyenne continues to enjoy the status of temporary capital of Wyoming. (Roberts 2001, p. 389).

Official State Designations

About the name "Wyoming"

The Wyoming Territory was given that name by Congress, named for the Wyoming Valley in northeastern Pennsylvania. The name was suggested by U.S. Rep. J.M. Ashbey of Ohio. The name was made popular by the poem "Gertrude of Wyoming," written in 1809 by British poet Thomas Campbell, about a clash of Native Americans and British colonists in 1778. "Wyoming" is from the Delaware Indian words *maugh-wau-wa-ma,* meaning "large plains" or "upon the great plain."

Capitol Building

The architecture of the Capitol is pseudo-Corinthian, something like the Capitol Building in Washington, D.C. The first two courses of the building are of sandstone from the quarries of Fort Collins, Colorado. Sandstone for the rest of the building came from quarries at Rawlins.

The central area and dome were completed in 1888. Small wings on the east and west ends of the original building were completed in April 1890 at a cost of $125,000.

The Tenth Legislative Assembly approved the project over the objections of Gov. Thomas Moonlight, who thought it too great a financial burden on state residents. State government soon outgrew the Capitol Building. In 1915, the Thirteenth State Legislature approved construction of the House and Senate chambers in the east and west wings for $140,790.

Each chamber has four large murals depicting Industry, Pioneer Life, Law, and Transportation, the work of Allen Tupper True. The Senate murals are "Indian Chief Cheyenne," "Frontier Cavalry Officer," "Pony Express Rider," and "Railroad Builders/Surveyors." The House murals are "Cattlemen," "Trappers," "Homesteaders," and "Stagecoach." (A photograph of "Homesteaders" is on the front cover of this book.) True was paid $5,200 for his work. (*Wyoming Blue Book* 1990, vol. 2, pp. 663-666).

The Capitol dome is covered in 24-carat gold leaf, which is visible from all roads entering the city. It was gilded in 1900 and has been gilded five more times since then, the last time in 1988. The peak of the dome is 146 feet high. The base is 50 feet in diameter.

In front of the State Capitol is a statue of Esther Hobart Morris. A replica is in Statuary Hall in the U.S. Capitol. She is reported to have played a prominent role in the Territorial Assembly's decision to grant women the right to vote. The act to grant women suffrage was introduced November 27, 1869, in the First Territorial Assembly. It was

Wyoming State Capitol in 2005.

signed by Gov. John A. Campbell on December 10, 1869. Morris, who lived in South Pass City, was appointed the first woman Justice of the Peace in 1870.

Wyoming State Seal

On Jan 10, 1891, the first State Legislature provided for a state seal that would differ from the Territorial Seal. It featured a landscape with a stream and valley down the middle. Cattle grazed and a farmer plowed along the stream. To the right of the valley was an oil derrick and tank. To the left was a mountain with mining works. On a platform above the landscape was a female figure with a broken chain dangling from an uplifted arm. On the platform was written the words, "Equal Rights." The figure pointed to a star on which was engraved "44." (Wyoming was the forty-fourth state to join the Union.)

The seal met with widespread disapproval, so the Second State Legislature approved another design on February 8, 1893. That is the one used today. It keeps the female figure with the broken chain. In her right hand is a staff and banner that reads, "Equal Rights." She is modeled after the statue of "Victory of the Louvre," the 1891 legislation says. To her right and left are male figures typifying the livestock and mining industries.

State seal commissioned by the First Wyoming Legislature in 1891, rejected in reaction to popular disapproval. (Wyoming State Archives)

Great Seal of the State of Wyoming, approved by the Second Wyoming Legislature in 1893, in use today. The Secretary of State is custodian of the seal.

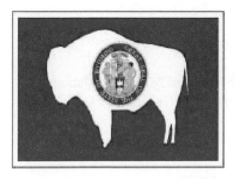

Wyoming State Flag

The 14th Legislature adopted a State Flag on January 31, 1917. The winning design was by Miss Verna Keays of Buffalo, Wyoming, selected from among 37 submitted in a contest by the Daughters of the American Revolution (*Wyoming Blue Book* 1990, vol. 2, p. 661).

Miss Keays wrote this legend for the flag:

"The Great Seal of the State of Wyoming is the heart of the flag.

"The seal of the bison represents the truly western custom of branding. The bison was once 'monarch of the plains.'

"The red border represents the Red Men, who knew and loved our country long before any of us were here; also, the blood of the pioneers who gave their lives reclaiming the soil.

"White is an emblem of purity and uprightness over Wyoming.

"Blue, which is found in the bluest of blue Wyoming skies and the distant mountains, has through the ages been significant of fidelity, justice, and virility.

"And finally, the red, the white, and the blue of the flag of the State of Wyoming are the colors of the greatest flag in all the world, the Stars and Stripes of the United States of America."

State Song

The official state song is "Wyoming," adopted by the Thirty-third Legislature in 1955. It is a poem written by Charles E. Winter in 1903, which was first set to song by Earle R. Clemens. The song won acceptance at the State Industrial Association in Sheridan that year and at the World's Fair in Saint Louis. Missouri, in 1904. It was used at the fair held in Portland, Oregon, in 1905 and again at the Panama Exposition in 1915.

In 1920, George E. Knapp, professor of music at the University of Wyoming, set the poem to a tune in march tempo and published it as "Wyoming March Song." This setting won popular approval and is the one adopted by the state.

Legal Holidays

Wyoming has ten legal holidays:
- New Year's Day, January 1
- Martin Luther King Jr.'s Birthday, third Monday in January
- Washington's and Lincoln's birthdays (President's Day), third Monday in February
- Memorial Day, last Monday in May
- Independence Day, July 4
- Labor Day, first Monday in September
- Veterans Day, November 11
- Thanksgiving Day, fourth Thursday in November
- Christmas Day, December 25

In addition, our state celebrates "Wyoming Day" on December 10 each year, to recognize "the action of the Wyoming territorial governor on December 10, 1869, in approving the first law found anywhere in legislative history which extends the right of suffrage to women (Wyoming Statutes 8-4-103).

The law says, "The day shall be observed in the schools, clubs and similar groups by appropriate exercises commemorating the history of the territory and state and the lives of its pioneers, and by fostering in all ways the loyalty and good citizenship of its people."

Wyoming also celebrates the birthday of Gov. Nellie Tayloe Ross, the first woman governor of any state. Her birthday, November 29, is a public holiday and should be "appropriately observed" in public schools, according to state law. The second Friday in May is "Native American Day" and should be observed in schools. Neither one requires closure of schools or courts.

Other State Designations

Nickname -- Equality State, Cowboy State
Motto -- Equal rights
State Flower -- Indian paintbrush
State Tree -- Plains cottonwood
State Bird -- Western meadowlark
State Dinosaur -- Triceratops
State Mammal -- Bison bison

State Fish -- Cutthroat trout
State Fossil - Knightia
State Gemstone -- Jade (nephrite)
State Reptile -- Horned lizard
State Grass -- Western wheatgrass
State Coin -- Golden Dollar
State Sport -- Rodeo
State Mythical Creature -- Jackalope

*Bronze statue of
Esther Hobart Morris
graces the front of the
State Capitol.*

License Plates

Wyoming began putting the "bucking horse" on its motor vehicle license plates in 1936. On the far left of the plates is a number representing the county where the vehicle is registered. The numbers were assigned to counties according to their total county property valuation. Obviously, the numbers were assigned before development of Campbell County's substantial coal deposits.

The numbers and corresponding counties are:

1 -- Natrona		13 -- Converse
2 -- Laramie		14 -- Niobrara
3 -- Sheridan		15 -- Hot Springs
4 -- Sweetwater		16 -- Johnson
5 -- Albany		17 -- Campbell
6 -- Carbon		18 -- Crook
7 -- Goshen		19 -- Uinta
8 -- Platte		20 -- Washakie
9 -- Big Horn		21 -- Weston
10 -- Fremont		22 -- Teton
11 -- Park		23 -- Sublette
12 -- Lincoln		

Chapter 4

Executive Branch

Wyoming state government is composed of three branches of government: executive, legislative, and judicial. The executive branch is charged with implementing the programs and policies adopted by the legislative branch. Executive officials also make policy and funding recommendations to the Legislature.

Article 4 of the Constitution of the State of Wyoming addresses the Executive Department. It establishes the top five elected officials: governor, secretary of state, state auditor, state treasurer, and state superintendent of public instruction. The governor's duties and powers are laid out in Article 4 of the Wyoming Constitution. Duties and powers of the other officials are described in law. Section 13 sets salaries for the five officials, although the amounts are updated by the Legislature and are put into statute. Annual salaries set by the Constitution in 1889 were: $2,500 for governor and $2,000 for the other officials. Salaries written into 9-3-101 of Wyoming Statutes for the top officials in 2002 were $105,000 for the governor and $92,000 for each of the other four top officials.

The term and qualifications for governor were laid out in the Constitution of 1889, Article 4, Section 2, and they have remained unchanged. A governor must be a United States citizen, a qualified elector of the state, 30 years of age, and a state or territory resident for the preceding five years.

Article 4, Section 11 of the Constitution sets out qualifications for the other four elected officials: they must be at least 25 years old, citizens of the United States, and qualified voters. Their terms are set at four years. The Constitution of 1889 prohibited the state treasurer from serving consecutive terms, although a treasurer could run again after spending four years out of office. This provision ostensibly protected the state's treasury from unscrupulous practices. The Constitution was amended to remove that restriction in 1982.

However, state law imposes term limits of eight years – two terms – on the governor and other four top elected officials. In 1992, voters approved a state law imposing term limits on legislators and the top elected officials. Affected legislators challenged the constitutionality of statutory term limits in 2004, and the Wyoming Supreme Court ruled in their favor. The Legislature repealed the limit on legislators in 2005. However, the Legislature let stand term limits for the top five officials, which remain in effect until repealed or challenged successfully in court.

The 1889 Constitution provided for a Board of Land Commissioners to have authority over the direction, control, care, leasing, and disposal of all lands in the state. Members were the governor, secretary of state, and superintendent of public instruction. A subsequent amendment added the state auditor and treasurer to the board. The Legislature passed legislation in 1921 to create the position of Land Commissioner.

If a governor is impeached or is displaced, resigns, or dies, or is for some other reason incapable of performing duties of the office or is absent from the state, the secretary of state acts as governor until the vacancy is filled or the disability removed.

If a governor dies, resigns, or for any other reason cannot finish a term, the succession to fill the vacancy is: secretary of state, president of the previous Senate, speaker of the previous House of Representatives, state auditor, and state treasurer. In most states, a lieutenant governor is elected and is first in the line of succession after the governor.

Article 4, Sections 4 and 5 of the Constitution lay out duties of the governor:

- Act as commander-in-chief of the military forces of the state (Wyoming National Guard).
- Convene the Legislature in special sessions. The Legislature also can call itself into special session.
- Address the Legislature at the beginning of sessions to discuss the condition of the state and recommend actions. for the session. It is called the "State of the State" address.
- Transact all necessary business with the officers of the government.

- Implement all measures resolved by the Legislature and take care that they be faithfully executed.
- Pardon or commute the sentences of convicted individuals. However, the Constitution was amended in 1994 to give the Legislature the power to create a criminal penalty of life in prison without parole and without the possibility of commutation by the governor.
- Veto legislative action. This includes "line-item" budget veto authority. That is, the governor can veto individual line items in budget bills. The Legislature can override a gubernatorial veto with two-thirds vote of both the House and Senate.
- Appoint office vacancies if no other method is provided for by the Constitution or law.

Article 4, Section 2 states that the governor shall not be eligible for any other office during the term. However, Gov. Francis Warren established a precedent when he accepted the appointment as one of Wyoming's first U.S. Senators. Over the years, four others have followed this precedent: John Kendrick in 1917, Lester Hunt in 1949, Frank Barrett in 1953, and J.J. Hickey in 1961. (Wyoming Official Directory 1989, p.267).

Article 4, Section 10 prohibits the governor from trading actions of his office in exchange for money or influence, and it prohibits him or her from using bribery or coercion to achieve certain legislative results. Governors are very careful not to threaten vetoes while the Legislature is considering proposals. This section has never been invoked.

The governor has many powers and duties granted by statutes, as well, which is the source of control over state government, including appointment and firing of heads of offices and agencies. Title 9 of Wyoming Statutes authorizes the governor to appoint an administrative assistant and state planning coordinator.

The constitutional prohibition against threatening vetoes is part of a tradition of a "weak" governor. Wyoming's chief executive also is in a position of having to share power with the other top four elected officials as they sit on various boards and commissions.

Nellie Tayloe Ross served as governor of Wyoming 1925-27, being the first woman to serve as governor in the United States. Her husband, William B. Ross, was elected goveror in 1922 but served just half his term. He died October 24, 1924, from complications from an appendectomy surgery. The Democratic Party nominated Mrs. Ross to run as the party's candidate in the election in November to finish the term. She was elected and took the oath of office January 5, 1925. She served until January 3, 1927. Ross was appointed the first woman director of the U.S. Mint in 1933, where she continued until her retirement in 1953.

All governors before and since have been men.

In 1989, the Legislature enacted the Wyoming Government Reorganization Act, which is in Wyoming Statutes, Title 9 "Administration of Government." It reduced the number of commissions, reorganized or consolidated several agencies, and attempted to set up a rational, efficient line of authority from the governor's office.

Gov. Ed Herschler, a Democrat, takes the oath of office to begin his third term in 1982. His wife, Casey, looks on. Herschler is the only governor to have served three terms. (Woming State Archives photo)

State Elected Officials:
Qualifications and Duties

Statutory duties and powers of the governor, secretary of state, auditor, treasurer and superintendent of public instruction are described at the beginning of Title 9 of Wyoming Statutes. Title 9 covers "Administration of the Government," and the first

chapter in that title deals with elected officials. The top five elected officials serve on the following boards and commissions:
- · State Loan and Investment board
- · Board of Land Commissioners
- · State Building Commission
- · State Canvassing Board

Votes of the boards and commission are made on a simple majority rule, giving the governor's vote the same weight as votes of the other officials.

Governor

Term limits for executive officials began with a two-term limit for governors enacted by the Legislature after Gov. Ed Herschler completed an unprecedented three terms 1974-1986. Term limits for the other top elected officials and legislators were imposed by voter referendum in 1992.

State law allows the governor to appoint an administrative assistant, a state planning coordinator, and a coordinator of state-federal relations. The law provides the other four officials authority to appoint their deputy officials.

The law gives the governor broad power to appoint the heads of certain agencies and departments and to approve their activities. The governor has direct or indirect responsibility for 174 boards and commissions in the executive branch. He appoints members to boards, commissions, councils, and committees associated with the Executive Branch. Of the boards and commissions appointments, 67 require confirmation by the Wyoming Senate. The governor makes 34 appointments for operating agencies and cabinet-level positions. The governor is responsible for hiring and firing agency and department directors and is responsible for seeing that the entities perform efficiently and economically. The governor's cabinet has 12-16 department heads. (See the Executive Branch organizational chart and agency division list on pp. 40-42.)

The governor is the visible symbol of the people of Wyoming inside and outside of the state. He is the head of the state, the head of his party, the person who deals directly with the federal government and commander-in-chief of the Wyoming National Guard. He formulates a proposed state budget and carries out the laws. He can lobby for bills and for his proposed budget. He can veto bills passed by the Legislature, but he is forbidden by the Constitution to threaten a veto. By proclamation he can declare special events and holidays.

The governor is Wyoming's representative in national and international affairs. Wyoming's governor is our chief trade representative to Australia and Taiwan. The governor also has ceremonial, social and political duties. By law, the state provides a residence for the governor and first family.

Secretary of State

The secretary of state serves as acting governor in the absence or indisposition of the governor.

The secretary of state is the custodian of the Great Seal of Wyoming, is chief elections officer for the state, and is administrator for all rules written by state agencies and all the codes and statutes that deal with Wyoming corporations.

The secretary of state's office certifies petition signatures gathered to qualify initiatives for the general election ballot, and it maintains a list of people who have registered to lobby members of the Wyoming Legislature.

The top elected officials come together to serve on several boards. Here, they meet as the State Loan and Investment Board in 2005 to consider a request from a water and sewer district for a grant to help pay for improvements. Left to right: Auditor Max Maxfield, Gov. Dave Freudenthal, Secretary of State Joe Meyer and Treasurer Cynthia Lummis. Not pictured is Superintendent of Public Instruction Trent Blankenship.

A major new responsibility was imposed on the secretary of state's office by the federal Help America Vote Act, which was passed by Congress in 2002. Secretary of State Joe Meyer and his staff worked with the county clerks and the public to develop a new state-wide voter registration and data system and to plan for the placement of electronic voting machines to comply with the law in all twenty-three counties by January 1, 2006.

As the state's record keeper, the secretary of state maintains records of administrative rules and regulations, oaths of office, facsimiles of signatures, discharges from state correctional institutions, proclamations, and executive orders. The secretary of state's office also publishes the Election Code (Title 22 of Wyoming Statutes), the Wyoming Constitution, and the Wyoming Official Directory. These are supplied to the public for a charge, and they also are available on the Internet (http://soswy.state.wy.us).

State Auditor

The state auditor is the state's chief accountant and chief payroll officer, responsible for writing the state's checks and monitoring spending by state agencies to make sure they are within legislative appropriations. The auditor is the only person with authority to sign checks drawn on the State Treasury. The auditor assesses the financial impact of various activities and provides that information to agencies, Wyoming Legislature, local governments, news media, and citizens.

The auditor serves on various boards and commissions with other elected officials and serves a chairman for the State Financial Advisory Committee.

The state auditor and the state treasurer maintain strict internal control by maintaining almost identical accounts, which are compared and reconciled daily.

Before the government reorganization of 1989, the auditor's office had two divisions: Audit and Accounting. A state Department of Audit was created in 1989 to conduct audits of state agencies and to keep track of mineral production on state and federal lands to ensure payment of mineral royalties to the state.

State Treasurer

The state treasurer receives and administers the state's money. The treasurer keeps accurate records, pays all warrants issued by the state auditor, and is the chief investment officer for state money.

The Constitution was amended in 1982 to allow the state treasurer to serve consecutive terms. Previously, the treasurer could serve one term of four years and then had to wait four years before seeking another term. Stan Smith, a veteran legislator from Thermopolis, was elected state treasurer in 1983 and served until 1999.

In 1995, Smith lobbied the Legislature successfully for a constitutional amendment to allow the treasurer to invest permanent funds in equity securities, which yielded more investment income than bonds. The amendment to Article 16, Section 6 was approved by the voters in 1996.

The state treasurer invests all the funds of the state, except for the State Retirement funds, and the Local Government Investment Pool, totaling about $5 billion in fiscal 2003. The treasurer also administers the Unclaimed Property Program and the College Achievement Program, which sets up future college tuition accounts. The treasurer serves on the following boards and commissions:

- State Loan and Investment Board
- Board of Land Commissioners
- State Building Commission
- Wyoming Community Development Authority
- Board of Deposits
- State Canvassing Board
- Wyoming Retirement System Board of Directors
- On-line Government Commission
- Financial Advisory Council

State Superintendent of Public Instruction

Wyoming is one of fifteen states that provide for the position of superintendent of public instruction by constitution. The office in Wyoming is more than just administrator for one of the state's largest agencies, however.

The person elected to this office administers the state Department of Education and is responsible for the general supervision of the public schools. Members of the State Board of Education are appointed by the governor. Trustees make policy, approve statewide academic standards, and approve statewide testing, and the superintendent executes those decisions with the professional staff of the Department of Education.

The superintendent represents the educational concerns of local school boards and administers federally funded education programs in Wyoming. By virtue of the office, the superintendent is a member of the Community College Commission, University of Wyoming Board of Trustees, State Board of Education, and School Facilities Commission. The 2006 Legislature acted to change the superintendent's status on the State Board from ex officio to voting member. ("Ex officio" means a member of a body by virtue of one's office, in an advisory capacity.)

Because state superintendents are elected, rather than appointed as are other agency heads, they are politicians. They enjoy some independence from the governor, although the governor retains the ability to recommend Education Department budgets to the Legislature for funding. Unlike other agency heads, state superintendents may use political clout to advocate for spending and other legislation, and their clashes with the governor or other elected officials can cause political controversy.

Superintendents' education credentials and experience have varied widely, as has their desire to get involved in day-to-day administrative duties. They may have advanced education degrees and previous experience as teachers or local school district superintendents or trustees. They may have no direct educational experience or credentials. It is difficult to say how the credentials or administrative abilities of candidates for the office figure into the voters' decisions.

Attorney General

In most states the attorney general is popularly elected and is largely independent of the governor. In Wyoming, he or she is appointed for a four-year term by the governor and is confirmed by the Senate. The attorneys general act as legal advisors to all executive branch state officers, and they render legal opinions at the request of legislators. They appoint the Chief Law Enforcement Officer for the State of Wyoming. They are empowered to prosecute and defend all lawsuits that may be instituted by or against the state and to represent

Wyoming State Government
Organizational Chart

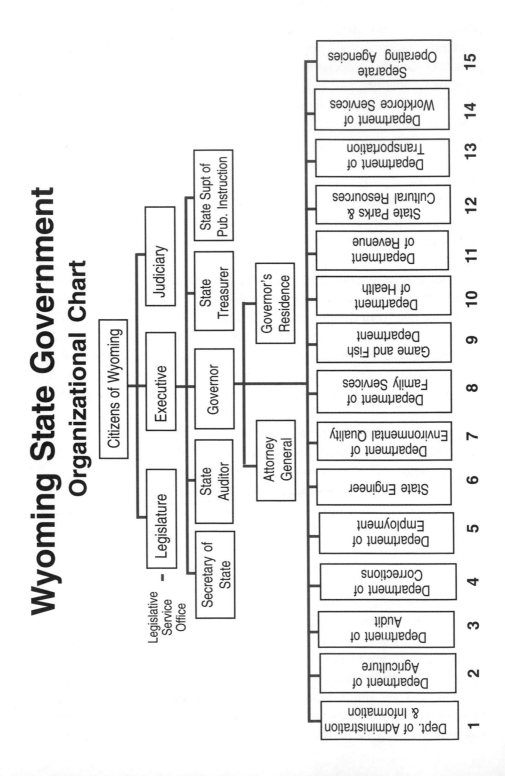

Citizens of Wyoming

Legislature · Executive · Judiciary

Legislative Service Office

Secretary of State

State Auditor

Governor

State Treasurer

State Supt of Pub. Instruction

Attorney General

Governor's Residence

1. Dept. of Administration & Information
2. Department of Agriculture
3. Department of Audit
4. Department of Corrections
5. Department of Employment
6. State Engineer
7. Department of Environmental Quality
8. Department of Family Services
9. Game and Fish Department
10. Department of Health
11. Department of Revenue
12. State Parks & Cultural Resources
13. Department of Transportation
14. Department of Workforce Services
15. Separate Operating Agencies

the state in all criminal matters in the Supreme Court. They may investigate any matter in any county at the governor's direction.

Special assistant attorneys general serve under the authority of the attorney general and work in either the Civil Division or Natural Resources Division.

The Division of Criminal Investigation (DCI) is a division of the Attorney General's Office. DCI provides criminal investigations, forensic laboratory services, telecommunications and other support services to local law enforcement officers, as well as other state and federal agencies in Wyoming.

The Law Enforcement Academy is located at Douglas. The academy provides education and training for all municipal, county, and state law enforcement officers. Officers must meet specific training requirements and complete continuing education courses every two years.

The Peace Officers Standards and Training Commission establishes and administers guidelines for Wyoming Peace Officer certification. The commission, which has a director and seven members, serves at the pleasure of the governor.

The Crime Victims Compensation Commission oversees implementation of the Crime Victim Compensation Act. It reviews crime victim's applications for financial compensation. The commission also holds public hearings four times a year during which the compensation awards are made. The three commission members are appointed by the governor for six-year terms.

Executive Agency Divisions

1. Administration & Information -- Administration, Budget, Economic Analysis, General Services, Information Technology, Human Resources, State Library

2. Agriculture -- Administrative Services, Analytical Services, Consumer Health, Technical Services, State Fair, Natural Resources

3. Audit -- Administration, Banking, Excise Tax, Mineral Audit, Public Funds

4. Corrections -- Prisons (Conservation Camp & Boot Camp, Honor Farm, Penitentiary, Women's Center) Field Services, Operations, Legal Services

5. Employment -- Administration, Economic and Admin. Services,

Employment Tax, Labor Standards, Mine Inspection & Safety, Unemployment Insurance, Worker's Safety and Compensation

6. State Engineer -- Board of Control, Board of Registration, Special Projects, Ground Water, Policy & Administration, Surface Water, Technical Services

7. Environmental Quality -- Abandoned Mine Land, Administration/ Outreach/ Air Quality, Industrial Siting, Land Quality, Solid Hazardous Waste Management, Water Quality

8. Family Services -- Protective Services, Financial Services, Juvenile Services, Information Services, Field Operations, Economic and Child Support, Enforcement Unit, Economic Assistance

9. Game and Fish -- Fish, Fiscal Services, Wildlife, Legal

10. Health -- Administration, Aging, Community &Family Health, Developmental Disabilities, Emergency Medical Services, Mental Health, Office of Health Facilities, Medicaid, Rural Health, Preventive Health & Safety, Substance Abuse, State Health Officer

11. Revenue -- Administrative Services, Ad Valorem Tax, Excise Tax, Technology, Liquor, Mineral Tax

12. Parks &Cultural Resources -- Administrative Services, Cultural Resources, State Parks & Historic Sites

13. Transportation -- Support Services, Aeronautics, Engineering & Planning, Highway Patrol, Technical Services, Chief Engineer

14. Workforce Services -- Employment Services, Administration & Support, business Training & Outreach, Quality Assurance, Vocational Rehabilitation

15. Separate Agencies -- Adjutant General's Office, Office of Administrative Hearings, Business Council, Community College Commission, Environmental Quality Council, Board of Equalization, Department of Fire Prevention & Electrical Safety, Geological Survey, Governor's Planning Council on Developmental Disabilities, Insurance Department, Livestock Board, Oil and Gas Commission, Public Defender, Public Service Commission, Retirement System, School Facilities Commission, Office of State Lands & Investments, University of Wyoming, Water Development Office, Licensing Boards and Commissions.

Attorney General's Office Divisions: Law Office, Division of Criminal Investigation, Peace Officers Standards & Training Commission, Victim Services, Wyoming Law Enforcement Academy

Chapter 5

Legislature

The Wyoming Constitution of 1889 created a bicameral legislature, having two chambers, to meet during a forty-day session every two years. Article 3 set legislative terms, requirements for members and for removal from office, and compensation. The Constitution required the Legislature to reapportion the House of Representatives and Senate after each U.S. census. It required redistricting "from time to time as public convenience may require." The Constitution also guaranteed each county its own seat in the House and Senate.

The guarantee of a House seat for every county was overturned by the courts 100 years later. Voters also amended the Constitution so the Legislature meets every year, alternating sessions devoted to the state budget and to "regular" lawmaking. These and other changes are discussed later in this chapter.

"Apportionment" is the fair division of a state's population among seats in the Legislature, so each seat represents about the same number of residents. The Wyoming Constitution requires the Legislature to "reapportion" itself during the budget session immediately after the U.S. census, to remain current with the growth, decline, or shifts of the state's population. Counties might gain or lose seats, if they have gained or lost population, or they might have to share a seat with another county. (Wyoming Constitution, art. 3, sec. 48)

"Redistricting"is the process of redrawing the geographic boundaries of legislative districts, which may be necessary to achieve fair apportionment. This process also provides the majority party the opportunity to assure continued dominance of the Legislature, by concentrating opposition party voters in a small number of districts.

Wyoming continues to have only one seat in the U.S. House of Representatives, because of its low population, so there is no need to redraw congressional district boundary lines or to increase the number of districts based on a larger population. The 2000 federal census counted 493,782 residents in Wyoming. Montana similarly has just one U.S. House seat with nearly twice that population.

At the writing of this book, the Wyoming Legislature had 60 seats in the House and 30 seats in the Senate. It meets for a total 60 days in a two-year period to pass laws: 20 days are allotted for budget sessions and 40 days for the regular sessions. The Legislature is not obliged to use all the days allowed, and legislative leaders have in recent years made an effort to complete sessions with a few days to spare, short of the maximum allowed. The money and days saved then are available for special sessions, if the Legislature or governor calls any.

The Legislature may override vetoes by the governor. The Legislature is able to place proposed legislation before voters of the state, and it also has the power to call itself into special session.

The legislative process provides the greatest opportunity for the state's citizens to have direct input in their state government, so it is important to understand how the process works and where the opportunities for involvement are.

Wyoming had 62,555 residents in 1890, according to the federal census. The 1889 Constitution laid out the following legislative representation, until a new apportionment by the Legislature:

Albany County – 2 senators and 5 representatives
Carbon County – 2 senators and 5 representatives
Converse County – 1 senator and 3 representatives
Crook County – 1 senator and 2 representatives
Fremont County – 1 senator and 2 representatives
Laramie County – 3 senators and 6 representatives
Johnson County – 1 senator and 2 representatives
Sheridan County – 1 senator and 2 representatives
Sweetwater County – 2 senators and 3 representatives
Uinta County – 2 senators and 3 representatives

These were the organized counties at the time of the Constitutional Convention. By the time of statehood, Weston and Natrona counties had organized, and they joined in voting in the first state elections. Big Horn County was created and was on the map, but it did not organize until 1897. The First Wyoming Legislature had 16 senators and 33 representatives. Carbon and Natrona counties shared two senators, and Crook and Weston counties shared one senator. In the

House, Natrona County took one of Carbon County's representatives.

The First Wyoming Legislature appointed the first United States senators from Wyoming, Francis E. Warren and Joseph M. Carey. The Legislature then turned to pressing state matters, many of which continue to be important to Wyoming more than a century later: roads, prisons, education, elections, and apportionment into legislative election districts.

Reapportionment and Redistricting

The Wyoming House has 60 members and the Senate 30. The Wyoming Constitution does not limit the number of legislative seats, although it does require a ratio between the House and Senate: Article 3, Section 3 says the number of House districts must be between two and three times the number of Senate districts. However, the size of the House and Senate chambers in the State Capitol puts practical limits on the number of desks that can be accommodated.

Wyoming legislators are elected from single-member districts, to comply with court rulings that required a revision of state districting laws in 1992. The House districts are "nested" within Senate districts. That means each Senate district contains two single-member House districts. This system is the result of a contentious reapportionment law passed in 1992, which reflects the power struggle in our Legislature between the Republicans and Democrats, between urban and rural interests, and between populous counties and sparsely-populated agricultural counties.

In 2002, former House member Matilda Hansen, a Democrat from Laramie, wrote the book *A Clear Use of Power,* about how legislative districts have been determined since statehood. Typically, the legislators in power are able to determine districts to preserve or enhance their own power and influence. Legislators who rise to positions of leadership in the House and Senate have great control over which laws get passed and how they are written.

The goal of apportionment is to have each House or Senate seat represent about the same number of residents, with less than 10 percent variance among the districts. That is the principle of "one man, one vote": no resident gets a disproportionately bigger voice than anyone else. This is the equal protection guaranteed in the Fourteenth

Amendment to the U.S. Constitution. The principle is established by the U.S. Supreme Court and is a necessary element of a constitutional districting plan.

The 1889 Wyoming Constitution guaranteed counties at least one seat in the House and Senate. There was strong sentiment that each county needed its own voice in the Legislature. To combine two counties would mean inferior representation for the less populous one, the reasoning went.

In 1965, a three judge federal panel reapportioned the Wyoming Legislature when the Legislature failed to reapportion itself. The court declared null and void the constitutional provision calling for one senator from each county. (United States Court of Appeals, Tenth Circuit, *Schaefer v. Thomson*, 251 F.Supp. 450, D.Wyo.1965)

The Wyoming Senate determined in 1971 that it had to create some multi-county districts to achieve roughly equivalent numbers with populous counties. However, the House kept insisting on its constitutional guarantee of one legislator for every county until it was declared unconstitutional by a three-judge panel of the U.S. District Court in Cheyenne.

The Wyoming League of Women Voters sued the state in 1982 to challenge the constitutionality of Wyoming's districting and apportionment. The League lost first in U.S. District Court (*Brown v. Thomson*, 536 F. Supp 780, 1982). The League appealed to the U.S. Supreme Court and lost there, as well. (*Brown et al. v. Thomson, Secretary of State of Wyoming et al.* Appeal from U.S. District Court for the District of Wyoming No. 82-65, decided June 22, 1983)

However, another challenge succeeded ten years later.

By 1991, there were great inequities in representation in the House, where the state still guaranteed each county its own House district. Niobrara County had one House member for 2,929 people, while Washakie County had one House member for 9,496 residents. In essence, that gave Niobrara residents three times the voice of Washakie residents in the Wyoming House. Yet the Legislature's reapportionment plan in 1991 still allowed Niobrara County to retain its seat in the Wyoming House.

Eleven citizens, led by then University of Wyoming graduate student Sarah Gorin, filed suit in U.S. District Court in Cheyenne to

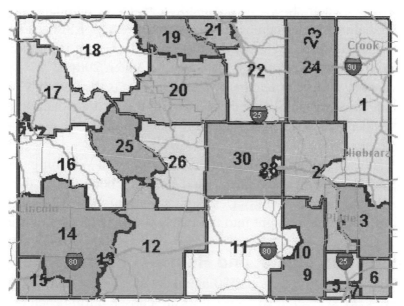

Wyoming House districts after 2002 redistricing. (Legislative Service Office)

Wyoming Senate districts after 2002 redistricing. (Legislative Service Offie)

challenge the 1991 law. (*Gorin vs. Karpan* 775 F. Supp. D.Wyo 1991)
A three-judge federal panel gave its ruling October 15, 1991, that the
new reapportionment plan violated the "one person, one vote" principle. In 1992, the Legislature reapportioned and redistricted the state.
The new plan redrew House and Senate district lines so the districts
had roughly the same number of constituents.

The plan created single-member districts. Previously, legislators
were elected at-large from a county. In Laramie County, for instance,
all candidates for the nine House seats ran in a pack and the top nine
vote-getters were elected. A system of single-member districts in use
today sets up one legislator per district, and district boundaries are
redrawn every ten years to make sure each district has about the same
number of residents. This system is intended to create more accountability of a legislator to a district's residents.

Critics of single-member districts say the system discourages
people from running, and they point to the number of legislative races
that lack enough candidates to give voters a choice in the primary and
general elections. However, an analysis of election data by the Equality
State Policy Center shows the decline in legislative candidates began
in 1986, before single-member districts were created. ESPC also found
the new system did not change the rate of re-election of incumbents.
(*Wyoming LAP Book*, Equality State Policy Center, 2004)

Another important feature of the 1992 plan is the "nesting" of
House districts within Senate districts. With this system, each Wyoming resident has one senator and one representative who are directly
accountable to him or her.

The history of apportionment and districting in Wyoming is one
of politics, personality, and power, and Hansen's book covers the topic
thoroughly, if from a patently Democratic point of view. Her account
provides fascinating insight into the inner workings of the Legislature.

Terms, Term Limits, and Removal From Office

The Wyoming Senate has 30 members elected for four-year terms.
The terms are staggered so 16 senators are chosen during each presidential election year, and 14 are chosen in off-year elections. The
Wyoming Constitution declares the number of members of the Wyoming House is never to be less than twice, nor greater than three times,

the number of members of the Senate. The Wyoming House has 60 members who serve two-year terms.

In 1992, Wyoming voters approved a law placed on the ballot by initiative to impose term limits on legislators: three terms for the House (six years) and three for the Senate (twelve years). The initiative was led by Jack Adsit of Sheridan, who contended the limit was necessary to avoid empire building by veteran legislators, even though very few lawmakers ever stayed for more than twelve years. The Legislature amended the law to make the limit twelve years for all legislators. Adsit responded with a successful petition drive to put an initiative on the general election ballot to restore the original three-terms-for-all limit. However, the voters rejected that in 1998. The Wyoming League of Women Voters lobbied the Legislature to repeal the term limit law, arguing it was an improper restriction on access to the ballot. However, Lawmakers deferred to what they considered the "will of the people," as expressed by the 1992 popular vote.

As legislators began running up against their term limits in 2004, three challenged the limits as an unconstitutional qualification to run for office. Such limits would require amending the Wyoming Constitution, they argued. The Wyoming Supreme Court agreed and declared the statutory term limit unconstitutional on May 4, 2004, with three weeks left in the time allowed to file with election officials to run for re-election. (*Cathcart v. Meyer*, 2004 WY 49, 88 P.3d 1050) (2004) The 2005 Legislature voted to repeal the limit on legislative terms, but they voted to continue the statutory two-term limit on the governor and the other top four elected officials.

There remains one limit on re-election that is imposed by custom: a representative who completes a term as speaker of the House does not run for another term. The Senate has a similar custom for president, but it is not followed strictly.

Otherwise, the Constitution imposes the following limitations on service:

Senate: At least 25 years old, qualified elector, citizen of the United States, resident in district for at least a year, term of four years.

House: At least 21 years old, qualified elector, citizen of the United States, resident in district for at least a year, term of two years.

Seats that become vacant during a term are filled by appointment.

The appointee must belong to the same political party as that of the person who left the seat vacant. County commissioners in the legislative district receive recommendations from the party precinct committeemen and committeewomen. Then the commissioners pick a replacement.

The Wyoming Constitution also gives the Legislature the power of impeachment. Article 3 lays out who may be impeached and how.

According to Section 18, the governor and other state and judicial officers except justices of the peace are liable to impeachment of high crimes and misdemeanors or malfeasance in office. Impeachment removes these officials from office and disqualifies them from holding any other office "of honor, trust or profit" under laws of the state.

Under Article 3, Section 17 of the Wyoming Constitution, the House of Representatives has the "sole power of impeachment." If a majority of House members vote to impeach an official, then the Senate members decide if the official is guilty, based on the law and evidence. When the governor is on trial, the chief justice of the Wyo-

The Wyoming House during a special session in July 2005 to consider bills and constitutional amendments to address health care availability in Wyoming. This was the first special session called by legislators themselves.

ming Supreme Court presides. Impeachment requires a two-thirds vote of the Senate.

Legislative Leadership

The Wyoming Senate and House of Representatives elect their own officers and establish their own rules.

The Senate elects a president by majority vote to preside over its sessions, and the House similarly elects a speaker, so the majority party controls selection of leaders.

The Senate president and House speaker preside over their chambers, assigns bills to committees, and signs bills passed by their chambers. They select members of conference committees and have a major role in selecting committee chairs. During sessions, they recognize legislators who wish to speak during debate.

In addition, the Senate selects a vice president, and the House selects a speaker pro tempore. They preside when the president and speaker are not in their chairs, and they generally move into the top position during the next session.

The majority and minority parties of both chambers also select their "floor leaders" and "whips."

The president of the Senate acts as governor if both the governor and the secretary of state are absent. If a vacancy occurs in both of those executive offices, the president of the Senate becomes the governor. The speaker of the House is next in line, after the president of the Senate, to act as governor.

Senate and House leadership can influence legislative actions by controlling how, when, and if bills will be considered. A bill may be expedited through the process or may die for lack of action in committee or while waiting on General File for debate in the full Senate or House. The president and speaker may decide a bill's fate by assigning it to a committee with a sympathetic or unsympathetic chairman.

The majority floor leader in each chamber exercises power by controlling the order of bills as they wait to be taken up each day on "General File." General File is the list of bills that have been reported out of committee and are ready for initial debate by the full chambers.

Controlling the progress of bills through the legislative process -- in committee or on General File -- is especially important during the relatively short sessions of the Wyoming Legislature. Deadlines for bills to pass through stages of the process come quickly, and many measures die because they simply run out of time. Majority floor leaders may kill a bill by keeping it at the bottom of the General File list.

Minority floor leaders are the chief spokesmen for their party.

Majority and minority whips serve as liaison between leadership members on the floor, and they make sure members are on the floor for key votes.

One effect of term limits was to shorten the patience of legislators who wanted to rise to leadership positions. The usual practice had been to bide one's time until one's seniority earned a position. After 1992, lawmakers with just a few terms of experience were vying for top spots, particularly in the House. Now, leaders are not necessarily the most senior members.

Sen. April Brimmer Kunz, R-Cheyenne, became the first woman to serve as Wyoming Senate president during the 2003-2004 sessions.

Legislative Sessions

The Wyoming Constitution was amended in 1972 to establish annual legislative meetings to total 60 days every two-year legislative term. In odd-numbered years the Legislature meets for 40 days to consider a full range of proposals, beginning on the second Tuesday in January. In even-numbered years, the Legislature meets for 20 days, primarily to consider budget issues, beginning on the third Monday in February. In each two-year period, the Legislature is allowed to meet for a total of only 60 legislative days, and a total of only 40 days in a single year.

With just 20 days to set the state's spending for the next two years, the Legislature requires a two-thirds vote of the House or Senate to introduce non-budget bills during the budget sessions. (Wyoming Constitution, art 3, sec. 6) The Senate and House have approved rules to limit bill introductions. Senate rules limit members to sponsoring seven bills in the regular session (rule 9-5) and three bills during budget sessions (rule 24-2-c). The House approved a rule in 2005 to limit its members to sponsoring five bills during budget sessions (rule 28-2-c). Legislators who hit their bill limit also may find colleagues to sponsor their proposals.

The number of bills introduced increases each session, even with the legislative limits. Legislators in recent years have bemoaned the lack of restraint by individual legislators to restrict bills during budget sessions to emergency matters. They equally bemoan the willingness of Senate and House members to allow introduction of the non-budget bills. This is considered more than just an inconvenience, because introduction votes on non-budget measures require time-consuming roll call votes, an estimated three minutes in the Senate and five minutes in the House.

In the 2004 budget session, House members sponsored 216 bills and 11 resolutions. House leadership let 54 of the measures die without bringing them up for a vote. Another three bills were withdrawn by their sponsors. Only 27 failed an introduction vote. Of the 143 bills and resolutions introduced, 80 passed and 63 failed. In the Senate, 99 bills and resolutions were prepared for the session. Of those, 58 passed, 27 failed, 10 failed introduction votes, and 4 were withdrawn. House and Senate members averaged about three bills per member and rejected introduction of about the same proportion, but House leaders also withheld a fair number of bills that were not considered.

Another development bemoaned by legislative leadership is the growing tendency to ask for appropriations during the regular, non-budget sessions. During the 2005 regular session, nearly 50 bills called for appropriations. Only two of them were official budget bills.

Recognizing the time constraints of budget sessions, the Legislature may finish its general session early and "save" some of its 40 days for special sessions or to add to the 20 days set aside for budget sessions. A special session is usually brief. It brings legislators back to the Capitol to take care of a single urgent problem.

The Wyoming Constitution provides that the governor may call a special session of the Legislature, outside the 60-day limit every two years. Governors have used this authority very rarely and in cases considered to be crises that could not wait until the next session, for instance in 1997 when the Legislature was working with a deadline imposed by the Wyoming Supreme Court to fix the state's school finance system.

Wyoming citizens amended the Constitution in 2002 to allow leaders of the House and Senate to call a special session, with the

approval of a majority of the members of both chambers. This amendment was seen as a move to increase the power of the Legislature, in
relation to the governor. The Legislature used this authority to call
itself into special session on July 12, 2004, to consider changes to state
laws and the Wyoming Constitution that would make health care
affordable and available in the state. The Legislature had finished up
its regular session with six days left in the two-year, 60-day limit, so it
had six days to work on the health care issue. The special session
resulted in several laws and one proposed constitutional amendment.
The amendment was rejected by voters in the 2004 general election.

All revenue-raising bills must originate in the House, according to
the Constitution. To help the budget process move rapidly during the
budget sessions, the Joint Appropriations Committee (JAC) holds
hearings on the budget several weeks before the sessions begin. In this
part of the process, executive agency administrators make their case
for their proposed budgets for the coming biennium. By Wyoming
Statute (28-1-113), the Joint Senate and House Appropriations Committee convenes in open session not less than 20 days prior to the
budget session to consider the budget. The committee prepares the
budget bills for introduction within five days of the start of the session
starts. Because of the length of time it takes to prepare the budget, the
JAC convenes in January, and then the legislative session opens on the
third Monday of February. (*Wyoming Manual of Legislative Procedures* 1989, p.4)

In the 1990s, the leadership of the House and Senate began the
practice of moving the budget proposal prepared by the Joint Appropriations Committee simultaneously through the House and Senate, as
so-called "mirror" bills. After the bills are debated, amended, and
passed in each house, they cross over in amended forms to be considered by the other chamber. This is intended to save time in the short
session, although it is difficult for citizens to follow the simultaneous
debate and to track the status of individual budget items.

Another consequence of the relatively short sessions in Cheyenne
is the extensive work by committees in the interim, i.e., between
sessions. The leadership of the House and Senate, sitting as the Management Council, assigns studies to standing and select committees.
The object is to thoroughly study issues and prepare legislation with

public input that can move swiftly through the process when the next session begins. Interim committees, aided by Legislative Service Office staff and consultants, typically will study reports and meet two to four times to take testimony and consider legislation.

The House and Senate adopt their own procedural rules. Both follow parliamentary rules of *Mason's Manual.*

Legislative Compensation

When Wyoming became a state, the Constitution set compensation at $5 for each day of a legislative session and 15 cents per mile for travel between the capital and home for the first session. The Legislature was to set compensation for future sessions.

The Constitution prohibits legislators from increasing their own compensation, so increases are made effective during a future session. (Wyoming Constitution, art. 3, sec. 6)

In 2005, a law took effect paying legislators $150 a day as salary during sessions. The 2005 Legislature approved several changes (to take effect in 2009) to compensate legislators for trips home during sessions and for legislative work during interims. (Wyoming Statutes 28-5-101). The provisions are:

- Mileage for one roundtrip a week between Legislature and home during sessions (rate per mile 35 cents)
- Daily salary four days a month for floor leaders and committee chairmen, six days a month for House speaker and Senate president, and two days for other legislators
- Daily salary for each day legislators do work for the Management Council or any committee assignment
- Half daily salary for each day of preparation for Management Council or committee work
- Half daily salary for each day of travel for interim meetings

Supporters said the new law, with its increased travel allowance and additional pay, recognized the increased responsibilities and work done by all legislators and especially by leaders between sessions. The burden of preparing for legislative sessions and the interim responsibilities have made the work of legislator nearly a year-round job, and serving in the Wyoming Legislature requires many days away from family and the workplace.

It is worth considering whether the financial sacrifices required of legislators, because of lost income while they serve during and between sessions, make legislative service practically impossible for most Wyoming citizens.

How a Bill Becomes a Law

The Wyoming Constitution provides for the passage of laws by the Wyoming Legislature through the proper introduction of bills into each house of the Legislature (Wyoming Constitution, art. 3, secs. 20-28). Bills may be introduced through either legislative chamber, except revenue-raising bills must must originate in the House of Representatives.

The Senate may amend revenue bills, as it does with all other acts (Wyoming Constitution, art. 3, sec. 33). No appropriation bill may be introduced within five days of the close of the legislative session, except by unanimous consent of the house in which it is introduced. To keep the traffic of bills moving smoothly, House and Senate rules establish a cut-off date for introducing all bills in the 40-day session, to allow enough time to be heard in committee, reported out of committee, and acted on by the full House or Senate and then sent to the governor before adjournment. Bills must be introduced by noon of the eighteenth working day, except by consent of two-thirds of the House or a unanimous vote of the Senate. During the budget session the introduction cut-off date is the fourth day in the House and the fifth day in the Senate. Non-budget bills may be considered only if a two-thirds majority approves introduction.

The Legislature is prohibited from altering or amending the original purpose of a bill during its legislative journey. (Wyoming Constitution, art. 3) This is very different from Congress, where members may attach completely unrelated "riders" to bills. In addition, before a bill can be considered by the Legislature or be allowed to become law, it must first be referred to a committee for investigation and discussion and then be approved. The measure is then returned from the committee in printed form for consideration by all legislative members. Each bill is further tested and refined as it makes its way through a series of debates and votes in both Senate and House. (See outline of the complete process on page 58.)

Photos from early session of the Wyoming Legislature -- Senate above and House below. However legislators may want to redraw district lines, they are constrained by the physical limits of the House and Senate chambers. Since these photos were taken, the House chamber has been remodeled to accommodate a growing number of representatives. The dais with the speaker's chair and the clerks' desk was moved back in 1975 to make more floor room, requiring the removal of offices and a gallery at the front of the chamber. The Senate chamber still has those features. (Undated Wyoming State Archives photos)

How a bill becomes law: *following House Bill 100.*

Conference Committee

HB100 returns to House, where members reject amendments adopted by Senate. Bill goes to "conference committee" to work out compromise.

House and Senate conferees present compromise bill to their chambers. HB100 conference committee report is adopted by roll call votes.

HB100 is printed as Enrolled Act 52. Signed by House Speaker and Senate President. Sent to governor for signature.

Governor

Governor signs EA52, and the higher speed limit becomes law on July 1, as specified in the bill. It is identified as Chapter 3 of Session Law.

Senate

HB100 introduced in Senate, 1st reading by title only. Senate President assigns to committee for study and recommendation.

Committee returns HB100 with recommendation that it pass, without amendments. HB100 put on Senate General File.

Senate, sitting as Committee of the Whole, debates HB100. Adopts committee amendments. HB100 advances to 2nd reading.

HB100 debated on 2nd reading. No amendments offered. Advances to 3rd reading in Senate.

HB100 3rd reading. Opposition surfaces. Fierce debate. Amendments pass to satisfy opponents. Passes roll call vote 16-14.

House

HB100 read in House by Clerk. House Speaker assigns to standing committee forrecommendation.

Committee recommends HB100 pass with amendments. Placed on General File, for initial debate by full House.

House, as Committee of the Whole, enjoys unlimited debate of HB100. Approves amendments. HB100 advances to 2nd reading.

2nd reading of HB100. Limited debate. No amendments offered. Advances to 3rd reading.

3rd reading of HB100. Amendments debated. One approved. Roll call vote. HB100 passes 40-20.

HB100 "engrossed" with amendments, printed and sent to Senate.

Each bill passed by the Senate and the House of Representatives may contain only one subject, which must be clearly expressed in the title of the bill. There are two exceptions: general appropriations bills and bills for the codification and general revision of the laws.

A majority vote of all House and Senate members is required for the passage of a bill. The final vote on each bill must be counted by "ayes and nays," and the names of those voting are entered into the Senate and House journals. Any member of the Wyoming Legislature who has a personal or private interest in any legislative measure must declare a conflict of interest and excuse himself from voting on that measure. Amendments to the Wyoming Constitution require a two-thirds vote of each chamber. Unless vetoed by the governor, proposed amendments go on the next general Eeection ballot for approval by the voters. Amendments must receive a majority approval by all the people voting in that election to be adopted.

Procedures of the House and Senate as they deliberate and make laws are all laid out in the "Wyoming Manual of Legislature Procedures," prepared by the Legislative Service Office (LSO) and reviewed every four years for revision. This document describes in detail the procedures that are set by the Constitution, by the House Rules and Senate Rules, and by custom and practice. It is written for the benefit of new legislators, but it also can be valuable for citizens who are following a bill through the process or just want to understand the legislative process they are watching. Both the manual and the rules can be found on the LSO's Web site http://legisweb.state.wy.us.

Here is a summary of the procedure for enacting a bill into law.

1. A legislator or legislative committee submits a proposed bill to the Legislative Service Office (LSO), where it is drafted into proper form so it may be added to Wyoming Statutes. All bills are written in an approved form, numbered, and stored in the LSO computer. Bills must be processed this way before being accepted for introduction. Bills must include a "Fiscal Impact" note if they require support from the General Fund. Legislators and LSO staff attorneys work in a confidential client-attorney relationship, so work done at this stage of the process is not public.

2. Bills are called Senate Files or House Bills depending on the body of introduction, and they are assigned a number. They are com-

monly referred to as "SF" or "HB," followed by a number, for instance, SF10 or HB15. After the sponsor signs the bill, it is introduced by the reading clerk by its title and sponsor(s) name only. (Non-budget bills submitted during budget sessions must receive a two-thirds vote at this point in order to be introduced.) The presiding officer immediately refers it to a standing committee. This is considered the "first reading" of the bill. The bill is then printed.

3. In committee, several things may happen to a bill. The chairman has the power to bring it up for consideration or to keep it on the bottom of the pile of the committee's bills. When a bill is considered, the committee usually hears testimony from citizens, lobbyists, and other legislators and gets information from government agencies. A committee member makes a motion on the bill – a motion to "do pass" or "do not pass" – which is seconded. The committee may amend the bill as it is being discussed, and then a roll call vote is taken of members. The committee then returns the bill to the chief clerk of the House or Senate with its recommendation to approve the bill as is or with amendments. The committee can return the bill "without recommendation," although that is very unusual. A bill may die in committee if it fails a "do pass" motion or if it receives no action at all. Bills that have failed votes or that have not been voted on are kept in committee and are finally returned to the presiding officer when time for consideration has expired.

4. A bill that is reported out with a "do pass" recommendation is placed on the General File of the House or Senate. There it waits, ready for the chamber's majority floor leader to bring it up for consideration by the full chamber when it acts as the Committee of the Whole. There, legislators give the bill a full debate and vote on amendments from the committee and offered by other legislators. After discussion, a vote is taken on whether to accept the bill for "second reading." Voting at this point and on amendments is by voice, and no official record is made. A legislator may call for "division," a standing count vote. A legislator may call for the "ayes and nays." If there is a second to the motion, the clerk takes a roll call vote, and the vote is made part of the bill's permanent record.

5. "Second reading" of the bill is by title and sponsor(s) name only. Amendments may be proposed, but debate is limited. Legislators

may speak only twice on each proposed amendment.

6. The next legislative day, all bills that have passed second reading are up for "third reading and final passage." A roll call vote is taken on final passage of the bill. It requires a majority vote of all members who have been elected, not just those present. Those who declare a conflict of interest do not vote.

7. The passed bill is printed up in "engrossed" form, with approved amendments included in the text, and is sent to the other chamber. There, it goes through the same process of first reading, committee work, second reading, and final passage.

8. If the second house amends the bill, it goes back to the house of origin. There it may be accepted as amended. If not, the bill goes to a joint conference committee made up of three members of each house, who, if possible, reconcile the differences between versions. The committee issues a conference report, and both houses vote by roll call to adopt or reject the committee report. If adopted, the bill passes. If not, the bill may go to subsequent conference committees until an acceptable compromise is reached. If none is reached, the bill is dead.

9. The bill that is passed returns to the house of origin where it is "enrolled," which means the LSO has finalized it with all amendments into an "act." The presiding officer announces the new number that has now been assigned to the act, the reading clerk reads it, and the presiding officer signs the act. Then the presiding officer sends it to the governor. The Wyoming Constitution gives the governor three days to sign a bill, veto it, or let it become law without signature. If the Legislature adjourns before the governor has had time to veto a bill and return it to both houses, it becomes law unless he files a statement of his objections within 15 days after adjournment. He does not have the power to veto resolutions, although the governor may veto proposed constitutional amendments. The Legislature may try to override a gubernatorial veto, which requires a two-thirds vote of both chambers. If the chamber where the bill originated votes to override, the second chamber must take an override vote.

An act becomes law 90 days after adjournment of the session unless a different "effective date" is specified in the bill.

Both chambers have rules prohibiting lobbying in the chambers. Senate Rule 21-1: "No person other than members and officers of the

Senate and House and legislative staff shall be admitted within the bar of the Senate, except by special invitation on the part of the Senate or President thereof; but a majority may authorize the President to have the Senate cleared of all such persons." House Rule 23-1: "Except for members, no other person shall engage in influencing the passage or defeat of legislation in the House Chambers."

Legislative Committees

Twelve standing committees operate in the House and twelve in the Senate. The Senate president appoints the chair and membership of the Senate standing committees. The House speaker appoints chairs and members in that chamber. The president and speaker have the advice and consent of the Rules and Procedure committees of their respective bodies. With some exceptions, committee membership is apportioned to reflect the percentage of the elected members' political parties in each house. It is customary for minority party leaders to participate in assignment of their party members to standing commit-tees.

This power to appoint standing committees and chairmen is substantial. Bills face their first real test of the legislative process in standing committees, where the bills might be left intact, changed greatly, expedited, delayed, or killed outright.

Standing committees combine into a joint committee to do in-terim work on legislation for the upcoming session. For instance, the House and Senate Education committees meet together as the Joint Education Interim Committee to study reports and hear public testi-mony and then write bills. The standing committees are:

1. Judiciary
2. Appropriations
3. Revenue
4. Education
5. Agriculture, Public Lands, and Water Resources
6. Travel, Recreation, Wildlife ,and Cultural Resources
7. Corporations, Elections, and Political Subdivisions
8. Transportation, Highways, and Military Affairs
9. Minerals, Business, and Economic Development
10. Labor, Health, and Social Services

11. Journal

12. Rules and Procedure

Much of the work on bills is done in committee, where a small number of lawmakers can learn about bills, debate them in detail, and hear from the public. Committee meetings give citizens their opportunity to "testify" about proposals, although chairmen may limit testimony. Most Senate committees have five members, and House committees nine members. The exceptions are the Rules and Journal Committees. Members of the full House and Senate rely heavily on their committees' recommendations.

On rare occasions, the full House or Senate may disagree with a committee's decision to kill a bill or otherwise keep it in committee. Rules allow the House or Senate to suspend the rules, by a two-thirds vote, to retrieve a bill from committee and have it heard in the Committee of the Whole (the full body). The Wyoming House took this action to hear a cigarette tax bill in 1989.

In addition, "select" committees are created by the Legislature for a limited time to study specific issues and make recommendations to a standing committee or the full Legislature. Select committees have equal numbers of senators and representatives. Legislation creating select panels specifies the number of members and how they are to be named.

Select committees in 2005 were: Select Committee on Air Transportation, Select Committee on Capital Financing and Investments, Select Committee on Legislative Facilities, Select Committee on Legislative Process, Select Committee on Mental Health and Substance Abuse Services, Select Committee to Study Developmental Programs, Select Committee on Higher Education Endowment Account Merit Scholarship, Select Committee on School Facilities, Select Committee on School Finance, Select Technology Committee, Select Committee on Tribal Relations, Select Water Committee, and the Select Committee on Wildlife and Natural Resources Fund.

The president of the Senate and the speaker of the House and members of the committees are officially named during the opening days of the session. However, they are actually chosen at party caucuses before the opening of the session.

The most powerful committee is the Management Council, which is composed of the majority and minority party leadership in the House and Senate, plus six others from House and Senate. The Management Council has the final word about all the work done by the Legislative Service Office. The Management Council has control over spending by standing committees. Occasionally, the Management Council will sponsor legislation it considers important to legislative operations. The director of the LSO answers directly to the Management Council. Management Council policies govern day-to-day activities by the LSO and legislators – everything from distribution of lawmakers' laptop computers, to handling sexual harassment complaints, to requests to the Wyoming State Museum for artwork for committee rooms. However, the Legislature has ultimate say over the policies. Chairmanship of the Management Council alternates between the House speaker and

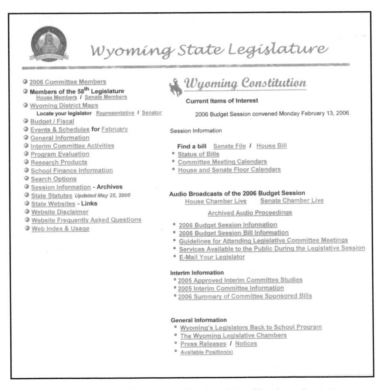

Legislative Service Office Web site, http://legisweb.state.wy.us. Anyone with access to a computer and the Internet can get up-to-date information on legislative action during sessions and on committee action during the interim (between sessions). Also, find on-line current versions of Wyoming Statutes and Wyoming Constitution.

Senate president. (*Management Council Policies* 2003)
Members of the Management Council are:
Senate: president, vice president, majority and minority floor
leaders of the Senate, plus two senators selected at large, only
one of them from the same political party as the president
House: the speaker, speaker pro tempore, majority and minority
floor leaders or their respective designees of the house, plus
two representatives selected at large, only one of them from
same party as the speaker.
At large selection: The four at-large members are selected by a
caucus of their political parties.
Finally, the twelve members listed above meet and select one
additional member from the chamber and the party that are not
those of the chairman.

The Legislature is exempt from the state's Open Meeting laws, so
it may close meetings for any reason. However, House and Senate
rules require the posting of committee meeting times, locations, and
bills being considered. This allows members of the public to monitor
committee deliberations and testify, if there is an opportunity to speak.

Legislative Service Office

One of the most dramatic changes in how the Legislature does
business and in citizens' access to the process was the creation of the
Legislative Service Office in 1971. The LSO is a professionally staffed
office with three main divisions: Budget, Audit, and Service. Legislative leadership, sitting as the Management Council, directs the LSO. It
appoints the director of the LSO and approves assistant directors of the
divisions. Staff members are hired without political consideration and
are governed by the office's Ethics and Conduct Guidelines. It states
that staff is to be "procedure oriented" not "issue oriented" and "shall
not be a source of inside information." LSO staff attorneys draft bills
and resolutions as requested by legislators. LSO auditors conduct
"management audits" of state agencies as requested by the Management Council, to assess efficiency.

LSO reports and its Web site are important sources of public
information about legislative work. During sessions, the LSO provides
copies of bills and amendments offered by legislators, "engrossed"

bills passed by each house (incorporating amendments), and enrolled acts as signed by the House speaker and Senate president and sent to the governor. The Web site reports interim work and provides background about the legislative process. (Find the site at http://legisweb.state.wy.us) Citizens can find bills from the current and recent sessions. They can access electronic versions of the Wyoming Statutes, the Wyoming Constitution, and documents relating to the operation of the Legislature, including the House and Senate Rules, the *Wyoming Manual of Legislative Procedures* and a calendar of events and committee meetings. Citizens who cannot be at the State Capitol in Cheyenne for the legislative sessions can go to the LSO Web site and listen to House and Senate debate carried live and also archived for a short while. In addition, the Web site provides contact information for each legislator, including e-mail addresses. In 2002, the state began providing laptop computers for all legislators, and most read and respond to e-mail several times each day during sessions.

It is difficult to overstate how much the LSO and technology have revolutionized citizens' access to the legislative process, especially for those who follow proposals from outside Cheyenne and who want to make comments in an effective and timely manner.

Nature of Wyoming Legislature

Those who serve in Wyoming's Legislature are, for the most part, hard-working people who sacrifice time from family and jobs to serve the state and its citizens. The job is increasingly difficult, in the amount of information they must process and the workload that extends beyond legislative sessions to fill the interims, which can deter people from serving in the Legislature. One solution, in the view of some, would be increased legislative pay, so more citizens could afford to serve.

The Legislature is a window on state government, where the public can watch the influence of politics and personalities on lawmaking. One House speaker might pressure members of his political party to adhere strictly to the party's position, while another might tolerate wide latitude in personal opinions or constituent service.

It is important for Wyoming citizens to realize how accessible the Legislature is and to understand opportunities they have to influence the legislative process. Citizens inform and persuade legislators during sessions, as they make laws and write proposed constitutional amendments, and when they are home between sessions. Interim committees meet in various locations around the state, and people who cannot come to Cheyenne may have a chance to testify closer to their home. The Legislative Service Office's Web site contains a wealth of information about the procedures and the work of the Legislature, including a complete history of every bill and resolution.

A major challenge to citizen participation that remained in 2005 was committee room logistics at the Capitol. Meetings may be open to the public, but citizens' ability to testify and listen to committee deliberations is severely curtailed if they cannot get into crowded meeting rooms. Rooms traditionally used for committees on the second and third floors of the Capitol are small and quickly fill with lobbyists, especially when controversial bills are being considered.

Another major challenge to legislative accountability is the number of important votes in the Wyoming Legislature that are not recorded. Roll call votes are taken on bills in committee, on bill introductions during budget sessions, on third and final reading ,and when a legislator requests that the chief clerk record "the ayes and the nays." Votes on amendment, however, are taken by voice only or by a standing head count (when a legislator requests it), and no permanent record is made of how individual legislators voted. (The Senate also requires roll call votes on amendments that spend public funds.) Some of these votes are very important. Yet citizens who are not present to witness the action or who do not have a lobbyist monitoring and reporting activity cannot track their legislators' voting. The Wyoming Legislature has rejected several proposals in the past to record all votes electronically.

In 2006, the Legislature passed a law making all communications and information used to draft legislation "privileged" and "confidential." and, therefore, unavailable to constituentsunless the legislators chose to disclose information. Gov. Dave Freudenthal vetoed the measure, calling it a barrier to transparent, accountable government. Legislators overrode the veto (Senate 19-1 and the House 43-14). They said they were preserving the "separation of powers" in resisting the governor's intrusion in how they made laws. They also said they were protecting sensitive information.

Citizens elect legislators, and they are answerable to the citizens of the state. Ultimately, people run for election to the Legislature and exercise their vote in the House or Senate.

Chapter 6

Judiciary

"Away from settlements the shotgun is the only law," Edward W. Smith of Evanston told the United States Public Lands Commission in 1879, writes Wyoming historian T.A. Larson.

"He was not far wrong," Larson wrote, "except that the rifle was used more often than the shotgun." (Larson 1978, p. 233)

Larson's description of "justice" far from any courtroom is consistent with the rough and ready reputation of life during early territorial days in the area that was later to become the state of Wyoming. This area included, at various times, parts of the Dakota, Nebraska, Utah, and Idaho territories.

Under the rule of the Dakota Territory, Wyoming was distant from the capital of Yankton. The weak judicial authority was unable to handle crime, and so "Judge Lynch" took command. (*Wyoming Blue Book* 1974, vol. 1, p. 111) A temporary government was set up in Cheyenne, without legal authority, and it tried cases not exceeding $2,000.

Even when disputes were settled in a court of law, the outcome could be unpredictable. Territorial judges were originally appointed by the United States president and Congress and were considered political appointments. Judges served for as long as their behavior was acceptable. Some judges had lawmaking duties, as well. (Hall 1981, p. 276)

By 1860, territorial judges were governed by rules and regulations set forth by Congress under Article 4 of the Constitution of the United States. At that time they began serving four-year terms. The pay was low and living conditions, like those for all Wyoming Territory settlers, were difficult. In 1867, the Dakota Legislative Assembly established a judicial district for the territory and set up a court in Cheyenne to be held annually.

The Organic Act of the Territory of Wyoming in 1868 set up a judicial system with a Supreme Court, district courts, probate courts, and justices of the peace. The Justice of the Peace system was finally phased out in 2003. The first justices appointed to the Wyoming Supreme Court were Chief Justice John H. Howe and Associate Justices William T. Jones and John W. Kingman. They were sworn in on April 6, 1869.

Wyoming territorial justices and judges generally included more prominent members of "society" who were better educated than most residents. During the period that Wyoming was a territory, between 41 percent and 51 percent of the appointees were college graduates. Approximately 26 percent attended college, and 33-39 percent attended secondary schools. These figures compare favorably with the federal judiciary of that time (Hall 1981, pp.277-282).

It was not unusual for Supreme Court justices, when not in session, to ride circuit as district court judges during territorial days. The story is told of Justice Jacob Blair, who was presiding over a murder trial in 1880. A gunsmith was called to testify and sat on the stand with the defendant's revolver in his hand. The judge turned to spit tobacco into a cuspidor and noticed the gun was pointed at him.

"Mr. Witness, is that gun loaded?" Blair asked.

"Yes, your honor," the gunsmith witness replied.

"Point it toward the lawyers. Good judges are scarce."

This story was told by pioneer lawyer A.C. Campbell in 1931 in an interview published in *Annals of Wyoming* in 1947. (*Wyoming Almanac* 2001, p. 212)

Wyoming courts are granted their powers and duties by Article 5 of the Wyoming Constitution. The Constitution also creates Wyoming's court structure: "The judicial power of the state shall be vested in the Senate, sitting as a court of impeachment, in a supreme court, district courts, and such subordinate courts as the legislature may, by general law, establish and ordain from time to time." (Wyoming Constitution, art. 5, sec. 1)

The judicial branch consists of the Supreme Court, District Courts, Circuit Courts, and Municipal Courts.

Selection and Tenure of Judges

Supreme Court justices and judges in other courts are appointed by the governor, with input from the Judicial Nominating Commission (to be discussed later). They serve a term and then stand for retention in a popular election if they wish to continue on the bench. Judges must file intent to stand for retention for another term between six months and three months before the General Election held prior to the expiration of the existing term. They run as non-partisan candidates, and they may not campaign.

However, the Wyoming State Bar Association publishes results of a "judicial advisory poll" in October of election years. Attorneys who are members of the Bar are asked to rate the performance of justices and judges on a range of characteristics, including knowledge of the law, diligence, courtesy, application of rules of evidence, and quality of judicial opinions. These results are used "to provide feedback to judicial officials about their performance on the bench and to help the public make more informed judgments in judicial elections." (*Wyoming Lawyer*, October 2002, p 16)

Supreme Court justices who are standing for retention appear on all ballots statewide. District and Circuit Court judges appear on ballots in their jurisdiction. If judges fail to file a declaration to stand for retention, or if a majority votes against retention, their seats are vacant.

Very rarely a judge or justice will lose a seat through the retention process. Typically, judicial retention gets little attention in an election season.

The Judicial Nominating Commission considers applicants for vacant judgeships on the Wyoming Supreme Court, the district courts, and the circuit courts. The commission then submits three names to the governor, who appoints one from the list for each vacancy.

The Nominating Commission has seven members. The chief justice of the Wyoming Supreme Court serves as chair. Three other members, who are selected by the Wyoming State Bar, must be attorneys in active legal practice. Three non-lawyers are appointed by the governor. Commission members serve four-year terms and are not eligible for a second term.

The Commission on Judicial Conduct and Ethics was created by constitutional amendment Article 5, Section 6 in 1996. The commission investigates allegations of judicial misconduct or disability against Supreme Court justices, district and circuit court judges, magistrates, municipal court judges, and other judicial officers. The commission may find a complaint untrue, may discipline a judicial official, or may recommend discipline of a judicial officer to the Wyoming Supreme Court or a special supreme court. The high court then makes a final determination: suspension, removal, or mandatory retirement.

The Commission on Judicial Conduct and Ethics has twelve members who serve three-year terms and are eligible for reappointment to a second term. Membership consists of:
- Two district judges and one circuit judge elected by their peers
- Three members of the Wyoming State Bar who have practiced law in Wyoming for at least ten years and are selected by its governing body
- Six citizens who are not judges or lawyers and are appointed by the governor and confirmed by the Wyoming Senate

The Judicial Council was created by order of the Supreme Court on June 8, 1981, to include all judges of all courts in the state. They are to meet each year at the annual Wyoming State Bar convention, where they exchange ideas and experiences.

The State Board of Continuing Legal Education is appointed by the Wyoming Supreme Court. The board supervises rules of the Supreme Court concerning requirements for continuing legal education for Wyoming State Bar members.

Supreme Court

The Supreme Court is the highest court in Wyoming. It is the highest court of appeal from rulings in lower courts in civil and criminal cases. It also has original jurisdiction in unusual cases that are filed and first heard there. Cases that involve a question of federal law can be appealed to the U.S. Supreme Court. Most cases docketed in the Wyoming Supreme Court are appeals by people who are challenging decisions of a District Court. Decisions by the Supreme Court are definitive statements on Wyoming law that are binding on all other courts and state agencies, unless changed by legislative action. (*Overview of Wyoming Courts* 2003, p. 1)

The Wyoming Supreme Court may rule in matters concerning the performance of duties by state officers, including the power to issue writs of mandamus. A writ of mandamus is an order to a lower court or

Wyoming Supreme Court Building is part of a complex of state office buildings in Cheyenne. It contains the State Law Library and the offices and courtroom for the Wyoming Supreme Court. In 2006, the bulding was renovated, and the State Library was moved out of the basement to a building that previously housed the Laramie County Public Library.

public official to perform a particular act. The Supreme Court specifies the number, selection, election, term, and quorum of justices for the Supreme Court. It sets the time period for the filling of vacancies on the bench and sets forth the rules and structure of the Judicial Nominating Commission and the Commission on Judicial Conduct and Ethics and their voting procedures.

The Supreme Court also exercises administrative supervision over the Wyoming State Bar. It regulates the practice of law in the state and admits new attorneys to that practice.

Rarely, the Supreme Court may decide that a statute or ordinance fails to meet requirements of the U.S. Constitution or Wyoming Constitution, and the justices will declare the law unconstitutional. The court did this in 1981 and 1995 with statutes governing financing of public schools. Opinions set into motion decades of legislative work and litigation in lower courts in an attempt to find a financing scheme that complied with constitutional guarantees to equal protection and to a "complete and uniform education." (Wyoming Constitution, art. 7)

The Supreme Court holds at least two terms annually in Cheyenne. Justices may determine their sessions by date and time.

Wyoming Supreme Court in 2006 Left to right: Justice Barton R. Voigt, Justice Michael Golden, Chief Justice William U. Hill, Justice Marilyn S. Kite, Justice E. James Burke   (Wyoming Supreme Court photo)

The five Supreme Court justices may serve until the mandatory retirement age of 70. They stand for retention one year after they are appointed and every eight years after that. They may not practice law while they are on the bench, and they must "recuse" themselves from cases they have been involved in, to avoid even the appearance of a conflict of interest.

The first woman named to the Supreme Court was Marilyn Kite, appointed by Gov. Jim Geringer. She was sworn in June 2, 2000.

The five justices select the chief justice, who serves for four years, presides at meetings of the court and in conference, and represents the high court on commissions.

Court staff includes a court coordinator and clerical assistants who are responsible for the court's budget, fiscal control, court technology, and purchase and maintenance of court property. The court appoints the Clerk of the Supreme Court, who collects fees and keeps records and papers of all cases. The clerk also distributes opinions and orders of the court. Staff attorneys help justices in legal research. (*Overview of Wyoming Courts* 2003, p. 2) (Also, see *Wyoming Court Rules Annotated* 2002)

One of the most important roles of Supreme Court is to guide decisions by lower court judges through the "precedents" set in the high court's opinions. A precedent is a decided case that furnishes a basis for determining a similar case that may arise later or a similar question of law. (*Dictionary of Modern Legal Usage* 1995, p.680)

Supreme Court rulings build on precedents set in rulings by previous Supreme Court justices. On rare occasions, justices will change a principle established by previous courts, and this new precedent becomes the law of Wyoming. Lower courts rely on Supreme Court opinions for guidance in their own rulings, so major changes by the justices can affect decisions throughout the court system in Wyoming

Supreme Court opinions are available in the State Law Library, housed in the Supreme Court building in Cheyenne, and in county law libraries. They also are published by the Wyoming State Bar Association in its bi-monthly magazine, *Wyoming Reporter.* Photocopies of rulings are available, for a fee, from the clerk of the Supreme Court.

One of Wyoming's outstanding jurists was Willis VanDevanter, the only person to be appointed to the U.S. Supreme Court from Wyoming.

As was true of all Wyoming justices during the first 60 years of statehood, VanDevanter was born and educated outside Wyoming. He was born in Indiana on April 17, 1859, and received his law degree at Cincinnati College in 1881. In 1889, President Benjamin Harrison appointed him chief jusice of the Supreme Court in territorial Wyoming. He was elected to the first Supreme Court of the state of Wyoming in 1890, although he served for just four days before resigning to resume private law practice. (In the early days of statehood, justices were popularly elected.)

Wyoming Republicans selected VanDevanter as chairman of the Republican Central Committee (1892-94), as delegate to the Republican National Convention in 1896, and as a member of the Republican National Committee (1896-1900). He was named Assistant U.S. Attorney General 1897, and he served until 1903, when he was named to the Eighth U.S. Circuit Court (1903-1910). VanDevanter then was appointed associate justice on the U.S. Supreme Court, where he served 1910-1937. (Miller 1981, p.172)

District Courts

District courts are the trial courts of general jurisdiction in Wyoming. District judges preside over felony criminal and civil cases, as

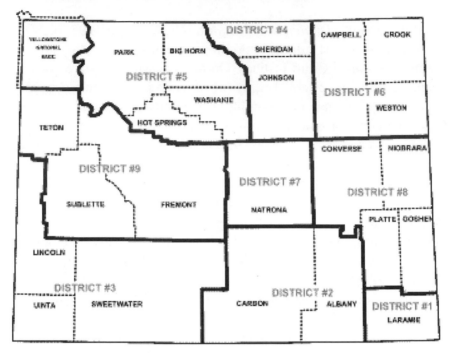

Nine judicial districts in Wyoming's State District Court system.

well as juvenile and probate matters and all initial appeals from the lower courts. The times for court sessions are set by the Legislature. Jurisdiction is unlimited, except that small claims and misdemeanors are heard in circuit courts. A provision is made for district court commissioners to perform chamber business and do other business outside of the court itself (Wyoming Constitution, art.5, secs. 10-14).

District judges stand for retention every six years. As with justices, they cannot practice law or hold any other office, and they may serve until age 70. A district judge must be an attorney, at least 28 years old, a U.S. citizen, and a resident of Wyoming for at least two years.

Wyoming is divided into nine judicial districts, served by 21 judges. Laramie and Natrona counties have case loads large enough to constitute their own judicial districts, with three judges each. Other districts include more than one county.

Judicial Districts:

First District -- Laramie County
Second District -- Albany and Carbon Counties

Third District -- Lincoln, Sweewater, and Uinta Counties
Fourth District -- Johnson and Sheridan Counties
Fifth District -- Big Horn, Hot Springs, Park, and Washakie Counties
Sixth District -- Campbell, Crook, and Weston Counties
Seventh District -- Natrona County
Eighth District -- Converse, Goshen, Niobrara, Platte Counties
Ninth District -- Fremont, Sublette, and Teton Counties.

District court is held in each county seat, so the judges must travel to all counties in their district to hear cases that arise there. In addition, district judges may be asked to help out and hear cases in other districts or to sit on cases in the Supreme Court, if a justice there has been excused from a case.

Each district judge hires a court reporter to keep a word-for-word record and prepare written transcripts of court proceedings. Each district court has a clerk to keep court records and maintain case files. Voters elect a district court clerk, who keeps a docket showing all cases filed and decided. The district court clerk also manages the calling and initial examination of jurors for the court.

Circuit Courts

Circuit courts have replaced the former county courts. The civil jurisdiction covers cases involving damages up to $7,000. Circuit courts also hear family violence cases and criminal cases involving misdemeanors. The circuit may also have the jurisdiction of a municipal court over ordinance violations if a municipality requests it, and if the Supreme Court consents to a consolidation of courts. The circuit court may set bail for a defendant, and it conducts preliminary hearings to determine if there is sufficient evidence for a person accused of a felony to stand trial in district court.

Circuit court judges are appointed by the governor, as are Supreme Court justices and district judges. They stand for retention every four years. They must be attorneys admitted to the Wyoming Bar and must be qualified voters. If a county has no resident circuit judge, the county commissioners may appoint a full-time magistrate. There are full-time magistrates in Johnson, Niobrara, Platte, Washakie, and Weston counties. Some magistrates are considered part-time and are not required to be trained in the law. They usually are located in remote, sparsely populated areas of the state. A law-trained magistrate may perform all the duties of the circuit judge.

Municipal Courts

The municipal court system is operated in all incorporated cities and towns. They deal with all ordinance violations. They have no civil jurisdiction. Municipal court judges may assess penalties of up to $750 and six months in jail.

Municipal court judges are appointed by the mayor with consent of the city or town council, which set the terms. Most municipal judges are part-time. About one-half are lawyers. A municipal court conviction can be appealed to the district court.

Justices of the Peace -- Gone

The Justice of the Peace courts ceased to exist in Wyoming in 2003, 136 years after the state's first Justice of the Peace, Robert Tate, received his appointment to serve Laramie County. He was appointed on January 9, 1867, by the Dakota Legislative Assembly.

The office of Justice of the Peace figured into Wyoming's history of women's rights. The Territorial Legislature enacted a bill granting women the right to vote in 1869. Just three months later, on February 17, 1870, Esther Hobart Morris was appointed Justice of the Peace in South Pass City, the first woman to hold the office.

In 1967, the Wyoming Constitution was amended to repeal sections that authorized Justice of the Peace courts, and the Legislature was given authority to establish subordinate courts. In 1971, the Legislature used that authority to establish the county court system, which it replaced in 2000 with the circuit court system. With these two court systems, counties had the opportunity to abolish the county-funded justice of the peace system and replace it with a court system funded by the state.

The justice of the peace system was criticized because the justices were not required to have legal backgrounds, and nearly anyone could be appointed a JP. Also, JPs in counties of fewer than 1,500 people were paid by the case, so a larger caseload meant more income. It implied a frontier flavor and was defended in the Legislature in the

1980s as a symbol of independence and a decentralized justice system.

By late 2002, only six Wyoming counties had justices of the peace: Johnson, Niobrara, Platte, Teton, Washakie, and Weston. In December of that year, they signed resolutions abolishing their justice of the peace courts. On January 6, 2003, all counties in Wyoming had circuit courts as courts of limited jurisdiction.

Wyoming State Bar

The University of Wyoming Law School is the primary source of lawyers in Wyoming. As in territorial days, the legal community is well educated, has diverse interests in the state, and has a strong commitment to Wyoming. Many attorneys serve on advisory boards and commissions as well as in the Legislature.

The Wyoming State Bar is the official organization of attorneys and judges in the state, and it officially acts under the authority of the Wyoming Supreme Court. An attorney must be a member to practice law in the state. To be admitted to the Bar, a person must graduate from a law school approved by the American Bar Association, pass the Bar examination, and have good character.

Through the Bar, lawyers make sure members of their profession adhere to a code of ethical standards, called the Code of Professional Conduct. Violation of these standards can result in censure or, in serious cases, disbarment. An attorney may be suspended for a period time or may be disbarred and permanently lose privileges to practice law in Wyoming.

Women in the Courtroom

The first woman admitted to the Wyoming Bar was Dr. Grace Raymond Hebard of Laramie, admitted on December 22, 1914. She had been admitted to practice before the district court in Laramie on November 18, 1898. The first woman to actually practice law in Wyoming was Grace McDonald Phillips, of Newcastle and Casper, who was admitted to the bar on April 19, 1920. That was one day before women were granted the right to vote by amendment to the U.S. Constitution. (*Wyoming Almanac* 2001, p. 210).

It took longer for the status of women as jurors to be settled.

The Organic Act of 1868, Section 9 relating to courts, made no provision for the qualification of jurors. The Legislative Assembly provided that juries be composed of "male" citizens, although an all-woman jury heard a trial in Laramie in 1870.

Twenty years later, the Wyoming Constitution was adopted to say in Article 1, Section 9, that a civil trial jury could consist of fewer than 12 "men."

In 1892, Wyoming Supreme Court Justice Herman V.S. Groesbeck considered an appeal that challenged the validity of a petit jury because it included no women. The appeal quoted Article 6, Section 1 of the Wyoming Constitution: "Both male and female citi-

The first Wyoming state court jury with women members pose after the trial of State of Wyoming vs. Otto Long on May 10, 1950, in Green River. Jurors are, left to right: (front row) Dona Schultz of Reliance, Kathryn Auld of Reliance, Mrs. John Wilde of Rock Springs, Mrs. Dave Rauzi of Rock Springs, Louise Graf of Green River (foreman); (back row) Mrs. Dan Marshall of Rock Springs, Frank Parton of Rock Springs, Hugh Sweeney, South of Rock Springs, Floyd Henry of Farson and Alva Qualls of Superior. Not pictured: George Palko of Rock Springs. (Wyoming State Archives photo)

zens of this state shall equally enjoy all civil, political, and religious rights and privileges."

Groesbeck said the right to vote and hold office did not include the right to serve as juror, and only a female defendant could demand a female jury.

Then in 1949, the Wyoming Legislature amended the law dealing with jurors' qualifications and referred to a juror's having possession of "his or her" natural faculties. The next year, the Wyoming Supreme Court upheld the law, saying the word "men" in the Constitution did not prevent the Legislature from passing the "Women on Jury Act." Justice Ralph Kimball wrote that, after all, women had served as jurors in territorial days.

On May 8, 1950, court convened in Green River to hear the trial of Otto Long, a coal miner accused of shooting another coal miner to death. One hundred men and women were called to be on the jury. After two days of testimony and one hour, 35 minutes of deliberation, the jury of six men and six women convicted Long of second degree murder. He was sentenced to 20-21 years in prison. Defense attorney Walter Muir Sr. had a reputation of seldom losing a criminal case and said afterward he would never have lost the case if it hadn't been for "those damn women on the jury." (*Wyoming Blue Book* 1974, vol. 3, pp. 422-425)

Public Defender System

An important part of the legal system in Wyoming rests with the public defender system. Its attorneys are charged with defending indigent persons (those who cannot afford representation) accused of crimes that could result in imprisonment. The Legislature passed the Wyoming Public Defender Act in 1978 to comply with rulings by the U.S. Supreme Court that the Sixth Amendment requires states to provide counsel to indigents charged with criminal offenses. The program also is responsible for representing juveniles charged as delinquents, people facing revocation of probation or parole, and those who are to be extradited to other states. Public defenders do not handle cases in municipal or federal court.

The Public Defender's Office is an independent agency in the executive branch of government, serving the public from 16 field offices. Public defenders are appointed by the governor. They must be members in good standing of the Wyoming State Bar. The judge presiding in a case also may appoint private attorneys who have volunteered to be available for these cases. Wyoming also provides a limited amount of civil legal aid assistance for people too poor to hire a private attorney.

Cameras in the Courtroom

Rule 53 of the Wyoming Rules of Criminal Procedure allows extended media coverage in both trial and appellate courts.

The judge may permit photographs in his or her courtroom during proceedings or radio or television broadcasting of the proceedings, with the following restrictions:

- Photographers must ask the judge for approval at least 24 hours before the proceedings, and they must get approval for use of their equipment. Requests are allowed only by representatives of accredited news media, and use for unrelated advertising purposes is prohibited.
- The judge may require that photographic and broadcast coverage of a trial be "pooled." That means one journalist records the proceedings and makes the material available to the others.
- Rules prohibit use of distracting sound or light, moving equipment during court proceedings, or entering the courtroom to take photographs or broadcast after the session has begun.
- Rules prohibit close-up photography of jurors.

Trial judges have broad discretion in limiting photographic coverage, as did Second Judicial District Judge Jeffrey Donnell for the murder trials of defendants in the slaying of University of Wyoming student Matthew Shepard in 1999. Judge Donnell limited media representatives to 24 seats in the courtroom in Laramie. He also prohibited cameras, audio recording, laptop computers, cellular phones, or other electronic equipment.

Judicial Procedure: Criminal and Civil

Most of the matters that come before the judicial system are in the form of cases, which are disputes to be resolved or complaints to be settled with the court's help. The two major categories of cases are criminal and civil. There also are juvenile matters and probate cases involving wills, trusts, and estates.

Criminal Cases

A criminal case develops through four stages before it is ready for trial: 1) investigation and arrest, 2) initial appearance, 3) preliminary hearing, and 4) arraignment. Alternatively, a district judge may summon a "grand jury" to hear evidence and return criminal indictments against individuals. (Wyoming Statutes 7-5-101) An indictment is considered sufficient grounds for taking the case to trial, and a preliminary hearing is unnecessary. The governor or attorney general may request a district attorney to summon a grand jury with statewide jurisdiction. (Wyoming Statutes 7-5-301)

Two counties have enough population (60,000 resident) to qualify as judicial districts in their own right: Laramie County and Natrona County. As such, they qualify for their own "district attorneys," to prosecute criminal cases. District attorneys are popularly elected in partisan races, and the expenses of their offices are covered by the state. Other judicial districts also may create a state-supported office of a district attorney. However, it requires the approval of the county commissions of all counties in the district. (Wyoming Statutes 9-1-801). The advantage to those counties would be having state resources to do a better job prosecuting criminal cases.

Criminal cases involve violations of the criminal law of the state. A felony is the most serious criminal offense. Felonies are offenses that may be punished by imprisonment for one year or longer. Misdemeanors include all other offenses, which can be punished by up to a year in the county jail.

Investigation and Arrest. The court begins its work on a criminal case after law enforcement authorities or the district or county attorney files a citation or an "information." An information is an accusation made under oath by a prosecutor. A circuit court judge or a magistrate may issue a search warrant if there is probable cause to believe the property to be searched contains evidence that a crime has been committed and a particular person committed the crime. These procedures are carried out in compliance with Article 4 of the U.S. Constitution and Article 1 of the Wyoming Constitution. These articles protect citizens from "unreasonable searches and seizures" and mandate that "no warrant shall issue except on probable cause."

As the criminal investigation proceeds, the district or county attorney files an information or citation with the circuit court, or the city attorney files a complaint in municipal court. If the information, citation, or complaint establishes probable cause that the individual has committed the crime, the circuit judge, magistrate, or municipal judge issues an arrest warrant.

Initial Appearance. The accused is arrested and brought before the circuit judge or magistrate without unnecessary delay. The judge informs the accused of the charge and of rights under the law. The accused has the right to counsel (an attorney). The state will provide an attorney if the accused cannot afford one, unless the defendant waives the right to counsel. The judge sets bail at the initial appearance. The judge may require sureties or bond to guarantee the defendant will show up for the trial. The judge also may restrict travel by the accused or order the accused to be put in detention pending the trial, if considered necessary to make sure the accused appears for trial.

Preliminary Hearing. A preliminary hearing is held to determine if there is enough evidence against the defendant to justify a trial. This step is to prevent the possibility of unjustified prosecution of an individual. If a circuit judge or magistrate is satisfied that probable cause has been established, the judge orders the defendant bound over to district court for arraignment and trial. If evidence does not establish probable cause, the judge dismisses the case, although the prosecutor can charge the person again for the same crime later.

Arraignment. The defendant is arraigned in the court where the trial will occur — in district court for a felony or in circuit court for a misdemeanor – and enters a plea. If the defendant pleads guilty, and if the judge accepts the plea, the case goes directly to sentencing. If the plea is "not guilty," the case goes to trial. Most cases do not result in full-fledged trials. Some are dismissed by the prosecutor or by the court. In other cases, the defendant pleads guilty. (*Overview of Wyoming Courts* 2003, 5)

Civil Cases

A civil action takes place between two or more persons. Government bodies, corporations, or businesses are included in the legal definition of "persons."

Pleadings. Initial papers in a civil case are called pleadings. The case begins when a plaintiff files a complaint against a defendant in the appropriate court, claiming some wrongful act or infringement of legal rights. Lawsuits are filed for damages. Cases include lawsuits for property damage or personal injury, disputes over contracts or real estate, divorces, and a wide variety of other controversies.

The court issues a summons to the defendant describing the complaint and requiring an answer. The defendant may also file a counter-claim.

Discovery. Fact-finding by both the plaintiff and defendant is called "discovery." It usually involves getting information about documents and witnesses, by oral and written questions, by a physical or mental examination, or by requests for documents or other physical evidence. Some information is privileged and cannot be required, including information from husband-wife, doctor-patient, or lawyer-client relationship.

Pretrial Conference. Either party may call for a conference before the trial to discuss matters that may simplify the dispute and save time in the trial. The parties may agree on a certain set of facts, amend the pleadings, or limit the number of witnesses. The court then issues an order that sums up actions of the conference.

Mediation. Court rules allow the district court to assign a civil case for mediation or arbitration, to dispose of the case more quickly and more cheaply than by a trial.

Trial

Trials are similar for civil and criminal cases. Opposing sides present arguments, evidence, and testimony, and the jury or judge decides the case. The right to trial by jury is widely preserved in Wyoming in both criminal and civil cases. Juries in criminal trials in district court consist of twelve persons. Civil trials in other courts usually have six jurors. The county clerk draws a pool of potential jurors, a "panel," at the start of a jury term. They are supposed to be representative of the whole population of the county. The court and attorneys select a jury from the panel, which is sworn in and the trial begins.

Plaintiffs (in civil cases) or prosecutors (in criminal cases) present their case first, and then the defendants presents their case. The judge or jury then gives a verdict. In criminal trials, the prosecutor must prove a case beyond a reasonable doubt, and jury verdicts must be unanimous. The burden is on the prosecutor; a defendant is not compelled to prove innocence.

Civil cases are decided by a preponderance of the evidence, and jury verdicts may be less than unanimous if the parties agree to a percentage. The judge or jury may find the defendants are not liable or determine they are responsible for the plaintiffs' injury. The judge or jury who finds civil defendants guilty will determine how much money they will pay. They do not face imprisonment. The court enters a judgment that contains the verdict or decision.

Sentencing comes next in the criminal process. The judge requests a presentence investigation in felony cases, to determine the appropriate sentence.

Appeal

The right to appeal in criminal cases is absolute. In civil cases, the right of appeal is governed by the law and court rules. Appeal of a death sentence is automatic.

District court decisions are appealed to the Wyoming Supreme Court. Circuit court decisions are appealed to district court. They can be appealed further to the Supreme Court, if the justices agree to the appeal and issue a "writ of certiorari." Appeals must be based on questions of law, and they must be based on what happened in the trial court. The party who loses a case and files an appeal is called the "appellant," and the other party is the "appellee." Usually the criminal sentence or civil judgment is delayed, or "stayed," while the appeal is pending. Both sides submit written arguments to the court and then make oral arguments, during which the justices may ask questions. This step is the most visible to the public in the appellate process.

In 1987, the Wyoming Supreme Court implemented the "expedited" docket procedure for cases that require a quick decision. Cases assigned to the expedited docket do not have oral arguments.

The five justices discuss the cases and reach majority decisions. One justice writes up the opinion and others in agreement sign it. Other justices may write dissenting opinions to say why they disagree, or they may write concurring opinions to say how they use different reasoning to arrive at the same conclusion of the majority. An opinion may affirm the decision of the trial court or reverse the decision -- or affirm in part and reverse in part. If reversed, the case may be "remanded" back to the trial court to be heard again.

Supreme Court rulings usually build on principles of law established in rulings by previous Supreme Court justices. These are called "precedents." On rare occasions, justices will change a principle established by previous courts, and this new precedent becomes the law of Wyoming. Lower courts rely on Supreme Court opinions for guidance in their own rulings.

Supreme Court opinions are available in the State Law Library and in county law libraries. They are published by the Wyoming State Bar Association, and photocopies are available from the clerk of the Supreme Court.

Special Cases

Courts hear a variety of special types of civil and criminal cases:
- Small claims of up to $7,000 constitute a special division of civil cases that can be decided according to informal procedures in the circuit courts.
- Juvenile matters, which include violations of criminal law or the juvenile code by persons under age 19, are heard according to procedures that are more informal than adult criminal procedures.
- County attorneys can decide if a case is to be heard in juvenile court, circuit court, or district court. When the juvenile defendant is older than age 17, most misdemeanors and major

crimes are heard in district courts; others automatically go to juvenile court. Juvenile proceedings may occur in a closed court room or in a judge's chambers. In all cases, the judge of district court may transfer any juvenile case to another court.

• Probate cases involve trusts and wills and estates of deceased persons. One kind of trust manages assets for minor children (minor is younger than 19 years old, which is the "age of majority"). When probate cases are contested, there can be a hearing as in other civil matters; otherwise, most probate matters are handled by judges and court clerks without formal hearings.

Federal Courts

Cases with federal jurisdiction fall in three basic categories::

• The cases involve federal questions. These involve the United States government, the U.S. Constitution, federal laws, or controversies between states or between the United States and foreign governments. For instance, the U.S. Attorney would prosecute violations of federal law in federal court. A person alleging violation of his civil rights or challenging actions by a federal agency would take the case to federal court.

• A case may go to federal court if it claims damages of more than $75,000 and the people involved are from different states or from the United States and another country. This is called "diversity of citizenship." A case would be in the U.S. District Court in Cheyenne or Casper if the case had a connection to Wyoming -- if one of the litigants or the event that caused the lawsuit were in Wyoming. For instance, a lawsuit involving people from different states who collided as they drove through Yellowstone National Park would be heard in U.S. District Court in Wyoming.

• Federal courts have jurisdiction over bankruptcy cases. Individuals or businesses that cannot pay creditors go to U.S. Bankruptcy Court in Cheyenne to seek a court-supervised liquidation of their assets, or they may reorganize their financial affairs and work out a plan to pay off their debts.

(*Source:* Administrative Office of the United States Courts)

The United States District Court has three judges who hear cases in federal courtrooms in Cheyenne and Casper. In addition, two federal appeals courts have jurisdiction in Wyoming. One is the U.S. Supreme Court in Washington, D.C., which is the highest and last court of appeal for every jurisdiction in the United States. The other is the Tenth U.S. Circuit Court of Appeals, one of eleven such courts in the United States. The court is in Denver, although it has two judges located in Cheyenne. The fourth element of the federal court system is the U.S. Bankruptcy Court, located in Cheyenne.

One other important court established in Wyoming in 1988 is the Shoshone and Arapaho Tribal Court on the Wind River Indian Reservation. It handles misdemeanors and civil cases arising on the reservation and enforces tribal codes. It is not connected with the state of Wyoming court system. (Read more about the tribal court in Chapter 11, Tribal Government.)

Chapter 7

Local Government

The political structure of the United States follows the principle of "federalism." At the top is a national government, organized by the U.S. Constitution, which is a union of 50 individual state and their governments.

Below that level are political subdivisions of the state – every county, city, incorporated and unincorporated town, school district, and special district within the state. They are formed according to the state Constitution and state laws and are subject to their restrictions, including open meetings and open records laws. The exception is "home rule," by which a municipality may exempt itself from a statutory requirement.

A subdivision of the State of Wyoming must have the following qualities, according to the Wyoming Supreme Court (*Witzenburger v. State ex rel. Wyoming Community Development Authority* 575 P.2D 110, 113). A subdivision:

1. Has a geographic area smaller than the state.
2. Is organized with officers elected by its inhabitants to carry on a governmental function.
3. Has a local purpose.
4. Has a provision for the levy and assessment of taxes to finance those purposes.

Political subdivisions can be general purpose or special purpose.

General purpose units are county and municipal governments. Special purpose units can be special districts or school districts. Special districts can form for soil and water conservation, recreation, weed and pest control, or other narrow purpose within a community. The state, through the Constitution and laws, sets forth the boundaries of the local government units and specifies their powers and functions, structure, ability to raise revenue, election processes and hiring practices. (Cawley et al. 1996, p. 127)

Local governments affect virtually every aspect of our day-to-day lives with law enforcement, fire protection, road construction and repair, public schools, drinking water, sewage, building codes, garbage pickup and landfill, utilities, hospitals, libraries, recreation centers, weed and pest control, and other services. Local government is the government closest and most responsive to the citizens, who can speak personally with the elected officials and appear at sessions where proposals are being considered. Citizens have the opportunity to participate in their local governments and to hold them accountable, although they do not always take that opportunity.

Local government is often where citizens first enter the political process themselves. Many members of the Legislature began their political careers on county commissions or school boards.

Local governments raise most of their revenue through property taxes and sales taxes. (See Chapter 15, "Revenue: Paying for Government.")

County Government

Counties were the basic administrative subdivision of territorial government, as they are now subdivisions of the state. Article 12 of the Wyoming Constitution gives the state the authority to create counties, draw their boundaries, designate a county seat, and define their powers and responsibilities. Wyoming had just four counties when it became a territory in 1869 and 13 at statehood in 1890. (See Appendix 2, "Counties As Created and Organized by Dakota and Wyoming Laws 1867-1923".)

The Wyoming Legislature created new counties as it thought necessary with growth in population and assessed valuation. The twenty-second and twenty-third counties were Sublette and Teton, created by the 1921 Legislature. Article 14 of the Constitution requires the state to designate county offices and fix salaries of the county officers.

A county is created when it is "organized." The process is laid out in Title 18, Article 3 of Wyoming Statutes:

- At least 300 qualified electors who are property owners must sign a petition to the governor to organize a new county and establish a county government. The petition asks the governor to appoint three commissioners.

- The proposed county must contain at least 3,000 residents and property value of at least $7 million.
- The action must leave at least 5,000 people and taxable property of at least $9 million in the county or counties from which the new county was formed.
- The commissioners named by the governor appoint a clerk and hold a special election among people in the proposed new county on the question of organizing..

Counties in Wyoming are governed by a board of commissioners, which are elected at large from the county. They run as representatives of political parties. The boards combine legislative and executive powers into one body: they make laws and carry them out. State law provides for boards of three commissioners, although the law allows voters to increase members to five. Five counties had five-member boards in 2006: Campbell, Fremont, Natrona, Teton, and Weston.

County governments have extensive authority. They make rules, regulations, and ordinances that govern the property of a county, and they may zone unincorporated areas of the county. They operate libraries and may create day care centers. They build and maintain roads and bridges. They raise money by levying taxes and issuing bonds. They spend county revenue and grant licenses and franchises.

Title 18 of Wyoming Statutes describes the duties and authority for the commissioners and seven county officers: assessor, attorney, clerk, sheriff, surveyor, and treasurer. The commissioners, assessor, clerk, sheriff, treasurer, and sometimes county attorney are elected. Briefly, their duties are:

- Assessor - The assessor maintains records on the ownership and assessed value of taxable property in the county.
- County and Prosecuting Attorneys – Every county may hire an attorney to represent the county in court and handle civil matters. If there is no district attorney in a county's judicial district, the county may elect an attorney to prosecute criminal matters.
- Clerk – The clerk keeps the seal and county records, keeps track of all county commission actions, and signs commission orders. The clerk also supervises elections and voter registration.
- Sheriff – The sheriff is responsible for keeping the peace outside incorporated cities and towns and for running the county jail.

- Surveyor – The surveyor is hired by the commission to conduct all surveys for the county and keep a plat of official surveys on file.
- Treasurer – The treasurer collects taxes and keeps accounts of receipts and expenditures for the county. The treasurer's office also registers motor vehicles and issues license plates.

In addition, every county elects a coroner, which is covered in Title 7 (Criminal Procedure) of state law. Most coroners are part-time and do not have medical training, although state law requires them to take a "basic coroner course." According to state law, coroners investigate deaths that involve violent or criminal action, apparent suicide, accident, apparent drug or chemical overdose or toxicity, someone who was not under a doctor's care, apparent child abuse, an unknown cause, or someone who was a prisoner or patient at a state facility.

Counties may issue revenue bonds but must observe a debt limit set by the Wyoming Constitution, which is 2 percent of assessed property value of the county. County governments can raise money with two optional one-cent sales taxes, with approval of the voters. They collect the property taxes assessed by the county government and by the various districts in the county, including the school district.

A major issue for county governments and residents is the ability of municipalities to annex an area of the county without the consent of the residents. When land becomes part of a city or town, the county no longer receives property taxes from that land.

Municipal Government

There were 98 municipalities in Wyoming in 2005, 17 of them classified as "first-class cities." The "first-class" designation is given to municipalities that have at least 4,000 residents and that apply for the status, according to the Wyoming Association of Municipalities (WAM).

Article 13 of the Wyoming Constitution directs the Legislature to write laws for the incorporation of cities, for the annexation of additional land to existing cities and towns and for procedures for cities and towns to merge, consolidate or dissolve.

Title 15 of Wyoming Statutes cover municipal government. This article was amended in 1972 to give municipalities the ability to assert "home rule." Before that time, they had only the powers given to them by the state. Under home rule, a city or town can approve a "charter ordinance" that exempts it from a particular provision of state law. The effect is to amend their municipal charter. It can be passed three ways. The governing body can pass a charter ordinance by a two-thirds vote. The residents may petition to put such an ordinance on the ballot and then pass it by a two-thirds vote. Or the governing body can put it on the ballot, and the voters can approve it with a majority.

Municipalities have no choice about the limits on indebtedness imposed by the state.

Cities have used the provision for home rule to create city administrator forms of government.

The state issues municipal charters of incorporation to areas that have a population of at least 500 people and cover an area of three square miles or less. The county then appoints three inspectors, who oversee an election by people in the area. If they approve the proposal to incorporate, they then elect officers, and then the incorporation is completed. The process also requires publication of the original request to the state and then the approval. The municipality remains incorporated, even if the population drops below 500, unless residents vote to dissolve the municipality.

People who live in municipalities live with restrictions imposed by the government and must pay to support the local government and its projects. They also get services: police and fire protection, water treatment and distribution systems, sewage treatment, garbage collection and disposal, health regulations, and weed and pest control. Municipalities also regulate land use through planning and zoning ordinances. They create and maintain streets, roads, alleys, bridges, and sewers. They also provide amenities, including parks, museums, recreational facilities, and cemeteries. They grant franchises to companies that provide telephone and cable services and telephone, gas and electric utilities.

Municipalities get revenue to pay for their services and projects from various sources: sales and property taxes, federal mineral royalties, license and user fees, federal and state grants and loans, bond issues and interest income. Municipalities are held to a debt limit imposed by the state, although their water systems are exempt. The 17 first-class cities in Wyoming in 2005 were Casper, Cheyenne, Cody, Douglas, Evanston, Gillette, Green River, Kemmerer, Lander, Laramie, Newcastle, Powell, Rawlins, Riverton, Rock Springs, Sheridan, and Worland.

The designations of "city" and "town" are based on population. They determine the size of the governing body, the terms of members and their duties and responsibilities. (Cawley et al. 1996, p. 136)

Cities and towns in Wyoming have four kinds of municipal governments:

- Mayor and City/Town Council
- City Manager
- City Commission
- City Administrator (requires passage of charter ordinance)

Organizational charts at the end of this chapter describe municipal governments used by four cities and towns in Wyoming: Cheyenne, Casper, Gillette, and Pinedale.

Mayor-Council

Most cities and towns use the mayor-council governing system,- known as the "strong mayor" system. Mayors are elected for two-year terms in towns and four-year terms in cities, and they serve as chief administrative officers. They oversee operations of municipal departments, they appoint and remove city officers, and they direct the budget process. (Cawley et al. 1996, p. 137) In 2005, three cities had full-time mayors with this form of government: Cheyenne, Sheridan, and Cody.

In this system, mayors also are part of the legislative process. They sit with the council members, preside over their meetings, vote on action items, and veto actions they oppose. It takes a two-thirds vote of council members to override vetoes.

Mayors also perform ceremonial duties of issuing proclamations, cutting ribbons, and greeting visiting dignitaries.

Members of both town councils and city councils serve four-year terms. Town councils have four members. The number of members on city councils depends on the number of wards in the city and the number of council seats assigned to each. For instance, Green River has three wards with two members each. Cheyenne has three wards with three members each. Councils enact ordinances, pass resolutions, approve mayoral appointments, set policy, adopt budgets, and authorize appropriations.

Council members may select a "president" from among themselves to preside when they meet as a "Committee of the Whole" or to preside at council meetings when the mayor is absent.

City Manager

In the city manager model of government – also called "council-manager" — city council members are elected, and then they hire an executive officer who is responsible to them. This model is similar to the parliamentary systems of Western Europe. Three Wyoming cities had this form of municipal government in 2005: Casper, Laramie, and Rawlins.

Voters elect a council to direct municipal policy. The number of council members depends on the population: municipalities with 4,000 residents have three council members; those with 4,000-20,000 have seven members; those larger than 20,000 population have nine members. They serve four-year, staggered terms. The council picks one of its members to be mayor, preside over council meetings, sign documents, and be the figurehead for the city.

The city manager is the chief executive officer, responsible for implementing actions by the council, hiring municipal employees except judges and city attorney.

Commission

Wyoming had no city commission forms of municipal government at the writing of this book.

Under this form of government, residents elect a mayor and two commissioners. It takes two votes to approve an action. The mayor cannot veto any measure, although every resolution or ordinance requires the signature of the mayor or the two commissioners to take effect.

Title 15, Chapter 4 of state law lays out the authority among the three. The mayor administers the department of public affairs and safety. The commissioner of finances and public property administers the department of accounts, finance, parks, and public property. This person also is the vice-president of the commission. The third commissioner administers the department of streets and public improvement.

They all hire the city clerk, attorney, treasurer, civil engineer, health officer, police chief, fire chief, and other officials.

City Administrator

The city administrator form is called the "weak mayor" system. The residents of a municipality elect a mayor and council. The mayor appoints a professional city administrator, who may be called a "manager," with the approval of the council. The administrator is responsible for the day-to-day management of city affairs, much like the city manager. The mayor has few executive duties.

In 2005, municipalities with city administrators were: Douglas, Gillette, Green River, Jackson, Kemmerer, Lovell, Lyman, and Powell.

Special Districts

Special districts are created to meet specific needs. Residents of a community who want new services or higher levels of an existing service form districts to serve the need. Residents pay for the new or enhanced services with a property tax. Special districts usually are created to provide one of three functions. They develop or maintain facilities, including bridges, airports, and parks. Or they provide services, including waste collection, health care, or weed and pest control. Or they engage in regulatory activity, including flood control or soil and water conservation. (Cawley 1996, p.142)

Districts authorized by state law are: special cemetery, conservation, fire protection, flood control, hospitals, improvement and service, special museum, rural health care, sanitary and improvement, water and sewer, watershed improvement, resort, and "other districts as specified by law." The resort special district was created by the 2003 Legislature to enhance facilities that serve tourists.

Special districts may cross county lines.

Laws governing the elections that form special districts are found primarily in Title 22 (Elections) and Title 18 (Counties) of Wyoming Statutes. State laws authorize formation of certain districts and specify the maximum property tax they can impose to support their activities.

Here is the process for creating a district:

• A petition to form a special district is filed with a county commission, signed by at least 25 percent of the landowners owning at least 25 percent of the assessed valuation of property in the area.

- The commission validates the signatures, checks the petition for accuracy, and evaluates the reason for the district. The commission also takes public comment on the proposal.
- If the commission approves the petition, the question goes on the ballot for all voters in the proposed district. The ballot includes election of officers and approval of a mill levy (property tax) to support the district's activities.

A petition to enlarge, consolidate, merge or dissolve a district must be signed by at least 25 percent of the voters owning at least 25 percent of the assessed valuation of property.

The mill levy must be reauthorized by voters in the district every two years on the general election ballot.

Forming special districts is a way for people in a given area to meet needs that are not covered by the general government of the county or municipality – needs that, in fact, might be peculiar to that limited area and group. Districts have the advantage of governing themselves, free of local partisan politics, and of raising their own revenue. Some have authority to impose a property tax, usually between 1 mill and 5 mills, and some may issue bonds. Special districts also can receive money from the State Board of Loans and Investments. People who live in a district must pay for the services, whether they voted for it or not.

Despite their potential to meet local needs, special districts tend to be a mystery to most voters, who are asked to elect officials and approve mill levies at election time.

Districts are governmental entities and are subject to legal requirements and restrictions, including open meetings and records laws, election procedures, bonding of treasurers, and handling public money. (Cawley 1996, p. 144)

School District Governments

School districts are the units of local government that operate public schools in Wyoming. Their particular kind of activity distinguishes them from other special districts.

The Tenth Amendment to the U.S. Constitution assigns responsibility for regulation of education largely to the states. Wyoming creates (and consolidates) districts and defines their boundaries so they can educate children in the district.

There are 48 school districts in Wyoming. They are governed by popularly elected boards of between five and nine trustees who serve four-year terms. The trustees run as nonpartisan candidates from the district at large or from single-member residence areas. School boards set policy, hire staff, buy textbooks, approve educational programs, determine the school calendar, and control the budget process.

The autonomy of school districts decreased after a Wyoming Supreme Court opinion in 1995 that clarified the state's constitutional responsibility to make sure public schools were funded adequately and equitably across the state. Several school districts, led by Campbell County School District One, had sued the state, claiming the system of financing schools violated the Wyoming Constitution. (*Campbell County School District v. State*, 907 P.2d) (Wyo. 1995)

The opinion was based on Article 1 of the Wyoming Constitution, which guarantees Wyoming citizens' right to an education, and Article 7, which requires the Legislature to "provide for the establishment and maintenance of a complete and uniform of public education."

The impact of the opinion was to declare that school district funding could not be based on taxes collected on the value of local property, which favored districts with mineral production. Previously, districts collected and spent local tax dollars, with some supplement from the state. This left great disparities among districts in money available to support education. The Supreme Court ruled property tax revenue collected locally must be available to all students across the state.

Over the years after the decision, the Legislature has struggled to devise a system to finance education and facilities to satisfy the constitutional mandate defined by the Supreme Court. As of 2005, challengers to the school finance system were individual school districts, the Wyoming Education Association, the Wyoming School Boards Association, and a coalition of small school districts. (School finance litigation is discussed more fully in Chapter 17.)

The Legislature set up a system to require collection of 25 mills property tax in each district. The Legislature devised a formula, roughly based on student enrollment and other cost considerations, to determine how much money each district should get. Districts that collected property taxes above the amount guaranteed to them by the funding formula had to send the extra revenue to the state School Foundation Account. There, the money was available to support other school districts.

With the new financing scheme came new requirements for accountability to the executive and legislative branches of state government, including statewide academic standards and testing, in addition to continuing accreditation requirements. While school districts lost some autonomy in making executive decisions, they received their funding as a "block grant" to be spent as district trustees thought best. However, legislators scrutinized local school district spending decisions to ensure good management.

Under the capital construction system crafted by the Legislature, districts no longer raised their own funds for construction. They also lost a great deal of autonomy over what kind of facilities were built, where they were built, and the programs they could offer as a result.

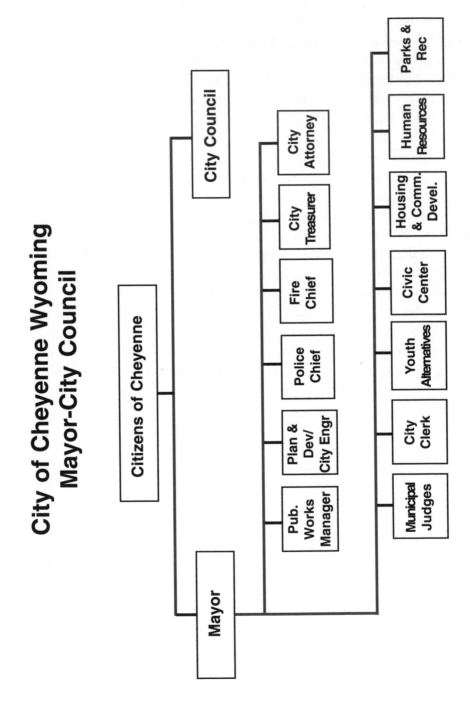

City of Cheyenne Wyoming
Mayor-City Council

Citizens of Cheyenne

City Council

Mayor

Pub. Works Manager

Plan & Dev/ City Engr

Police Chief

Fire Chief

City Treasurer

City Attorney

Municipal Judges

City Clerk

Youth Alternatives

Civic Center

Housing & Comm. Devel.

Human Resources

Parks & Rec

City of Casper, Wyoming Council-Manager

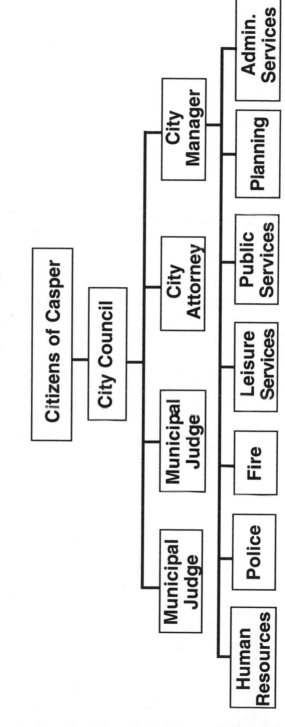

City of Gillette, Wyoming City Administrator

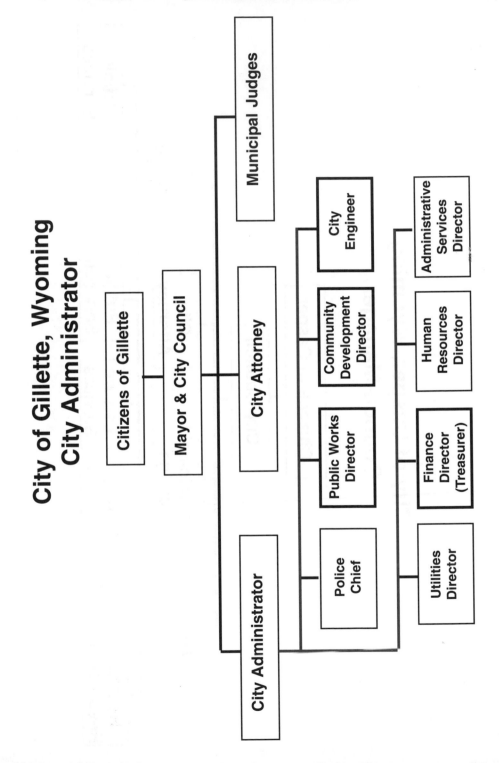

Town of Pinedale, Wyoming
Mayor-Town Council

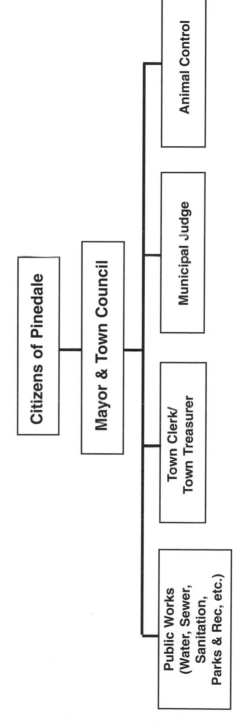

Citizens of Pinedale

Mayor & Town Council

Public Works
(Water, Sewer,
Sanitation,
Parks & Rec, etc.)

Town Clerk/
Town Treasurer

Municipal Judge

Animal Control

Chapter 8

Good Government

"Good government" describes laws, rules, and other measures intended to make government – state and local – open, accessible, accountable, and responsible to the people who are constituents of that government.

They include:

- Measures to require disclosure and reporting by officials, with the idea that the public should understand the interests and potential conflicts of the people who run for office and who serve them.
- Laws to address disclosure and reporting by lobbyists, whose job is to inform and influence the legislature and government agencies as they make rules and enact laws. Disclosure may reveal the influence of certain interest groups in the legislative decision-making process.
- Measures to prohibit certain behavior by legislators, elected officials, and public employees.
- Recording of votes and other actions by elected officials and making the records easily accessible to the public.
- Campaign finance reporting to enable voters to understand the financing of efforts to influence them. Candidates for state and local offices file reports with the Secretary of State's Office. Candidates for U.S. Senate and House file with the Federal Election Commission.
- Laws to require public access to public records and access to meetings where governmental bodies debate and vote.

Government Ethics

Title 9 of Wyoming Statutes, "Government Ethics," lays out the following prohibitions on behavior by public officials and employees:

- They may not use their position for private benefit, defined as a gift that resulted from their position. This excludes food or beverages. It also excludes entertainment, recreation, and tickets to an event with a value of $250 or less. The law specifically exempts attendance at conferences or other meetings they attend as elected officials.
- They cannot get involved in the hiring, promotion, supervision, or discipline of a family member in a position of the state, county, municipality, or school district. They cannot advocate for a family member to be appointed to a board or hired for a public position. A family member can work in the elected person's office, but not under that person's direct supervision.
- They may not use public funds, time, personnel, facilities, or equipment for private benefit, including campaign activity, unless the use is incidental to a public action and it is reimbursed. This is considered a "misuse" of office.
- They must abstain from decisions and votes in which they have a personal or private interest. This can be a judgment call, so the law provides some direction: officials should consider the importance of representing their constituency, and they must abstain "only in clear cases" of self interest. The law forbids participating in decisions that give officials direct financial benefit, except in cases of tax cuts that affect everyone.

A "personal or private interest" is direct and immediate, not speculative and remote. Legislators may vote on issues that would affect them only as part of a general class of people. So, a rancher who leases state land for grazing can vote on public land issues, and a teacher may vote on a public school funding formula.

Legislators with a conflict of interest on an issue may still testify on the matter in committee. They just may not vote on the matter. They may abstain from voting on a particular section of the biennial budget bill, but they may vote on the whole measure.

They must abstain from taking official action or voting on matters affecting someone who is talking to them about hiring them.

The law requires a financial disclosure statement every year from legislators and the top five elected officials – governor, secretary of state, treasurer, auditor, and superintendent of public instruction. This statement includes: 1) a list of all offices, directorships, and salaried jobs held in any for-profit business enterprise; 2) a list describing sources of income (not amount). The disclosure form is due January 31. Violation of the act is a misdemeanor with a maximum fine of $1,000 and removal from office or job. (Wyoming Statutes 9-13-101-109) (*Ethics Brochure for Legislators*, Legislative Service Office)

Other laws cover conflict of interest by Downtown Development Authority members (Title 15) and municipal officials (Title 16).

House and Senate Rules

The Wyoming House and Senate rules also govern members concerning conflict of interest. The chambers adopt rules at the beginning of sessions and may change them any time, but changes typically are minor from session to session.

House and Senate Rules in effect for the 58th Legislature (2005-2006) required members to announce personal or private interest in any proposal during initial debate in Committee of the Whole or the first time they are aware of the conflict.

In cases of budget bills or bills recodifying an entire title of state law, House members may limit their declaration of conflict to individual sections.

Both House and Senate rules provided for noting declarations of conflict of interest in the House and Senate journals at the time they were made. Journals also noted if legislators later declared no conflict on the same matter.

"Personal or private interest" is defined in House Rules as a direct financial gain or loss if the measure is enacted. It does not include gain or loss a House member would experience as a "substantial class of persons," for instance an increase in teacher salaries.

House and Senate members who are uncertain if they should abstain from voting may ask their chamber's Rules Committee for recommendation. (*House Rules of the 58th Legislature*, 17-3, "Time of Declaring Personal or Private Interest;" Senate Rules of the 58th Legislature, 14-7, "Disclosure of Personal or Private Interest; 23-1, "Code of Ethics")

House and Senate rules give broad discretion to legislators to decide if they have conflicts of interest and should abstain from voting, and lawmakers do not challenge each other on their judgment of whether they should have abstained or not. Legislative work is only part-time, so most legislators have full-time employment elsewhere and have direct knowledge and interest in many proposals that cross their desks. That is often viewed as a strength of a "citizen Legislature," but it also creates situations where a decision to abstain from a vote is a matter of individual perception.

For example, should a legislator who is near the end of his term and will soon take an executive position with a special interest group be voting on a bill directly affecting that interest group? This situation arose with a member of the Wyoming Senate in 2004, and he decided in favor of voting.

Lobbying and Lobbyist Disclosure

"Lobbying" encompasses all the efforts by individuals or groups to influence government decisions. That could include law-making decisions by the Legislature or regulations and rules-making by executive agencies. The term "lobbying" comes from the practice of talking to legislators in House and Senate chamber lobbies, although the activity takes place anywhere but in the chambers themselves, which is forbidden by House and Senate rules.

Lobbyists advocate the interests of themselves and their groups, and so their information and arguments are typically one-sided. It is the job of decision makers to listen to all sides and weigh the merits of those arguments with other information that may come from their own experience, their constituents, or government agencies. Lobbyists may be paid or may be volunteers.

Individual citizens always may communicate with legislators and other officials any time to express opinions on pending or past issues. They may also be members of a common interest group, for instance the American Association of Retired Persons, which hires a lobbyist to attend legislative meetings and sessions to monitor action and testify on issues of concern to the group. Or one lobbyist might work for several smaller groups.

Wyoming's part-time legislators, who must make decisions during short, intense sessions without a large staff to do research for them, rely heavily on information provided by lobbyists.

There is a danger when legislators or other decision-makers rely too much on lobbyists to get information and get a sense of public opinion on certain issues. Lobbyists are advocates for a particular viewpoint and interest, and they may not represent all the important interests and viewpoints that legislators need to consider for a decision that serves the best interests of Wyoming's residents. One argument against term limits related to the importance of legislators' "institutional knowledge," which is the experience and knowledge they have from previous sessions. When they have little experience at the Capitol, they can become too reliant on lobbyist-provided information.

The Secretary of State's Office maintains a public list of registered lobbyists, the groups they represent, and contact information.

Factors that influence the effectiveness of lobbyists include the reliability of information they provide, their knowledge of procedures and opportunities to advocate, and the personal rapport they establish decision-makers. One of the most valuable commodities for a lobbyist is credibility. Lobbyists who lose credibility by giving unreliable or misleading information may lose their ability to influence others.

Lobbying can be intense on issues of importance to the state or a particular group, but pressure can be counter-productive. The following comments from Govs. Ed Herschler and Stan Hathaway are from interviews by Professor John T. Hinckley of Northwest Community College in 1977.

Governor Herschler, a veteran of the Legislature, served as governor from 1974 to 1986. He described to Professor Hinckley his reaction to high-pressure lobbying:

"There is a lot of pressure applied both to the Legislature and to the executive branch, I think. Some of the lobbying is very beneficial because, actually, some of the lobbyists are able to give you insight on bills and the ramifications of things that perhaps an individual never thinks about. Even in my office, where I have people that are able to do research for me, we sometimes completely overlook something. That [kind of lobbying] is very helpful. But by the same token, I have had special interest groups come in and not only lobby but threaten. So my position is, 'I'm sorry, but my feeling is that the program I have is for the best interest of the state, in my judgment, and I

can't go along with you and I don't mind telling you."
(Miller 1981, p. 66)

Governor Hathaway, 1966-74, described a vehement rejection of high pressure tactics. Shortly after his first legislative session began, he was visited by about 15 lobbyists "mostly on the economic side -- oil industry, stockmen, Farm Bureau, railroads, etc." They were unhappy with his agenda for the session and reminded him they had contributed to his gubernatorial campaign, and they expected results. He described the rest of the exchange:

> "They said they didn't think I represented the Republican party. And I said, 'Well I've just spent eight months out talking to 150,000 people, and I think I've got a pretty good idea... . Besides, I'm not governor of just the Republicans, anyway.' Then they said something that really infuriated me. They said, 'Well if you continue on the path you're on, you have no political future.' I stood up, pounded my desk and said, 'Don't ever come in here and threaten me with my political future. In the first place, I never expected to be governor of Wyoming. But I'm here and I'm going to do what I think is right while I'm here. And you'll get nowhere threatening me with my political future.' They didn't come around the rest of that session."
> (Miller 1981, p. 65)

Governor Hathaway went on to be re-elected.

In 1998, Wyoming became the last state in the nation to require lobbyist disclosure, whose purpose is to make this aspect of legislative influence more transparent to the public. The law specifically states that the law does not restrict the right of citizens as individuals to contact legislators, and it doesn't apply to any public officials acting in their official capacity.

Title 28 of state law, which deals with the Legislature, devotes Chapter 7 to requirements for lobbyists to register with the secretary of state and report spending on legislators. Lobbyists who are compensated at least $500 a year must pay a registration fee of $25 fee. Others pay $5. The list of lobbyists and groups they represent is available to the public at the Secretary of State's Office.

The law has penalties: a $200 fine for failing to register and $750 for failing to report activity. A second failure to report is punished by revocation of the right to register as a lobbyist for two years. However, it does not specifically address how the law will be enforced. The Secretary of State's Office receives the reports and makes them available to the public, but it is not an enforcement agency.

Lobbyists or their employers must report:

- Funding sources.
- Loans, gifts, gratuities, special discounts, or hospitality greater than $50 given to legislators, elected officials, or state employees acting in their official capacity.
- Special events for legislators that cost more than $500, along with a description of the group of legislators invited.
- Receipts and expenditures by any group that bought advertising to influence legislation.

Wyoming's lobbyist disclosure law is the least complete among states in the region. State law does not deal with expenditures by lobbyists to influence rulemaking by government agencies. It does not require lobbyists to disclose how much they are compensated in salary or expenses. Only about 10 percent of the 447 lobbyists filed spending reports as required by law on June 30, 2004. Lobbyists testified in a legislative committee during the 2003 session that reporting of salary and expenses would be intrusive and burdensome.

Access to Legislature

The ability of citizens to participate in their government and hold their elected officials accountable depends on their ability to track decisions by members of the Legislature, county commissions, city councils, and boards.

Work of the Legislature has become much more accessible in the past 25 years, thanks to a great extent to computer technology, which makes votes and other actions quickly and easily available to the public. The Legislature also has instituted policies of publicly posting committee meetings and agendas as soon as they are scheduled.

Citizens can become involved in legislative actions by being represented by a lobbyist or by attending sessions and committee meetings personally to monitor debate and votes, to provide information, and to advocate for their interests.

All legislators are provided laptop computers and individual e-mail accounts, and nearly all lawmakers use e-mail frequently during sessions. However, the ease of using e-mail has resulted in a new phenomenon -- the inundation of lawmakers with communications when controversial issues are coming up for important votes. Some legislators complain they cannot keep up with the flow, and they read only the e-mail from people they know.

Citizens may use the Legislature's "Voter Hotline" to leave messages for legislators. Citizens may send letters through the U.S. Postal Service. If they are at the Capitol, they may send short written notes in to legislators while they are in session, or they can meet personally with legislators.

Contact information for all legislators during sessions and at home is available from the Legislative Service Office.

As part of its service to the Legislature, the LSO also provides a wealth of information to the public that allows Wyoming citizens to participate from a distance as the Legislature conducts its business in Cheyenne. A key tool is the LSO Website (http://legisweb.state.wy.us). Some information available there includes: all bills in original and amended forms as they make their way through the legislative process; amendments that have been offered to the bills; recorded roll call votes; House and Senate schedules for the day; schedule of committee meetings and agendas.

In 2001, the Senate began to use microphones during debate. House members already were using microphones. This allowed people watching the sessions in person to hear the debate. It also allowed the LSO to broadcast House and Senate debate live on the Web site and to make a whole day's worth of debate available to download.

The LSO Website provides many additional documents and features that help the public understand the legislative process and contact the legislators. The site provides the full text of the Wyoming Constitution, Wyoming Statutes, House and Senate rules, and the Wyoming Manual for Legislative Procedures.

The LSO should be credited as an agent for "good government" in its support for Wyoming's part-time Legislature. LSO staff draft bills, do research, analyze data, store and retrieve information, brief new legislators on historical issues, and perform other jobs in a nonpartisan fashion that enables Wyoming to have a citizens' Legislature that meets just 60 days during a two-year period.

The major exceptions to this extraordinary access is the inability of Wyoming citizens to learn about legislation while it is being drafted and the inability to track many of the votes taken during a session.

Votes are recorded when the clerk of the House or Senate takes a "roll call" vote, calling each legislator by name in alphabetical order and recording the votes on a computer touch screen. Roll call votes are automatically taken when a bill is on third reading and when the House and Senate are voting to introduce non-budget bills in a budget session. In the Senate, roll calls also are automatic on amendments that increase or cut money from a bill.

Otherwise, bills are advanced and amendments are voted up or down based on just a voice vote or a head-count. Sometimes the amendments can drastically change the direction of legislation. A legislator can make a special request for a roll call vote, but this is rare. Meanwhile, people who cannot come to Cheyenne and personally observe sessions are at a great disadvantage to follow measures they care about and to know who supported them. Even professional lobbyists watching from the House and Senate galleries have difficulty tracking how legislators are voting, without an official record.

Bills face their first tests in House and Senate committees, where roll call votes are recorded for all bills that are "moved" by members for approval. The votes are announced publicly and officially recorded when the bills are returned to the House speaker or Senate president. For bills that succeed, this is right away. However, bills that fail in committee are not returned, and votes are not publicly reported, until the time for consideration in committee expires. That means the public does not learn of a bill's demise until it is too late to work for its revival, unless the vote is unofficially reported by someone who witnesses the action. It is difficult for people who rely on official reports to discover that the bills they were following have died in committee.

Public Records, Open Meetings

Citizens are able to participate in their government when they can see what their government is doing, in the form of public records and meetings. Open records and meetings are guaranteed in Title 16 of state law, Chapter 4, "Public Records, Documents and Meetings."

The laws for public records and open meetings apply to all levels of government, although the Legislature exempted itself from public meetings requirements. Violations are misdemeanors punishable by a fine of up to $750.

Public Records

The Wyoming Public Records Law allows anyone to ask to inspect public records, regardless of his purpose. This includes all public records of government agencies, the Legislature, and the courts (except juvenile proceedings). It also covers advisory boards and commissions. (Wyoming Statutes 16-4-201–205)

The law says "public records" includes "the original and copies of any paper, correspondence, form, book, photograph, photostat, film, microfilm, sound recording, map drawing, or other document, regardless of physical form." The Legislature also has classified electronic mail concerning government business as "public records."

The ease of using electronic mail for both formal and casual communication prompted the Management Council, composed of legislative leaders, to propose a law in 2006 that would have allowed any government employee or elected official to delete "transitory" e-mail thought to have no lasting value. Representatives for the League of Women Voters of Wyoming, the Wyoming Press Association, and the Equality State Policy Center lobbied against the proposal for the broad discretion it gave any person in government to determine what might be important in the future. They argued in favor of archiving all government-related electronic mail to create a complete record. The bill died in the House Rules Committee 5-4.

A companion measure, also by the Management Council, was approved to make all communications and information involved in drafting legislation privileged and confidential and, therefore, unavailable to the public.

A person asking to see the records may be charged a "reasonable fee" for the agency's time in finding and copying the documents and for the copies themselves.

The law gives officials some leeway in releasing documents.

In *Sheridan Newspapers, Inc. v. City of Sheridan,* the Wyoming Supreme Court said the custodian of the records "must weigh the competing interests." The custodian must determine "whether permitting inspection would result in harm to the public interest which outweighs the legislative policy recognizing the public interest in allowing inspection." (660 P.2d at 798) (Wyo 1983)

In *Houghton v. Franscell,* the Wyoming Supreme Court balanced the public's right to know against invasion of privacy. The court defined invasion of privacy as "unwarranted publicity, unwarranted appropriation or exploitation of one's personality, or the publicizing of one's private affairs with which the public had no legitimate concern." (870 P.2d at 1055) (Wyo 1994)

Some records are never released unless another law requires it: medical records, adoption records, personnel files, letters of reference, trade secrets, and other confidential documents.. (*Tapping Officials' Secrets*, 4th ed, 2001, The Reporters Committee for Freedom of the Press)

Open Meetings

The state Open Meetings law begins with the statement of purpose: "The agencies of Wyoming exist to conduct public business. Certain deliberations and actions shall be taken openly as provided in this act." (Wyoming Statutes 16-4-401) Until 2005, violation of the law carried no penalty.

The law applies to governing boards of all state and local government agencies – all multi-member bodies created by the Wyoming Constitution, state law, or ordinance. The law specifically mentions open meetings for school boards. Another section of state law includes a requirement for county commissioners that dates back to territorial days: "They shall sit with open doors and all persons conducting themselves in an orderly manner may attend their meetings." (Wyoming Statutes 18-3-506)

The Wyoming Legislature is exempt, but the law applies to committees that include legislators and non-legislators.

The law does not apply to nongovernmental bodies, unless they include government officials.

What is a "meeting?" According to the law, it is an assembly of at least a quorum of the governing body of an agency which has been called by proper authority of the agency for the purpose of discussion, deliberation, presentation of information, or taking action regarding public business. (Wyoming Statutes 14-4-402) The Open Meetings Law covers just about any gathering of a quorum where official business is discussed, although it does not address such discussions held by electronic mail, telephone, or video conferencing.

Public notice requirements for regular, special, and budget meetings are covered in Section 404.

Section 405 of the law specifies eleven reasons for a governing body to close a meeting to the public and go into "executive session:"

- To meet with officers of the law (attorneys, sheriff, police) to discuss security.
- To consider hiring, disciplinary, or other personnel matters.
- To consider litigation that involves or may involve the governing body.
- To consider matters of national security.
- As a licensing agency, to prepare, administer, or grade examinations.
- To consider and act on the term, parole, or release of a person from a correctional or penal institution.
- To consider purchase of real estate, when publicity would increase the price.
- To consider acceptance of donations which the donor has requested in writing to be kept confidential.
- To consider information classified by law as confidential.
- To discuss proposed wages, salaries, benefits, and terms of employment during negotiations.
- To consider disciplinary action against students.

Knowing and willful violation of the Open Meetings Law is a misdemeanor punishable by a maximum fine of $750, paid by the offending official, not the governing body. (Wyoming Statutes 16-4-408). In 2005, the Legislature added the penalty, required a majority vote to go into executive session, and required minutes be taken to record an official's objection to an improper discussion.

The Legislature has exempted itself from the open meetings requirements, but it generally tries to give adequate notice of meetings and to meet in an accessible location. The challenge is for meetings of conference committees, which are called with little forewarning in the final days of legislative sessions, to work out compromises in versions of bills that have come from the House and Senate. In recent years, however, conference committee chairmen have tried to post meeting information as soon as it was available on bulletin boards at the entrances of the House and Senate chambers.

Members of the Legislature's Democratic Caucus open their meetings to the public. Republican caucuses are closed.

Although legislative committee meetings are open to all people, meeting rooms on the second and third floors of the Capitol Building are small, which effectively excludes anyone who is not there early to get a seat. The problem worsens when committees are considering controversial bills with a great deal of public interest.

Political Campaigns

The Legislature has enacted laws that restrict contributions to political campaigns and require reporting of both contributions and expenses. They are in Title 22 (Elections Code) in Chapter 25, which is entitled "Campaign Practices." The Secretary of State's Office also has written a "Wyoming Campaign Guide" to help candidates.

The Campaign Practices Act applies to candidates for the top five elected offices, the Wyoming Legislature, district attorneys, county offices, school district boards, community college boards of trustees, municipal offices, and magistrates. The top elected offices are governor, secretary of state, treasurer, auditor, and superintendent of public instruction.

Campaign Practices apply to judges who stand for retention to the Wyoming Supreme Court, District Court, and Circuit Court. A year after judges are appointed by the governor to those state courts, Wyoming citizens vote to retain them on the bench or to remove them.

Campaign Practices Act
- There are no limits on campaign spending.
- Individual contributions are limited to $1,000 per candidate per

election. There is no specific limit on contributions to a political action committee. However, an individual is limited to giving $25,000 total during a two-year election period.

- The exception to this restriction is a member of the candidate's "immediate family," who may contribute without limit. The law defines "immediate family" as spouse, parent, sibling, child, or other person in the candidate's household.

- Corporations, unions, partnerships, professional associations, or civic, fraternal, or religious groups are prohibited from making contributions to candidates or political parties. However, they may make contributions to support or oppose ballot issues or a petition drive to put an issue on the ballot.

- There is no limit on contributions to candidates from political action committees and political party committees. Groups mentioned in the item above may form political action committees so they may contribute to election campaigns.

- A chapter of the Election Code prohibits electioneering within 100 yards of a polling place on election day. That includes displaying campaign signs or distributing campaign literature. The law prohibits polling voters, except by news media.

- Campaign Practices forbids written campaign advertising on property of the state or political subdivisions (counties, municipalities, and special districts), except for colleges and schools as permitted by their trustees. Political advertisements may be placed on fairgrounds and municipal street rights-of-way.

- Rates for political advertisements cannot be higher than rates for similar local advertising.

- A law called "Offenses Against Public Peace" (6-6-104) prohibits anyone from using an automated telephone system to select and dial numbers and play recorded messages, if the purpose is related to a political campaign.

- Those who violate the Campaign Practices Act may be guilty of a misdemeanor or felony, punishable by fine and/or incarceration.

- A candidate, political party, or prosecuting authority can seek a civil penalty of up to $10,000 for violations by a corporation, person or organization.

Campaign Finance Reporting
Candidates

- Candidates do not need a committee, but they must keep accurate records of receipts and expenditures. They may take contributions and begin spending them before filing for office.
- ALL candidates file a report, whether they win or lose, regardless of whether they received or spent any money on the campaign.
- As of 2004, candidates must report their receipts at least a week before an election. Complete receipt and expenditure reports are due 10 days after any election – primary, general, or special. A handful of legislative candidates missed this deadline in 2004, a violation that was punishable by refusal of election officials to certify the offender as the winner. However, the state attorney general said that penalty probably was unconstitutional and unenforceable. (The 2005 Legislature removed that provision of the law.)
- Reports must itemize all receipts over $25, including date received and the name, city, and state of the contributor. Contributions less than $25 must be reported but not itemized. If a contributor gives several small amounts that total more than $25, the total must be itemized. Reports must itemize ALL expenditures of any amount.
- Contributions include fund-raising tickets and in-kind donations.
- A candidate may call a contribution "anonymous" only if the candidate truly does not know who gave the money.
- The Wyoming Election Code does not say how funds left over after a campaign must be used.

Political Action Committees

- A political action committee (PAC) means any group of two or more persons associated for the purpose of raising, collecting, or spending money for a campaign. PACs are formed because corporations, unions, and most other organizations may not contribute directly to candidates. So they form PACS, which receive contributions from individual members and do other fund-raising. Wyoming law puts no limit on the amount of money PACs may contribute to legislative races.
- A PAC must file a "Statement of Formation" within ten days after

formation. The chairman and treasurer of the PAC must be separate individuals. PAC filings are public record, available from the Secretary of State's Office.

- If a PAC is working to elect a candidate, it may not receive money from a corporation, partnership, trade union, professional association, or civic, fraternal or religious group. If the PAC is working for or against a ballot issue, the contributions are fine.
- PACs may terminate when their debts are cleared. Otherwise, active PACS must file a report by December 31 of off-numbered years (non-election years).

Organizations

- The Election Code requires a campaign report by any "organization" that receives or spends money on a ballot issue or petition, when that organization exists for a purpose other than the campaign. An example provided by the Secretary of State's Office is a tobacco company that spends money to defeat a ballot proposal to ban smoking in all public places.
- Any organization that supports or opposes a petition drive or ballot issue must file a statement of receipts and expenditures within ten days of an election or ten days after the petition is submitted to the Secretary of State's Office.

Political Party Contributions

- A political party may not spend money to help the nomination of one person against another of the same party in the primary. In the general election, however, a party may contribute to its candidate for office.
- A party must file a campaign finance report, with receipts and expenditures, within ten days after the general or special election. The report must include all operating expenses for any party activity since the previous report in the previous election year.
- Reports must specify which expenses supported which candidates.
- The Secretary of State's Office advises that the Young Democrats, county Republican Women's Club, or other clubs should check

with their party authority to determine their power to contribute directly to a candidate.

Removing Elected Officials

Opportunities to remove officials from office in mid-term are very limited in Wyoming.

The Wyoming House may impeach certain state officials, and the Senate follows with a trial to determine if the impeached officials should be removed. There is no state law providing citizens the means to recall state or local officials whose performance is considered unsatisfactory, except in cities and towns that use the commission form of government. (Wyoming Statutes 15-4-110) No municipality in Wyoming currently uses that form of government.

Chapter 9

Initiative & Referendum

Citizens in Wyoming may participate directly in their own government by writing and passing their own city ordinances and state laws through the "initiative" process. They also may approve or reject action by a law-making body with a "referendum."

The Legislature must approve constitutional amendments by a two-thirds vote before they are put to a popular vote. Amendments must receive majority approval from all voters participating in that election.

These activities are governed by Title 22 of Wyoming Statutes, "Election Code."

Ordinance by Initiative and Referendum

Residents of an incorporated city or town with a commission form of government may circulate a petition and get signatures from 10 percent of registered voters to put a proposed ordinance on the ballot. The petition goes to the governing body, which can pass the ordinance or put it on a ballot. If approved by a majority of voters, the proposal becomes an ordinance, which cannot be repealed or changed except by the voters.

Residents of a municipality can challenge an ordinance if they gather signatures of 10 percent of registered voters and file a referendum petition with the city or town clerk within 10 days of the ordinance's publication. The ordinance is suspended until the governing body repeals the ordinance or puts it on the ballot. Residents of Laramie used this provision in 2004 to challenge a city ban on cigarette smoking in restaurants and bars. The ordinance subsequently was approved by the voters.

State Law by Initiative and Referendum

Citizens who wish to put a proposed state law before the voters or to challenge a legislatively-passed law must submit their proposal to the Wyoming Secretary of State's Office with petitions signed by registered voters equal to 15 percent of the number of people voting in the previous general election. Petitions must say if the people gathering signatures are being paid for their work.

The fact that few sponsors get their initiative and referendum proposals on the ballot indicates the difficulty of the process.

Initiative and referendum procedures and requirements are in Wyoming Statutes Title 22, Chapter 24, and in the Wyoming Constitution Article 3, Section 52.

Two restrictions have been added to statutes and the Wyoming Constitution since the Initiative and Referendum processes were enacted in 1968. Both actions were taken after initiatives that were unpopular with many legislators made it to the ballot:

- The 1985 Legislature amended the initiative and referendum law to limit signature-gathering to 18 months and to define a political action committee to include any group organized to support or defeat an initiative or referendum petition drive. This came after sponsors for an in-stream flow law won a court ruling that they could continue gathering signatures after initial petition efforts fell short.
- In 1997, the Legislature approved a constitutional amendment to add a hurdle to gathering the necessary number of signatures: sponsors had to get 15 percent of the voters in 2/3 of the counties (16 of 23 counties). This action followed the success of petitioners for a legislative term limit law. Legislators said they feared petitioners were gaining ballot access with heavy participation from a few populous counties. They said they wanted to make sure any ballot proposition had broad support from across the state. The proposed amendment was on the 1998 general election ballot, where voters approved it.

A bill in 2002 that would have removed the two-thirds requirement failed introduction in the House by a whopping 5-54 vote.

The change had been proposed by the Joint Corporations Committee, which attempted another bill to give voters greater say in amending the Wyoming Constitution. That would have let voters petition to put amendments on the ballot themselves. If approved by two-thirds of the people voting in that election, an amendment would be submitted to the Legislature for ratification by a simple majority. That proposal also failed.

Voters also rejected a proposal in 2002 that would have bypassed the governor in sending constitutional amendments straight from the Legislature to the ballot.

Wyoming has one of the most restrictive initiative/referendum laws in the country, and few proposals make it to the ballot. Most sponsors never submit petitions to the Secretary of State's Office for verification of voters' signatures, or they fall short of the 15 percent needed.

A complete list of initiative attempts is on pages 132-138.

One initiative that qualified for the ballot was a proposal to preserve minimum in-stream flows. This would have changed Wyoming water law to consider in-stream flows of water as a beneficial use of water, along with agricultural use. It was filed May 23, 1982, by Tom Dougherty of Cheyenne for the Wyoming Citizens for Committee for Instream Flow. The Secretary of State's Office verified voters' signatures and ruled on January 6, 1984, that the initiative fell short of the 25,810 required signatures. The state attorney general ruled the group could continue gathering signatures, which it did, and 4,370 additional signatures were submitted November 5, 1984. The signatures were verified, and the proposal was ready for the 1986 ballot, but the Legislature enacted similar legislation in 1985, which made the ballot issue unnecessary.

The Legislature then imposed an 18-month circulation limit.

One successful initiative prohibited triple trailers in Wyoming. John Rogers of Cheyenne filed the proposal on August 27, 1990, and was notified in January that it had qualified for the ballot, with 27,962 signatures. It appeared on the 1992 general election ballot and passed.

Another successful initiative set term limits for legislators. However, the Wyoming Supreme Court ruled in 2004 it was unconstitutional because it imposed a restriction on legislative candidacy outside the requirements listed in the Wyoming Constitution.

Dave Dawson of Casper was the sponsor of the term limit initiative. He filed in 1991, and it was on the 1992 ballot. It was approved by 77 percent of the people who voted on the question. The voter-approved law limited House and Senate members to three terms each. House terms are two years, and Senate terms are four years. The result was unequal limits -- six years for the House and twelve years for the Senate. The Legislature amended the new law to set the limit to twelve years for all. Again, term limit advocates circulated petitions for a referendum to repeal the legislative action and reinstate the three-term limit. Sponsor Jack Adsit of Sheridan succeeded in getting the question on the 1996 ballot, but it failed.

Term limit proponents acted further. They wanted to require candidates for legislative office to have a statement by their names on the ballot indicating their support for a congressional term limit. The proposed law also would have instructed legislators to call for a federal constitutional convention. Supporters gathered more than 30,000 signatures and qualified for the 1996 ballot. This proposal also failed.

In 1997, a group circulated petitions for an Ethics in Government law, to establish ethical standards and outlaw certain acts by public employees, officials, and other public members. It would have required financial disclosure by officials and close family members. Sponsors were Curt Kaiser, League of Women Voters of Wyoming President Angeline M. Kinneman, and Nyla Murphy. Sponsors did not submit petitions by the end of the 18-month circulation period.

People may use the initiative process to demonstrate public support for legislation. Rep. Ann Robinson, a Casper Democrat, tried for years to win support for a proposal to remove sales tax from food purchased for home consumption. In 2005, she began circulating petitions to put the question on the ballot. By the 2006 legislative session, she said she had gathered about 19,000 signatures, and she filed a bill to remove sales tax from utility bills for two years and from groceries permanently. The bill failed in the House Revenue Commit-tee, 5-4. Subsequently, the House and Senate put a two-year grocery tax exemption in the biennial budget bill. Robinson said she planned to continue gathering signatures.

The initiative and referendum process gives Wyoming citizens the means to make and change laws on their own. However, it is very difficult to qualify proposals for the general election ballot, particularly by groups who rely on volunteers, instead of paid workers, to gather signatures on petitions.

Initiative Process
A guide by the Wyoming Secretary of State's Office

Anyone considering filing an initiative application should consult the Wyoming Constitution and the Election Code in Wyoming Statutes. Electronic versions of both the Constitution and statutes are available at the Legislative Service Office's Web site: http://legisweb.state.wy.us. Paper copies were available from the Secretary of State's Office for $3.00 per copy in 2005.

Governance
Wyoming Constitution, Article 3 Section 52, and various state laws, particularly Wyoming Statutes 22-24-101 through 22-24-125.

Requirements
The initiative must be in bill form (refer to W.S. 8-1-101 through 8-1-108). The bill must be on legal size paper, attached to the application form. The entire subject of the bill must be included in the title. The enacting clause must read: "Be it enacted by the people of the state of Wyoming". The bill must have an effective date. The application must be filed with the Secretary of State. A fee of $500 must accompany the application.

Restrictions
The bill may not contain more than one subject. The bill may not dedicate revenues. The bill may not make or repeal appropriations. The bill may not create courts, define the jurisdiction of courts, or prescribe their rules. The bill may not enact local or special legislation. The bill may not enact anything that is prohibited by the Constitution. The bill may not be substantially the same as that defeated by an initiative election within the previous five years.

Committee
There must be a committee of three people who will be the main sponsors of the initiative. These committee members will be the contact people for the initiative. They may be served with legal notices and will be responsible for statutory fees and costs.

Certification for Circulation
After the application is filed, the Secretary of State will hold a conference with the sponsors to discuss possible problems with the format or contents, fiscal impact to the state, and the initiative amend-

ment process. The sponsors may then amend the initiative language. If the proposed bill will not be amended, the committee of sponsors shall submit the names, signatures, addresses, and the signing dates of one hundred (100) qualified electors to act as sponsors supporting the application in its final form to the Secretary of State. If the application meets all constitutional and statutory requirements, the Secretary of State will certify the application as filed. If the application is denied, the Secretary of State will notify the committee in writing of the grounds for denial. Denial of certification is subject to judicial review if any aggrieved person files an application within thirty days of the notification.

Petitions

The Secretary of State will develop the petition form, which is the only form that may be circulated. The Secretary of State shall print and number the petitions for distribution, but the cost of petition preparation is the responsibility of the sponsors.

Circulation

Sponsors have 18 months from the initial date the petitions are delivered to the sponsor to file the petitions for verification. Petitions are to be circulated throughout the state only by a sponsor and only in person. The committee may designate additional sponsors by giving written notice to the Secretary of State of those names and addresses. Sponsors will be required to submit an affidavit upon submission of each petition he/she circulated. Sponsors must submit registered voter signatures representing fifteen percent (15%) of those who voted in the preceding general election and fifteen percent (15%) of those resident in at least two-thirds of Wyoming counties. Failure of a petition to qualify as of the filing date voids the future use of all signatures.

Circulators may not be paid based upon the number of signatures gathered nor shall a circulator pay or offer to pay any compensation to another person for that person's signature. Any person who signs a name other than his own or who knowingly signs his name more than once or who signs knowing that he is not a qualified registered voter or who makes a false affidavit or verification, upon conviction can be fined up to $1,000 or imprisoned up to one year, or both.

Certification for the Ballot

Within 60 days after the filing of the petition, the Secretary of State will notify the committee of whether or not enough valid signatures had been obtained. If so, the Secretary of State will prepare a proposition and ballot title summarizing the proposed law. The proposition will then be voted on in the first statewide election held more than 120 days after adjournment of the legislative session. If the Legislature enacts substantially the same measure before the election, the petition is void.

Enactment

The measure is enacted if it receives approval of more than 50 percent of those voting in the general election. Election results are certified by the State Canvassing Board. An initiated law becomes effective 90 days after certification. It is not subject to veto, and it may not be repealed by the Legislature within two years of its effective date. It may be amended at any time.

Initiative & Referendum
Summary Sheet

Citizens of Wyoming have had the privilege of proposing and enacting laws by the initiative, or rejecting acts of the legislature by the referendum, since December 1968.

The first amendments to the initiative and referendum law were made by the 1985 Wyoming Legislature. An 18-month circulation period was established, and the definition of a political action committee was amended to include any group organized for the support or defeat of any initiative or referendum petition drive.

Below are all past initiatives/referenda filed in Wyoming, as reported by the Secretary of State's office.

1.   Declaring gambling to be lawful. Filed May 8, 1970. Principal sponsor: Harry Poulos, 6902 Bomar Drive, Cheyenne, WY 82009.

2.   Disclosing private interests by certain public officials; requiring such disclosure and providing penalties for failure to disclose and for false disclosure. Filed July 9, 1973. Principal sponsor: Rodger McDaniel, P.O. Box 1707, Cheyenne, WY 82003.

3.   Relating to private ownership or possession of big and trophy game animals and importation of same into Wyoming. Filed September 19, 1973. Principal sponsor: Dick Sadler, 2626 Bonnie Brae, Casper, WY 82601.

4.   Providing for a constitutional amendment on the general election ballot to create the office of Lt. Governor. Filed May 14, 1976. Principal sponsor: John Jacobs, P.O. Box 98, Gillette, WY 82716. (In Wyoming the initiative process cannot be used to propose an amendment to the Wyoming Constitution.)

5.   Imposing a 23% severance tax on the value of coal produced by open mining. Filed November 23, 1976. Principal sponsor: Donald Shanor, 5001 Sagebrush, Cheyenne, WY 82001.

6. **Authorizing the issuance of malt beverage and wine permits by cities and counties to restaurants.** Filed August 31, 1978. Principal sponsor: Bob Hulburt, 162 N. Beech, Casper, WY 82601.

7. **Imposing an additional 5% severance tax on the value of coal produced.** Filed September 22, 1978. Principal sponsor: Bob Burnett, P.O. Box 1123, Laramie, WY 82070.

8. **Preserving minimum in-stream flows.** Filed October 20, 1980. Principal sponsor: Dr. Charles Stebner. Petitions filed December 11, 1981. Verification completed Jan. 26, 1982 and the Secretary of State notified the sponsors that the initiative fell 1,266 signatures short of the 27,154 needed.

In February 1982 the In-Stream Flow Committee filed an action for review of the Secretary of State's determination. On May 10, 1982 the action was heard in District Court. The decision handed down by Judge Alan Johnson on August 12, 1982 reversed the letter decision of the Secretary of State.

9. **Replacement of exported groundwater.** Filed June 22, 1981. Principal sponsor: Winslow Taylor, P.O. Box 39, Story, WY 82842.

10. **Deposits in credit unions.** Filed March 3, 1982. Principal sponsor: Roshara J. Holub, Wyoming Credit Union League, Inc., 864 Spruce St, Casper, WY 82601.

11. **Constitutional Amendment** - Article 3, Section 52(c) and (f) on initiative. Filed June 16, 1982. Principal sponsor: Sweetwater County Rep. James Roth, P.O. Box 432, Green River, WY 82935. Amending constitutional provision on initiative process and lowering signature requirement for placement of an initiative on the general election ballot from 15% to 10%.

12.   Instream flows as a beneficial use of water under Wyoming law. Filed May 23, 1982. Principal Sponsor: Tom Dougherty, Wyoming Citizens for Committee for Instream Flow, P.O. Box 15732, Cheyenne, WY 82003. Initial verification by Secretary of State completed January 6, 1984. Initiative fell short of the 25,810 required signatures. Because of a February 1984 ruling by the Attorney General, 4,370 additional signatures were submitted on Nov. 5, 1984. The Wyoming Citizens Committee for Instream Flow was notified on Nov. 13, 1984 that the initiative petition had been properly filed and qualified for ballot placement in the 1986 general election. However, this initiative did not appear on the 1986 general election ballot as legislation passed in 1985 was determined to be substantially the same.

13.   Water storage for instream flows. Filed August 22, 1983. Principal sponsor: Gilbert Engen, Wyoming Citizens for Wyoming Water, P.O. Box 1348, Laramie, WY 82070. Failed to file petition by the December 16, 1983 deadline for placement on the 1984 general Eeection Ballot. The Committee continued to gather signatures for the 1986 general election ballot. However, failed to file the requisite number of signatures by February 17, 1986, the first day of the legislature. (Note: An Attorney General's opinion issued January 10, 1986, stated an initiative petition need not be verified 60 days prior to a legislative session but rather, the initiative petition must only be deposited prior to the convening of the legislative session.

14.   Election of Public Service Commission Members. Filed July 11, 1985. Principal Sponsor: Fremont County Sen. John P. Vinich, P.O. Box 67, Hudson, WY 82515. The 18-month circulation period established by the 1985 legislature expired January 11, 1987.

15.   Link Deposit Program. Filed July 15, 1988. Principal sponsor: Russ Donley, 1120 Ivy Lane, Casper, WY 82607. The 18-month circulation period expired with the sponsors filing 267 verified signatures. 1990 ballot placement required 27,962 signatures.

16.   Local Option Gambling. Filed July 15, 1989. Principal sponsor: Mary Allison, P.O. Box 775, Dubois, WY 82513. The 18-

month circulation period expired with the sponsors submitting 11,787 signatures. 1990 or 1992 general election ballot placement required 27,962 signatures.

17.   Prohibiting triple trailers. Filed August 27, 1990. Principal sponsor: John Rogers, 2909 Capitol Avenue, Cheyenne, WY 82001. The sponsors were notified January 4, 1991 that the Secretary of State had verified 27,962 signatures. The initiative appeared on the 1992 general election ballot and was passed: Yes votes - 165,879; No votes - 31,997.

18.   Term Limitations. Filed September 13, 1991. Principal sponsor: Dave Dawson, 3518 Partridge, Casper, WY 82604. The sponsors were notified February 4, 1992 that the Secretary of State had verified 24,646 signatures. The initiative appeared on the 1992 general election ballot and was passed: Yes votes - 150,113; No votes - 44,424.

19.   Railway Safety. Filed October 31, 1991. Principal sponsor: Tom Jones, 215 Lakeshore Drive, Cheyenne, WY 82009. The sponsors were notified February 14, 1992 that the Secretary of State had verified 24,646 signatures. The initiative appeared on the 1992 general election ballot and was passed: Yes votes - 130,803; No votes - 52,835.

20.   Abortion Restrictions. Filed August 8, 1991. Coordinator: Richard Grout, 4950 Antelope Drive, Bar Nunn, WY 82801. The sponsors were notified on December 8, 1992 that the Secretary of State had verified 24,646 signatures. The initiative appeared on the 1994 ballot. The initiative was defeated: Yes votes - 78,978; No votes - 118,760. Total votes cast were 204,025.

21.   Local Option Gambling. Filed October 30, 1991. Principal sponsor: Leo McCue, 4 Corthell, Laramie, WY 82070. The sponsors were notified April 19, 1993 that the Secretary of State had verified 24,646 signatures and April 23, 1993 that the Secretary of State had verified 30,540 signatures. The initiative appeared on the 1994 general election ballot. The initiative was defeated: Yes votes - 61,980; No votes - 137,379. Total votes cast were 204,025.

22.   Invest in Wyoming. Filed May 17, 1993. Principal sponsor: Russ Donley, 1120 Ivy Lane, Casper, WY 82607. 30,540 signatures of registered voters needed for ballot access. This petition reached the appropriate number of signatures and appeared on the 1994 ballot. The initiative was defeated: Yes votes - 75,547; No votes - 114,273. Total votes cast were 204,025.

23. Legislative Accountability. Filed August 19, 1993. Principal sponsor: Betty Jo Beardsley, 814 Hillcrest Road, Cheyenne, WY. 30,540 signatures needed for ballot access. The initiative failed to gather enough signatures to qualify.

24.   Term Limits. An application for a referendum to repeal Senate Enrolled Act 4 was certified March 14, 1995. Principal Sponsor: Mr. Jack Adsit, 73 Metz Road, Sheridan, WY 82801. 30,604 signatures were needed to make the 1996 ballot. The needed signatures were gathered and filed by the deadline. The question appeared on the 1996 ballot, but failed: Yes votes - 104,544; No votes - 90,138.

In order to pass a constitutional amendment, initiative or referendum it must receive a majority of the total votes cast in the election. The total votes cast was 215,844. Therefore, the majority needed was 107,923.

25.   Term Limits. An application for an initiative was certified. This initiative was to require candidates for a legislative office to have a statement next to their name on the ballot indicating their support of congressional term limits by past votes or a signed pledge. It also would instruct the legislators to call for a federal constitutional convention. 30,604 signatures were needed to make the 1996 ballot. Sponsors were Jack Adsit, Jim Brady and Steve Richardson. This petition gained the appropriate number of signatures and appeared on the 1996 ballot. The initiative was defeated: Yes votes - 105,093; No votes - 89,018. Total votes cast were 215,844.

In order to pass a constitutional amendment, initiative or referendum it must receive a majority of the total votes cast in the election. The total votes cast was 215,844. Therefore, the majority needed was 107,923.

26. **Denturity.** An application for an initiative was certified by the Secretary of State's Office on April 18, 1997. This initiative would have established professional licensure of denturists; require the Board of Dental Examiners to regulate denturists, dental hygienists and dentists and to function with a lay person majority vote; and repealing the authority of dentists to make and repair dentures, bridges and appliances. Sponsors of the bill were Billy M. Strickland, Christine L. Conley and Marilyn V. Anderson. 32,377 signatures were needed to make the 1998 ballot. The 18-month circulation period established by the 1985 Legislature expired October 18, 1998.

27. **Ethics In Government.** An application for an initiative was certified by the Secretary of State's Office on September 3, 1997. This initiative would have established ethical standards and specify unlawful acts for specified public employees, officials and other public members; require financial disclosure and other filings; provide for enforcement; provide definitions, procedures, penalties and remedies; authorize investigations; make conforming amendments; and provide for an effective date. Sponsors of the bill were Curt Kaiser, Angeline M. Kinneman and Nyla Murphy. 32,377 signatures were needed to make the 1998 or 2000 ballot. The 18-month circulation period established by the 1985 legislature expired March 3, 1999.

28. **Surface Owners' Accommodation.** An application for an initiative was certified by the Secretary of State's Office on May 14, 2004. This initiative would have required surface owners and oil and gas operators to enter into good faith negotiations for a surface use agreement to compensate the surface owner for reasonable damages, if any, to the surface estate, that may be caused by the oil and gas operations. Such agreement may include reclamation requirements. Upon failure to reach such agreement, the oil and gas operator would provide financial assurance to the Wyoming Oil and Gas Conservation Commission, in an amount not less than $5,000 nor more than $500,000, to pay for reasonable damages to the surface estate which may occur. Sponsors of the bill were John G. Andrikopoulos, Bill Garland, and Laurie D. Goodman. 38,866 signatures were needed to make the 2006 ballot. The 18-month circulation period established by the 1985 Legislature expired January 20, 2006. The Legislature passed similar legislation on February 24, 2005 (Senate File 60), and the initiative was withdrawn.

29.   Food Tax Exemption. An application for an initiative was certified by the Secretary of State's Office on May 19, 2005. This initiative would remove the sales and use tax on food for domestic home consumption as defined by Revenue Department rule and regulation. Sponsors were Rep. Ann Robinson of Casper, Kenilynn Zanetti of Rock Springs, and Dr. John Millin of Cheyenne. 36,868 signatures were needed to make the 2006 ballot. The 18-month circulation period was scheduled to expire December 1, 2006.

Chapter 10

Voting & Running for Office

Voting

The right of citizens to vote is their right to determine the government that makes their laws, levies their taxes, and spends their money. It is a precious right that is, sadly, unappreciated by many. This chapter begins with an illustration of the importance of a vote.

In 1994, Republican Randall Luthi, an attorney living in Freedom in far western Wyoming, faced Independent Larry Call for a seat in the state House to represent Lincoln County. They tied with 1,941 votes each. The tie remained after a recount. To decide the winner, pingpong balls with the names of the contenders were put into the cowboy hat of Wyoming Gov. Mike Sullivan. In a drawing before the State Canvassing Board, the pingpong ball with Luthi's name was pulled out, and he was declared the winner.

Ten years later, Randall Luthi was Wyoming House Speaker, the most powerful person in that chamber.

One of the most notable voters in Wyoming history was Louisa Swain of Laramie, the first woman to exercise her right to vote under the woman's suffrage law passed by the first Legislative Assembly in 1869.

Who May Vote

According to the Wyoming Election Code, Title 22 of Wyoming Statutes, a person is eligible to register and vote if he or she is:
- A citizen of the United States
- A resident of the State of Wyoming
- At least 18 years old on election day
- Not a felon

· Not adjudicated mentally incompetent

Once registered, a person will stay registered if he or she voted in the previous general election. People who move to a different precinct or change their names must notify their county clerks, who are the chief election officials for the county. People who move to a different county must re-register in the new county.

Wyoming has 345 polling places in 483 precincts in twenty-three counties.

The Election Code is Title 22 of Wyoming Statutes, which covers requirements for political parties, voter registration, voting, campaign practices, and elections on state and local levels.

Wyoming is liberal about letting anyone vote absentee who is unable or simply prefers not to vote on election day. Once the voting period begins, anyone can go to the county clerk's office and cast an absentee ballot in person. People who are voting outside Wyoming must ask for an absentee ballot from their county clerks and make sure they are delivered to the clerk's office no later than 7 p.m. on election day, which is when the polls close. Absentee ballots are counted on election day.

Under state law, people who require assistance to vote because of a disability or because they cannot read or write may bring a person with them to the polling place to help. People may bring sample ballots or notes with them into the voting booth to help them mark their ballots.

A prohibition on voting by convicted felons was amended by the Legislature in 2003. The law now allows people who were convicted of one nonviolent felony, who have served their sentences, and who have not had any other convictions for at least five years to apply for restoration of their voting rights. Previously, ex-felons lost their right to vote permanently. They could ask the governor to restore voting rights, but granting the request was completely at the governors' discretion, and their policies varied widely. The law sets out qualifications and specifies the petition will be considered by the State Parole Board. (Wyoming Statute 7-13-105)

Wyoming allows citizens to register at the polls on election day. Voters also are allowed to change their party affiliation on election day and switch back again before they leave the polls. This creates the opportunity for people to participate in the primary of another political party and thus have a voice in deciding that party's nominees for the general election.

Wyoming's Election Code requires employers to give workers an hour off work to vote, aside from a meal break. People whose jobs include a break of at least three hours do not get an additional voting break.

Help America Vote Act

Congress passed the Help America Vote Act (HAVA) in 2002, in response to the experiences of the presidential election of 2000, when problems with voter registration and faulty voting procedures cast a shadow over election results in Florida. (Public Law 107-252)

The law requires a statewide voter registration system and use of electronic voting machines, called "DRE." That stands for "Direct Recording Electronic" voting machine. Voters directly enter their votes, which are recorded electronically. Most DREs have touch screens. A few have knobs or switches instead of touch screens. DREs have the advantage of letting voters know right away, before they finish voting, if they have "overvoted" (filled in too many candidates). They can accommodate voters with hearing and vision problems.

Previously, county clerks ran each county's voter registration system and kept their own records. They forwarded voter lists to the Secretary of State's Office, but methods of keeping lists up-to-date varied from county to county.

The Wyoming Legislature began incorporating HAVA requirements into the Election Code in 2003 with new voter registration requirements.

Voter registration requirements are now uniform statewide. Voter records are computerized and accessible by county clerks and the Secretary of State's Office. This benefits voters who show up at the wrong polling place, so poll workers can verify they are registered but must go to another location to vote.

Wyoming law authorizes the secretary of state to verify voter registration information by comparing it with the Department of Transportation's driver's license data, with information maintained by the Division of Criminal Investigation, with records of the State Board of Parole, and with death records of the Office of Vital Records Services. This verification process also is intended to assure that if a voter is an ex-felon, voting rights have been restored properly. The process checks information provided during registration and makes sure deceased voters are removed from voting lists.

Residents must produce a photo identification when registering to vote. If they have registered by mail, they must produce the photo identification the first time they vote.

Every voter has a unique voter identification number – a driver's license number or last four digits of a Social Security Number. A voter who has neither is assigned a number by the voter registration system.

County clerks may try to verify if people are providing accurate information by checking where they live, work, register their vehicles, or own property. People who are denied registration may appeal to a Circuit Court. (Wyoming Statutes 22-3-104)

Anyone who was registered and voting before the new system was created remained on the rolls and did not have to be verified.

Another requirement of the Help America Vote Act is availability of provisional ballots, so people whose voter registration is questioned on election day may go ahead and vote. Their ballots are put aside for a day until their status as valid, registered voters is verified. People who cannot provide proof of identification may use the provisional ballot and then present documentation by the end of the following day to the county clerk establishing eligibility to vote in the precinct.

A person who is challenged and wants to use a provisional ballot must sign the following oath before an election judge:

"I do solemnly swear (or affirm) that I am the person I represent myself to be and that I am a qualified elector entitled to vote in this precinct at this election and that this is the only ballot I have or will vote in this election.".

....
Signature of voter

....
Signature of judge

....
Precinct and District No.
(Wyoming Statutes 22-15-105)

The county's canvassing board decides if the information provided is valid.

A person challenged on the ground that his or her name does not appear on the registry list may vote if an election judge obtains verification from the county clerk that the person is entitled to vote in that election within that county. That is the benefit of having complete, up-to-date computerized voter lists available to every election judge in every precinct on election day.

The Help America Vote Act also includes requirements for voting machines. The Secretary of State's Office reported that in the 2002 General Election, Wyoming had 101 precincts still using punch card or lever machines. At least six counties counted their optical scan ballots at a central location, instead of at each polling place. Both of these situations would have violated the Help America Vote Act. Only a few precincts had voting systems that could be used by disabled voters.

The Help America Vote Act required states to replace all punch card, lever, and central-count optical scan voting systems by January 1, 2006.

Wyoming also planned to provide one DRE voting machine in every polling place. The state planned to establish a computerized statewide voter registration system that met HAVA requirements by January 1, 2006. (*Help America Vote Act: Wyoming's State Plan*)

Running for Office

Our representative form of government depends on people who take the time, effort, and expense to campaign for office and then devote two or more years to public service. A candidate must be a qualified elector, who is eligible and registered to vote.

Wyoming Campaign Practices are in the state's Election Code, which is Title 22 of Wyoming Statutes. The Secretary of State's Office also has published a "Wyoming Campaign Guide" that summarizes and highlights requirements for candidates. (The guide is described in Chapter 8.)

Candidates for statewide and legislative offices must file for office with the Secretary of State's Office. Candidates for county, municipal, school, and other local government office must file at their county clerk's office.

The filing fee for candidates running for statewide office is $200. That applies to the offices of governor, secretary of state, treasurer, auditor, and superintendent of public instruction. The fee for candidates for the Legislature and for local government office is $25. There is no fee for candidates for committeeman and committeewoman. (Wyoming Statutes 22-5-208)

By law, an application for nomination must be filed between 96 days and 81 days before the primary election. (Wyoming Statutes 22-5-209) In the nonpartisan races for school board and community college board of trustees, candidates file with the county clerk after the primary.

Candidates for U.S. Senate and U.S. House of Representatives must file with the Federal Election Commission in Washington, D.C.

All candidates may purchase a list of registered voters in their election district from the Secretary of State's Office. This list is useful for contacting voters by mail or for "walking the district" to visit voters at home.

Candidates are not required to form a campaign committee, but if they do, they must file a "statement of formation" within ten days of doing so. Every candidate and every candidate's campaign committee must file a report before the election on campaign contributions and after the election on both receipts and expenses. That includes candidates who lose and candidates who have neither contributions nor expenses.

Candidates are forbidden by law to use automated systems to dial telephone numbers and play recorded messages related to their political campaigns.

Candidates or their committee chairs should read Wyoming's campaign practices laws to make sure they comply with limitations on sources and amounts of campaign donations. They should take careful note of requirements to report contributions and to acknowledge in advertisements who has paid for the ads.

State law requires candidates seeking a seat in a legislative district to have lived in that district for at least a year.

Citizens who want to vote for someone who is not on their ballots may "write in" the name of that person. A person who gets "write in" votes and wants them counted must file an application for candidacy and a filing fee with the appropriate filing officer within two days after the election. In partisan races, where a nomination is being decided for a political party for the general election, the person must get at least 25 write-in votes. In nonpartisan races, where political party is not an issue, the person must get at least 3 percent of the votes.

A candidate who loses a primary election race cannot be a "write in" candidate for the same office in the general election.

A person who wants to be nominated for an office and win a spot on the general election ballot as an independent candidate must use the petition method. That means getting signatures from registered voters equal to 2 percent of the votes cast in that election district for Congress in the previous election.

Bronze sculpture of Louisa Swain, recognized as the first woman to exercise the suffrage rights given to women by the First Legislative Assembly of the Wyoming Territory in 1869. Swain cast her vote in Laramie in 1871. (Photo by Grayson Baird. Courtesy The Foundation of Laramie.)

Chapter 11

Tribal Government

The Wind River Reservation encompasses 2.3 million acres, about 3,800 square miles, in central Wyoming. It is home for two American Indian tribes: Northern Arapaho and Eastern Shoshone. Currently, 5,953 Arapaho and 2,650 Shoshone tribal members live on the reservation. The reservation is sparsely occupied: 6.7 people and 2.7 housing units per square mile of land. (U.S. Census Bureau, U.S. Department of Commerce)

This chapter describes the history of the reservation and how these two tribes came to the Wind River Reservation. It describes development of tribal government on the reservation, both executive and judicial, as influenced by traditional tribal culture and the federal government.

A major source of information for this chapter is *Tribal Government – Wind River Reservation*, written by Janet Flynn with the assistance of Scott J. Ratliff, a member of the Eastern Shoshone tribe and a former member of the Wyoming House of Representatives. Historical information is taken from *People of the Wind River,* by Henry E. Stamm IV, and from *Arapahoe Politics 1851-1978*, by Loretta Fowler. Fowler's book explains the guidance of elders in Northern Arapaho society and religion, the role of intermediaries in dealings with non-Indians, and the impact of ruling by consensus. John Washakie, descendent of Eastern Shoshone Chief Washakie, also lent valuable insight to this chapter.

Tribes on the Wind River Reservation

The main Arapaho tribe probably came from what is now northern Minnesota, moving south and west about 1600. In the 1860s, the tribe split. The Southern Arapaho accepted a small reservation in "Indian Territory" in the central part of the country in 1865, and in 1867 the tribe agreed to a reduction of that area. The Northern Arapaho

Eastern Shoshone Chief Washakie

One of three 11-foot-tall bronze sculptures of Eastern Shoshone Chief Washakie by Dave McGary. One statue is in the rotunda of the Wyoming State Capitol, a second in the Statuary Hall at the U.S. Capitol and the third at the Joint Shoshone and Arapaho Tribal Complex at Fort Washakie on the Wind River Reservation. (Photo courtesy: Dave McGary Studios)

resisted pressure to leave their hunting grounds in what is now Wyoming and Colorado.

"Age grading" was an important part of Northern Arapaho life. It is the custom of granting status and power based on achievements within age groups. (Flynn 1991, p. 11). The highest status and authority was given to the oldest men and women, who alone were allowed to perform certain religious and ceremonial rituals. Tribes and bands maintained a common purpose and value system of reaching decisions by consensus and respecting the wisdom of elders. Age grading created bonds among age groups and among different families, and it enhanced unity and reduced conflict. (Flynn 1991, p. 18) Younger generations were expected to learn new social skills and introduce new ideas, with the approval of elders. This system reaffirmed the authority of elders, while it legitimized change and enabled the Northern Arapaho to adapt to reservation life. (Fowler 1982, p. 9)

The Shoshone Indians ranged from California through Wyoming as early as the 1500s. They acquired a reputation for horsemanship and for being fierce fighters in conflicts with other tribes and with non-Indians over game and land. They had a warrior society among the men. They did not have formal age grading, as the Arapahos had, but they valued the wisdom of elders. The general pattern of Shoshone traditional tribal government was to have several bands within a tribe, each with a "headman" to negotiate with other bands or tribes. Dealings with Europeans and early American government representatives required tribes to establish single chiefs as designated, centralized leaders. The U.S. government later required tribes to establish government by councils.

Both the Shoshones and Arapahos found they had to adapt their political organization to accommodate dealings with the federal government, which wanted intermediaries or "chiefs" who could speak for tribal members and who had authority to sign treaties and other agreements. The Shoshones had been accustomed to living independently in bands of about 100-200, coming together only rarely for tribal decisions that required everyone's cooperation. On the

Chief Washakie

Photographic portrait of Chief Washakie. (Courtesy Wyoming State Archives)

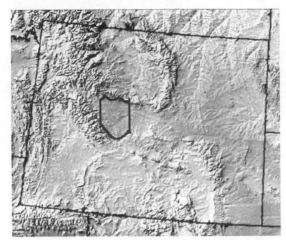

Topographical map of Wyoming showing original area of the Shoshone tribe in the second Fort Bridger Treaty of 1868.

reservation, all 1,000 tribal members were under one chief and a centralized government. The Northern Arapaho maintained separate communities on the reservation, with their individual headmen.

Chief Washakie, whose name means Rawhide Rattle, earned the status of statesman as he negotiated treaties for the Eastern Shoshone Tribe, and he became a respected figure of authority on the Wind River Reservation. He was born about 1810 to a father from the Flat Head tribe in Montana and a Shoshone mother from Idaho. During adolescence, while living in Idaho, he joined a passing band of Shoshone and Bannock that considered the Green River Basin area home. There, in about 1826, he joined a band of Eastern Shoshones and rose to prominence in that culture, while dealing with white trappers, including Jim Bridger. (Stamm 1999, pp. 25-27) Non-Indians began referring to Washakie as a leader in the 1840s.

Washakie is recognized as one of the most respected leaders in the American West, for his exploits in battle and for his statesmanship on behalf of his tribe. When he died February 20, 1900, at age 102, he was given full military funeral, unique for an Indian chief.

Treaties & the Shrinking Reservation

The first treaty between the U.S. government and American Indians was the U.S.-Delaware Treaty in 1778. A treaty is a contract between two sovereign nations, and it is the supreme law of the land. The U.S. Supreme Court has ruled treaties to be grants of rights from Indians, not to them. So, a right that is not expressly outlawed by a treaty is reserved to the tribe. This is the "reserved rights" doctrine.

A treaty with an Indian tribe recognizes the tribe's status as an independent nation, and early treaties did put tribes and the colonial government on equal footing. Colonists wanted Indian land and cooperation. Tribes wanted colonies' goods and services.

The last treaty was in 1871. After that, Indian matters were handled by legislative and executive branches of the federal government, and formal consent by tribal leaders was not required because Congress no longer viewed Indian tribes as sovereign nations. When land was transferred from tribes to the U.S. government, transactions were referred to as "agreements" and not "treaties." (Fowler 1982, p. 59)

As non-Indians moved westward to settle, prospect, and build railroads, Indians lost their bargaining position, and many of the treaties were not voluntary. The treaties resulted in Indian tribes' relinquishing land and being confined to reservations, sometimes far from their homelands.

It is difficult to determine how many treaties were voluntary, mutually understood, and favored by both governments. One problem was that negotiators for the U.S. government sometimes did not understand tribal leadership structure, and agreements were struck with the wrong individuals. Indians who seemed to ignore treaties may not have agreed to them in the first place. Or they may not have known exactly what was in the treaties, which were written in English and may have been amended after negotiations ended.

In 1851, federal Indian commissioners asked to meet with representatives of several tribes at Horse Creek, 35 miles east of Fort Laramie, in hopes of an agreement to keep the peace among the tribes and to ensure the safety of U.S. citizens. The agreement was signed September 17, 1851, by representatives of the Arapahos, Cheyennes, Sioux, Arikaras, Mandans, Gros Ventres, Assiniboines, Crows, and Shoshones. Under the agreement, the United States could establish roads and posts through Indian territory, and tribes would make restitution for damages to people passing lawfully through Indian country. To compensate for prior damage to hunting grounds, the U.S. government agreed to give the some 50,000 tribal members involved in the agreement $50,000 a year for 50 years, to be spent on provisions and merchandise, domestic animals, and agricultural implements. Arapahos and Cheyennes were assigned a large swath of land between the Arkansas River and the North Platte River, in northeastern

Colorado and southeastern Wyoming. (Fowler 1982, pp. 29-35) This agreement is sometimes referred to as the Fort Laramie Treaty of 1851.

As immigrants and settlers moved across and into Shoshone territory, and as clashes with Indians worsened, the U.S. government proposed the Treaty of Fort Bridger in 1863, which set aside more than 44 million acres of "Shoshone country" west of the Wind River Mountains and north of main immigrant trails. The area included parts of Colorado, Utah, Idaho, and Wyoming. The treaty established peaceful relations between the Shoshone tribe and the U.S. government. It provided for safe travel through the territory and settlement by the military. It compensated the Shoshones for loss of game, totaling $200,000 over 20 years to be paid in "articles the President of the United States may deem suitable to their wants." (Flynn 1991, p. 33)

The Arapaho and Shoshones looked forward to peaceful years ahead. However, white settlers continued their westward expansion throughout the 1860s. Game the tribes had relied on in their traditional hunting areas became scarce.

Shoshones, who had hunted in the Green River Valley, turned to hunting in Crow tribal territory to the north. Meanwhile, the government desired to provide stability for settlers in the Green River Valley and to maintain the railroads. Conflicts over land use became a major political issue under terms of the 1863 Treaty. This led to the second Treaty of Fort Bridger in 1868, which was signed by Chief Washakie and other leaders of the Eastern Shoshone and the Shoshone and Bannock Bands. The 1868 Treaty firmly established the Eastern Shoshone Indian Reservation, the "Shoshone Indian Agency," in Wyoming and the Fort Hall Indian Reservation at Fort Hall, Idaho. In 1871, the federal government established the military base of Camp Brown, renamed Fort Washakie in 1878, to protect the agency against Sioux warriors, and Chief Washakie and his Shoshones moved onto the reservation. The Bannocks moved in 1872 to Fort Hall in eastern Idaho. (John Washakie) (Stamm 1999, pp.57-85)

Under terms of the 1868 Treaty, the U.S. government was to give the Indians clothing and farming equipment and supplies for 30 years and to provide a teacher, carpenter, doctor, and other skilled individuals to help the Indians convert to a new lifestyle. In return, the

Shoshones agreed to stay on the reservation and not take up arms against the United States. The treaty also established the first federal government agent on the reservation.

Similarly, the Northern Arapahos found the Fort Laramie Treaty of 1851 did not ensure the peaceful future they had hoped for. In 1865, they lacked hunting and provisions and were wracked by disease. "These were disturbing times for the Araphos; they were aware that they could not hope to prevent white encroachments and that they could not survive without aid from whites," writes Loretta Fowler in *Arapahoe Politics 1851-1978.* (p. 37) On May 10, 1868, 150 lodges of Northern Arapahos and Northern Cheyenne met with an Indian Peace Commission that was assigned the job to settle tribes in areas where they would not conflict with settlement of the West. The commission also was to "obtain consent to a program of civilization," which would replace hunting with agriculture. (Fowler 1982, p.46)

Northern Arapahoe tribal intermediaries worked at cultivating good relations with Army officers so their tribe would not be settled with the Sioux or Cheyenne or with the Southern Arapaho in Indian Country, which had shrunk by this time to approximately present-day Oklahoma. The Northern Arapaho held out hope for their own reservation in the Powder River area of northern Wyoming. Black Coal and other tribal intermediaries referred to the Northern Arapaho as the "peace tribe" and "good Indians," and they expressed the tribe's willingness to adapt to an agricultural way of life. They gave up claims to the hunting privileges in land outside reservations defined in the 1868 treaty. (Fowler 1982, pp. 56-59)

Black Coal met with U.S. President Rutherford B. Hayes and Secretary of the Interior Carl Shurz in the fall of 1877. He recalled how Northern Arapaho scouts had helped the U.S. Army subdue hostile Indians. The Northern Arapahoe had made peace with the Shoshones, and they would be "good Indians" if they were placed in Wyoming on the Shoshone reservation. Black Coal said, "You ought to take pity on us and give us good land, so that we can remain upon it and call it our home. If you will give us a good place to stay where we can farm – we want wagons and farming implements of all kinds; provisions and annuities of all kinds – all to be given to us as we want them." (Fowler 1982, pp. 64-65)

In 1878, about 1,000 Arapaho Indians were brought by military escort to the Shoshone Agency as a temporary home.

In the first few years after arrival at the Shoshone Agency, Arapaho council chiefs worked to ensure the tribe's location in Wyoming was secure, by pressing the federal government to resettle them in northern Wyoming and later by resisting efforts by the Shoshones to have them removed. In 1885, Indian Agent Sanderson Martin advised the Arapaho tribe it would not get another reservation: "Here you must stay and die."

Treaties and agreements with tribes that restricted Indian activities included promises by the federal government to supply food, livestock, agricultural equipment, and other supplies. Typically, the Indians did not receive what was promised.

In a speech in 1878, Shoshone Chief Washakie said the white man's government had not kept its word. "The white man kills our game, captures our furs, and sometimes feeds his herds upon our meadows," he said. The government had failed to fulfill commitments to provide seed, farming tools, breeding stock, and schools the tribe could not provide itself on the reservation. "I again say, the government does not keep its word. And so, after all we can get by cultivating the land, and by hunting and fishing, we are sometimes nearly starved, and go half-naked, as you see us! Knowing this, do you wonder, sir, that we have fits of desperation and think to be avenged?" (Flynn 1991, p. 16)

Chief Washakie and Arapaho council chiefs Black Coal and Sharp Nose appealed to Indian agents to supply the promised provisions, as game became increasingly scarce. Members of the two tribes killed 2,400 bison in 1882, 1,500 in 1883, 500 in 1884, and none in 1885. They could not hunt outside the reservation boundaries. (Fowler 1982, p. 81) In "Historical Highlights" in the back of Volume 1 of *Wyoming Blue Book* (1979), events of 1889 include, "Last wild buffalo is killed in Wyoming."

In 1889, each person on the reservation who was entitled to rations received one pound of beef and 10 ounces of flour once a week. (Fowler 1982, p. 88)

Meanwhile, the reservation shrank considerably over the years. The first great reduction was the Brunot Cession of 1872, named for Felix R. Brunot, head of the federal Board of Indian Commissioners.

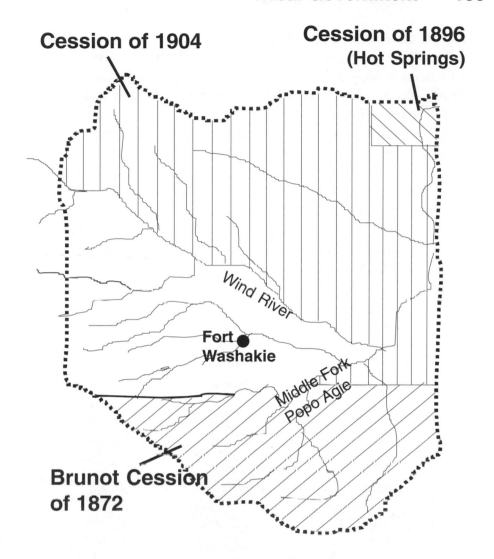

Cession of 1904

Cession of 1896
(Hot Springs)

Wind River

Fort Washakie

Middle Fork
Popo Agie

Brunot Cession
of 1872

Map of Shoshone Agency as created by the 1868 Treaty of Fort Bridger, later named Wind River Reservation, showing loss of land through cessions in 1872, 1896, and 1904. (Congress amended the 1904 agreement in 1905 before approving it.)

Source: Adapted from a map by Wyoming historian Grace Raymond Hebard. (Courtesy Wyoming State Archives.)

The Shoshones ceded the southern third of the reservation, the 700,000 acre Popo Agie valley, which already had many white settlers. Lander was founded in 1874 just 15 miles south of the new southern border. In exchange, the Shoshones received $20,000 worth of cattle and $5,000 in cash. (Stamm 1999, pp. 79-96)

It was another land cession that really established the Northern Arapahos as full partners in the reservation.

In 1891 and again in 1893, the two tribes negotiated with federal Indian Commissioners to cede about half the reservation to the United States, but Congress and the tribes could not agree.

In 1896, in the first McLaughlin Cession, the Shoshones and Arapahos accepted an agreement presented by Indian inspector James McLaughlin to cede to the government about 10 square miles of hot springs near what is now the city of Thermopolis. In return, the tribes were to receive $50,000 in cash. The Arapahos were to receive $10,000 in cattle and the Shoshones the same amount in cattle or cash. The $50,000 was to be spent on the tribes at the discretion of the Interior secretary in five annual installments. It is noteworthy that the government negotiated separate agreements with the tribes (how they would take the $10,000), and men from both tribes voted on the proposal. Of 457 men over age 18 on the reservation, 180 Shoshones and 93 Arapahos signed the agreement. Chief Washakie insisted the springs be open to the public, a condition still honored today. The tribes saw little of the promised $50,000. (Stamm 1999, p. 243) (Fowler 1982, p. 93)

Representatives of Eastern Shoshone and Northern Arapaho tribes sign the 1904 Land Cession Agreement, also known as the Second McLaughlin Agreement, which was amended and approved by Congress in 1905. Photo by J.E. Stimson. (From the collection of Evelyn Bell, courtesy of the Chief Washakie Foundation.)

In 1904, McLaughlin proposed another cession of land, which was needed for white settlers. Under the second McLaughlin Cession, the U.S. government negotiated with the Shoshone and Arapaho tribes to open 1.48 million acres north of the Wind River for purchase by homesteaders to farm the land. From the proceeds, the tribes were to receive a minimum $150,000 for an irrigation system, $50,000 in livestock, $50,000 for a school fund, and $50 for each member of the tribes. (Flynn 1991, p. 34) Congress amended and ratified the agreement in 1905 to include all the land north of the Wind River to the junction of the Popo Agie and from the mouth of the north fork of the Popo Agie to the southern boundary of the reservation. (Fowler 1982, p. 95)

This resulted in the founding of the town of Riverton. Hundreds of white settlers moved onto prime irrigable lands, and the federal government began pouring money into water development programs. (Stamm 1999, p. 243)

It was several years before the Indians and their children received the promised $50 per capita payments. The government sold land for $1.50 an acre for two years, then for $1.25 an acre for the next three years, for not less than $1 an acre for the next three years, and subsequently to the highest bidders. Proceeds went to the tribes' accounts, after deductions to pay for $85,000 in per capita payments, $35,000 to survey the ceded lands, and $25,000 for irrigation work.

The second McLaughlin Cession left the reservation with 808,500 acres, although the tribes later bought back much of the land that was lost.

Participation by Arapahos in the hot springs deal gave them legal and political legitimacy at Wind River.

In 1927, the Shoshone Business Council sued the U.S. government for giving a portion of the reservation to the Arapaho without permission or compensation. In 1939, the lawsuit was settled with the payment of $4.5 million to the Shoshones. The Joint Business Council used the money to buy back as much of the ceded land as possible. The Arapaho were not entitled to settlement money, so they borrowed $500,000 from the Shoshones to participate in the buy-back.. By 1940, about 1 million acres were returned to tribal ownership.

In 1955, the Arapaho and Cheyenne tribes brought suit against the U.S. government through the Indian Claims Commission for compensation for land that was granted to them in the Fort Laramie

Treaty of 1851 but was lost to non-Indians. The claim was paid in 1961, and the Northern Arapaho received a one-quarter share. The U.S. government kept the money as reimbursement for money paid to the Shoshones for one-half of the reservation.

Tribal Politics

When the Shoshones and Northern Arapahos had their first contact with representatives of the federal government, they did not have individuals who ruled over the entire tribes. Tribal bands had headmen, who later rose to "chief" or "intermediary" status in dealings with the federal government and other whites.

For the Northern Arapaho, leaders were men who were brave and good, generous, even-tempered, conciliatory, and respectful toward elders. They were mature men who ruled by persuasion and consensus, not assertion. In dealings with the federal government, they became intermediaries for their bands and the whole tribe. Tribal members expected these intermediaries to represent the desires of the tribe, not to make decisions independently. They gained stature by bravery in battle and then, later, by defending the interests of the Arapaho tribe in dealings with the federal government and the Shoshones, getting provisions and money promised by treaties.

When they settled on the Shoshones' reservation, council chiefs emerged as leaders in Arapaho politics. They were expected to obtain concessions and benefits for their tribe, to resist the government's attempts to undermine tribal institutions, and to exhibit the qualities of "good men." Those qualities were generosity, bravery, respect for elders, and responsiveness to group consensus. They represented themselves to whites as reliable allies of the government. Black Coal and Sharp Nose were particularly adept at showing bravery in confrontations with whites and Shoshones, while demonstrating to tribal members the high regard they held among federal officials. (Fowler 1982, p. 70)

The influence of elders helped maintain social stability and preserve religious ceremonies during the traumatic decades of the 1880s and 1890s.

The Arapahos have retained their political system of consensus and respect for elders, even as they have adopted political innovations initiated by the federal government. These innovations include

Northern Arapahoe Leaders

Black Coal and Sharp Nose emerged as chief intermediaries for the Northern Arapaho tribe in dealings with the U.S. government the years around the settling of the tribe on the Shoshone Agency in 1878. As a boy, Friday lived with non-Indians in St. Louis 1831-1834 and was very important as intermediary and translator.

These images appeared in the March 1880 issue of Harper's New Monthly Magazine, for an article by U.S. Army Lieutenant H.R. Lemly. (Courtesy of Cornell University Library, Making of America Digital Collection. Lemly, H.R.. "Among the Arrapahoes." Harper's New Monthly Magazine, Vo. 60, Issue 358, March 1880 pp. 494-501)

Black Coal

Sharp Nose

Friday

selection of leaders by voting, political centralization, and directive leadership. (Fowler 1982, p. 13)

Shoshone tribal politics worked differently. Chief Washakie had great personal influence and had authority to make decisions on behalf of his tribe. He was respected as a wise leader and advocate for his tribe. After his death in 1900, 120 members of the Shoshone tribe petitioned the federal Indian Office to select a new chief or chiefs. (Fowler 1982, p. 104)

A letter written in 1889 by the Rev. John Roberts, Episcopalian missionary on the Shoshone Agency, related the tribe's "pitiful" condition and Washakie's advocacy:

> "These Indians are passing through, just now, the most trying time they have ever experienced for the reason that the wild game which hitherto has been their support, is now very scarce. They have not yet learned to farm and raise crops. However, they are, this spring, fencing in small farms and the Shoshones have raised a small amount of wheat for the last four years. So far, they have no means of having it ground. They pound it with a stone, roast it or boil it but in such a way that is not palatable. They need a mill. … I heard Chief Washakie tell an inspector, 'I have waited a long time to hear the rumble of a mill. It is one thing to hear before I die.' When Washakie consented to settle on a Reservation, he was promised a mill, schools, and protection from his enemies. In the early days great injustice was done the loyal Shoshones by allowing the hostile, troublesome tribes much more than was allowed those who had been loyal to the government. […] (Markley and Crofts 1997, p. 23)

Relationship with U.S. Government & History of Tribal Government

Relations with the federal government have depended on tribal sovereignty recognized by the government and courts. Relations also have relied on prevailing politics in Washington, D.C, which have ranged from assimilation to tribal autonomy.

Over the years, the governments of Shoshones and Arapahos on the Wind River Reservation have evolved to a blend of traditional tribal ways and systems that accommodate the respective cultures.

Changes have been influenced by the requirements of sharing a reservation, by federal agents, by pressures to adopt non-Indian ways, and by the allotment program, which broke up traditional family units. (Flynn 1982, p. 20)

In the 1850s, the federal government began creating reservations for American Indians, with the goals of avoiding conflicts with white settlers and cultivating self-sufficiency. (Cawley et al. 1996, p. 147) In 1871, however, the mood in Washington, D.C, favored assimilation of Indians into the wider American culture and to limit tribal sovereignty. Treaty-making with tribes ended.

Life on the reservation was fundamentally changed with the federal General Allotment Act of 1887, also called the Dawes Act for sponsor Sen. Henry Dawes of Massachusetts. Previously, land was owned communally, and the notion of individual ownership ran counter to traditional cultural values and work ethic. This new law allowed ownership of land by individual tribe members: a quarter-section (160 acres) to heads of families and smaller parcels for single tribal members and children. Land not settled by Indians could be purchased by non-Indians. Indians who occupied their land for 25 years received title to the land. Until then, land was held in trust by the federal government. Those who accepted allotments became U.S. citizens.

Supporters saw the Allotment Act as a way to speed up assimilation of Indians into the Anglo-American culture. Some genuine friends of Indians hoped their treaty land would be secure, protected from exploitation by non-Indians, railroads, and the government. They also hoped the philosophy of individualism and the hard work of farming would help Indians prosper and succeed in the American culture.

The real effect of the Allotment Act was an assault on the history of the tribes and Indian culture. Directly or indirectly, the Allotment Act determined how much land the tribes would keep and how much could be acquired by non-Indians. It determined citizenship rights, which were tied to land ownership instead of traditional ways of determining tribal membership. Reservation land that had been owned communally by tribes was divided into parcels owned by individuals. This all affected how authority was shared between individuals and the tribe. (Flynn 1982, p. 24)

In fact, in the 47 years between 1887 and 1934, tribal lands shrunk from 138 million acres to 48 million acres nationally. The Wind River Reservation is now a fraction of its original size. Much of the land, including the city of Riverton, was sold to non-Indians, as a result of the Allotment Act. (See map on page 153.)

The Eastern Shoshone and Northern Arapaho previously enjoyed a nomadic life of hunting and gathering food, and reservation land was held by all tribal members. The Allotment Act tied individuals to parcels of land they were to cultivate, and tribes had to concern themselves with inheritance and issues of land ownership. When the federal government put the allotment policy into effect on the Wind River Reservation, the Commissioner of Indian Affairs treated the Northern Arapahos as if they had equal rights on the reservation. (Trenholm 1970, p. 306)

With the new century came a new role for leaders of the two tribes, who formed chief's councils. Instead of appealing for increased rations, they focused efforts on increasing tribal income from leases and gaining control over expenditure of that income. (Fowler 1982, p. 130) In 1908, at the insistence of the Indian Office, the tribes began electing six-member Business Councils to conduct tribal business. However, the Business Councils followed the desires of all tribe members, who comprised the tribes' General Councils.

The Shoshones and Arapahos had not received full payment for the lands ceded in 1904. They did not receive the cattle they were promised nor the irrigation system and water rights they had expected, and the government was withholding the $50 per capita payments to minors. Many Indians sold or leased their allotments at amounts far below their value and took wage work, while the money was held in a trust account or was released as purchase orders at stores owned by non-Indians. Indians on the Shoshone Agency were living in extreme poverty, most still living in tents and brush shelters. The tribes were particularly frustrated at the Indian Office's insistence at allowing only minimal and occasional per capita payments, for instance, only $12 in 1920 and $20 in 1921 for Arapaho tribal members. (Fowler 1982, p. 130-134)

The Shoshones and Arapahos sent delegations to Washington, D.C., in 1903, 1913, and 1928 to seek more control over mineral lease income and the unfulfilled promises of 1904. They continued to lobby for per capita payments.

The Bureau of Indian Affairs had been created in 1824 by Secretary of War John C. Calhoun. Congress formalized the BIA in 1832 and moved it to the Interior Department in 1849. Most of the dealings were payment for lands, settlement of claims, and accounting of money to civilize Indians. The BIA assumed governmental duties on reservations to provide subsistence aid and administer allotment-related activities, which included land sales and enforcement of land dealings.

With the federal Snyder Act of 1921, the BIA assumed formal authority over most legal and business affairs on reservations. The BIA had custody of individual and tribal money, approved wills and heirs, prosecuted criminals, and aided development of agriculture.

The Indian Citizenship Act of 1924 made all American Indians citizens of the United States, while they kept tribal affiliation. They became citizens of three sovereign entities: their tribe, their state, and the United States.

In 1934, Congress passed the Indian Reorganization Act (IRA) at the urging of federal Indian Commissioner John Collier, who wanted to restore the power of tribes to manage their own affairs. The IRA, also known as the Wheeler-Howard Act, called for preservation of tribal land and resources and economic development to help the tribes. Reservation lands were to be held by tribes in trust, instead of being allotted to individuals. Congress also wanted to lessen influence of the BIA over tribal affairs and to strengthen tribes' autonomy by allowing them to write their own constitutions

The IRA included several reforms that tribes could adopt individually. Under IRA, tribes could reassert control over their own resources, establish economic development projects, create legal codes and tribal courts, and promote projects to improve health, education, and welfare on reservations.

However of the 181 tribes that voted on IRA provisions to reorganize and incorporate, only 103 voted "yes."

The Wind River tribes were among those who opted to stay under direction of the BIA, perhaps because of a reluctance to trust the U.S. government to honor its treaties and agreements involving water rights and oil leases. The tribes were still pressing for per capita payments. In 1935, they received $5 in cash and $40 in store orders. Tribal members were reluctant to change the ownership and use of their lands. They counted on individual allotment of lands for the security for the elderly and children on the reservation. Members of both tribes resisted persuasion by the BIA. When the official vote was taken in 1935, many Shoshones had a change of heart, and the tribe approved the reform agenda by a one-vote margin. However, the Arapaho soundly defeated it. Lacking approval by both tribes, the reorganization failed.

In 1908, the Shoshone and Arapaho tribes each had a general council, composed of all tribal members. Each tribe also selected a business council of six members to deal with tribal affairs. To deal with issues affecting both tribes, the business councils regularly met together as a Joint Business Council. There also was a Court of Indian Offenses to handle judicial functions.

The U.S. government preferred to deal with business councils instead of general councils, where tribes made decisions by consensus and where issues usually involved mediating disputes. Use of business councils had the effect of "detribalization," which was the process of weakening traditional culture and government. This further had the effect of increasing federal officials' control over the tribes in getting access to tribal resources.

Arapaho council leaders usually served until death or until disabled by old age or illness. During the years 1908 to 1936, the six seats on the Arapaho Business Council were held by just 22 men. Shoshone leaders tended to be younger, to serve shorter terms, and to be of "mixed blood." They also tended to be more assertive in dealings with federal officials. Despite their cultural differences, though, the tribes realized the benefit of joint negotiations when dealing with the U.S. government. (Flynn 1991, pp. 39-40)

In the 1920s and 1930s, federal authorities tried to pressure the tribes to adopt non-Indian methods of government. Shoshone Agency Superintendent Reuben Haas persisted in attempts to detribalize the reservation. He tried to remove the Shoshone Business Council chairman, Charles Driskell, because of his resistance to Haas' ideas, but the joint tribal council refused to support the action. Haas urged young men – in their 20s and 30s – to run for business council elections, and he promoted ill-fated farming and ranching operations. (Fowler 1982, p. 154)

Haas pushed the tribes to adopt a constitution and by-laws that undermined traditional governing systems by increasing the power of business councils over the tribal members. He insisted that tribes select council members by balloting in 1930. Only half the eligible Arapaho voters participated, and they re-elected three of six from the previous council. The three were aged 50, 60, and 64 years old.

The Wind River tribes do not have a constitution, although they benefited from other reforms under the Indian Reorganization Act of 1934, which was intended to reduce the influence of the federal government and dependence on the Bureau of Indian Affairs. The law gave tribes the power to control their own resources, to incorporate, and to give final approval over disposition of tribal money and income-producing holdings.

Under the Indian Reorganization Act of 1934, there was an effort to "modernize" the Joint Business Council in 1937. Arapahos Bruce Groesbeck and Robert Friday and Shoshones Irene Meade and Lynn St. Clair were appointed by agency Superintendent Forrest Stone to prepare a constitution and by-laws to give the council new powers. The Joint Business Council approved the documents in 1938 but then rejected revisions proposed by the BIA in 1939. However, the business councils of both tribes adopted some provisions:

- Elections were held every two years in November.
- The business councils appointed election judges and clerks.
- The six elected members of the Arapaho and Shoshone business councils came together to form a Joint Business Council, whose chairman's seat is held alternately by the chairmen of the Arapaho and Shoshone councils.
- Meetings were conducted according to parliamentary rules. Minutes were recorded.
- Only enrolled tribal members at least 21 years old were allowed to run for office or vote.
- Reservation resources were divided equally between the tribes.
- The Joint Business Council was authorized to conduct programs to protect tribal customs and religious freedom, to guard tribal rights and property, to conserve natural resources and use them

for the greatest good, to retain tribal lands in tribal ownership, and to make recommendations on federal government programs.

The tribes ignored other provisions of the proposed constitution:

• A primary election in October would select twelve candidates for the November business council elections. (The Arapahos used "nomination meetings," where candidates were generally selected by elders.)

• Twenty-five percent of eligible voters could sign a petition to hold a referendum vote to revoke a council decision.

• A majority of Joint Business Council members could vote to dismiss a member who missed three consecutive meetings without an excuse or who was guilty of misconduct. Council members' behavior that was deemed inappropriate was handled by pressure from tribal leaders.

(Fowler 1982, pp. 187-188)

The 1930s was a decade of struggle between attempts to keep important old ways while adopting practices that dealt with political realities on the reservation. BIA personnel succeeded in shortening the terms of business council members from four to two years and in making the Joint Business Council more representative and more powerful. Conflict arose between young Indians eager to adopt non-Indian ways and older tribe members who criticized lack of loyalty to traditional values.

Other attempts by the BIA to detribalize the reservation focused on cultural and religious practices overseen by tribal elders. The Sun Dance, one of the most important religious ceremonies, was prohibited in 1913 but allowed again in 1923, when it included Christian symbols. The government also prohibited the Ghost Dance, a ceremony practiced by many Plains tribes to describe the end of white occupation and the return of land to Native Americans. The Shoshones and Arapaho practiced the dance for a short time in the late 1800s.

Participation by Arapahos in the hot springs deal of 1896 gave them legal and political legitimacy at Wind River, but it was a court case settled in 1937 that gave them equal status on the reservation.

In 1927, the Shoshone tribe won congressional consent to file a claim for damages against the United States for violation of the 1868

Two women stand with three three children outside a structure on the reservation known as the Shoshone Reservation ca. 1925. The reservation was renamed the Wind River Reservation 14 years later. (Photo courtesy of Bureau of Indian Affairs)

Cattle crew at Wind River Agency, ca. 1943. (Photo courtesy of Bureau of Indian Affairs)

Treaty. Under terms of that treaty, the Eastern Shoshones relinquished a reservation of 44,672,000 acres in what are now the states of Colorado, Utah, Idaho, and Wyoming. In return, the United States pledged the Shoshones would have exclusive occupation of the 3,054,182-acre Shoshone Agency in Wyoming. In 1878, the commissioner of Indian affairs allowed the Northern Arapaho to settle on the Shoshone Agency, where they shared in payments from land cessions of 1896 and 1904 and in the allotment of lands.

Shoshone attorney George Tunison won the case in 1937, and the Eastern Shoshones were awarded $4.4 million in damages. The agency was officially renamed "Wind River Agency." It is commonly known as the Wind River Indian Reservation.

By a congressional act on July 27, 1939, the Shoshones received $4.2 million, after addition of $155,080 in interest and subtraction of attorneys' fees. Of the total, $1 million was designated to buy land. Each Shoshone received $2,450: $100 in cash; $1,350 in credit to be used to buy land, housing, equipment, seed, and livestock, or to support the elderly and disabled; and $1,000 to individual Shoshone accounts for purposes approved by the Interior secretary. The money also included $125,000 loan fund. The rest of the money was put in a capital reserve fund to be used with the consent of the Interior secretary. Reservation lands were put in trust for both tribes. (Fowler 1982, pp. 196-197)

The Arapaho, not entitled to settlement money, borrowed $500,000 from the Shoshones at 4 percent interest to participate in the buy-back of land from non-Indians. On April 17, 1940, the Interior secretary signed an order of restoration that returned about 1.25 million acres of ceded land to joint tribal ownership. (Fowler 1982, p. 196)

The BIA engineered the major land purchase of the Padlock Ranch in the northeastern corner of the reservation, with the idea the two tribes would own the land but the Arapahos would run the ranch and generate income for the tribe. The Arapaho Ranch began operations in 1941 with 4,939 head of cattle. By 1947, the Arapaho tribe had repaid the Shoshones the money borrowed to buy the land. The ranch started with a non-Indian manager named by the BIA. In 1948, the Arapaho Business Council succeeded in obtaining the authority to select the manager and make policy decisions, including the hiring of Arapahos to work the ranch. Under the management of a board of three Arapaho trustees, the ranch encompassed 343,000 acres of range and 4,500 acres of irrigated land. (Fowler 1982, pp.198-199)

In 1946, Congress created the Indian Claims Commission to handle claims from Indian tribes for land taken illegally by the U.S. government. Awards were based on the value of land at the time it was taken, and the federal government reduced money it had already spent on the tribe. (Cawley et al. 1996, p. 149)

Congress began in 1947 to "terminate" American Indian tribes. This meant the federal government cut its programs and services on the reservations, and tribes were freed from supervision and control. Federal termination policies 1947-58 had serious consequences:

- For the first time, states could exercise jurisdiction over Indians.
- Termination policies ended many special federal programs for Indians.
- Termination ended the trust relationship between some tribes and the federal government.
- Termination policies raised questions about tribal sovereignty in dealings with the federal government.

In 1954, a congressional committee recommended termination for the Shoshone and Northern Arapaho. The Joint Business Council sent Arapaho Nell Scott and Shoshone Bob Harris to Washington, D.C., and they argued successfully for continuing federal aid. Congress abandoned the termination effort for all tribes in 1968. President Richard Nixon officially ended the policy in 1970 as "morally and legally unacceptable."

The Indian Self Determination and Education Assistance Act of 1975 transferred more authority to the tribes. It encouraged a system of government that enabled the tribes to contract for their own programs and services.

The Bureau of Indian Affairs originally exercised direct supervision and control of tribes. Now, it is primarily a contracting agency, with indirect oversight over programs. However, the influence and direct involvement of the BIA in tribal government depends on the wishes of the tribes. In Wyoming, the Shoshone and Arapaho tribes prefer a more traditional relationship with the BIA, with more direct administration of tribal programs and services. (Flynn 1991, p. 28)

By 1950, individual business councils and the Joint Business Council became effective governmental bodies in dealings with the U.S. government. They negotiated agreements on regulation of oil and gas leases, treaty violation claims, and distribution of tribal income that had been held in trust. The councils defeated attempts to end federal aid to the Wind River tribes. They dealt with economic development and protection and control of tribal resources.

The tribes had argued for decades, loudly but without success, for the federal government to share more of the tribal income with members in the form of per capita cash payments to relieve some of the deep poverty on the reservation. A BIA survey in 1940 of 218 Arapaho homes found 69 households were using a one-room log house, and 62 households lived in tents. The domestic water supply was the river or an irrigation ditch. The agency superintendent reported in 1943 that 77 percent of the Indian families had an average income of less than $1,000 a year, which was up from previous years but far below that of neighboring non-Indians, including those with agricultural operations on leased reservation land. (Fowler 1982, pp. 201-202)

Then in 1947, a delegation consisting of the Arapaho Business Council, three Shoshone councilmen, and two tribal attorneys went to Washington, D.C., to plead their case once again. Wyoming Congressman Frank Barrett had introduced a bill to pay out two-thirds of tribal money in per capita payments and to retain one-third of joint funds in trust under BIA control. Arapaho council member Nell Scott was the main spokesman for the tribes, and she testified before the House Subcommittee on Indian Affairs. She and the others testified that BIA management was inept. (Fowler 1982, p. 203-206)

In May 1947, Congress authorized payments for a five-year trial period. Payments averaged about $550 a year per enrolled Arapaho and a little more for Shoshone members, because there were fewer of them.

In 1951, Congress renewed the semi-annual payments and specified that tribal income from sources other than oil royalties was to be distributed in the same fashion. In 1953, Congress acted to increase the proportion of tribal income distributed to members to 80 percent. In 1955, Congress provided for quarterly payments, so they became a more regular source of income. The proportion was raised to 85 percent in 1956, and in 1958 Congress amended the law so that payments were monthly and the Interior secretary could not exercise liens on the payments to minors.

Per capita payments vary with the income and enrollment of the tribes. In 2005, payments were about $325 a month for members of the Eastern Shoshone tribe and $140 a month for Northern Arapahos.

With the beginning of per capita payments in 1947, the Wind River tribes acted to better define tribal enrollment. Previously, adherence to tribal customs and culture was enough to be considered a member. Over the years, the Shoshone and Arapaho tribes have tightened criteria, which is still a concern for them.

As the tribes' business councils gained political power to make laws, set policy, and administer life on the reservation, the tribes created "social committees" to organize and coordinate tribal social functions and celebrations. In recent years, the Shoshone tribe has shifted power to enact legislation from the Business Council to the Shoshone General Council, which includes all tribal members.

As the tribal government grew stronger, it came to more closely resemble the government of the non-Indian culture. In 1972, the Arapahos adopted a primary to reduce the field of business council candidates to twelve for the general election. The Shoshones began primaries in 1990. (Flynn 1991, p. 65)

Government structures on reservations continue to change. Modern tribal government evolves as it accommodates the larger American culture and tribes' distinct native cultures and customs. Over the years, tribal governments generally have become more sophisticated and more formal. Another dynamic influence on tribal government is the interaction among federal government, the states, and Indian tribes.

The Wind River tribes won significant court victories in 2005 that supported a claim of unpaid royalties and affirmed their right to run casino-style gambling free of state regulation.

On April 18, 2005, the U.S. Supreme Court let stand a federal appeals court ruling that the U.S. government mismanaged oil, gas, timber, and grazing royalties on the Wind River Reservation between 1946 and 1973. The government paid a $12 million claim to the tribes.

On July 14, 2005, the Tenth U.S. Circuit Court of Appeals affirmed a ruling by three of its judges eight months earlier that the

Northern Arapaho tribe did not need approval by the Wyoming state government to operate a Las Vegas-style "Class III" level casino. The tribe accused the state of failing to negotiate in good faith to enter a compact to set up a gambling operation on the reservation, while allowing gambling elsewhere for social or nonprofit purposes. That ruling allowed the tribe to seek Class III casino gambling authority from the Interior Department under the federal Indian Gaming Regulatory Act of 1988. The request was granted September 23, 2005. Then the Shoshones announced their own plans for a casino. On April 19, 2006, Wyoming and tribal officials signed a gaming compact to allow the Eastern Shoshones to operate a Class III casino on the reservation.

During the litigation, members of the Northern Arapaho tribe said the tribe needed the income from gambling to alleviate poverty on the reservation, and they predicted the communities of Fort Washakie, Riverton, and Lander would benefit economically as well. Burnett Whiteplume, chairman of the Northern Arapaho Gaming Agency, was quoted in the online publication "Gambling Magazine" as saying, "We just want to be able to take care of ourselves."

Questions of Sovereignty

The U.S. Supreme Court wrote three key opinions to define lines of authority and sovereignty of Indian tribes:

- In 1823, the Supreme Court case of McIntosh vs. Johnson dealt with the relationship between the federal government and Indian tribes. Chief Justice John Marshall affirmed tribes were separate political bodies, but their land could be claimed by the U.S. government when its military forces conquered the tribes.
- In 1831, the Supreme Court decided in Cherokee Nation vs. Georgia that Indian tribes had limited sovereignty as "domestic dependent nations" under federal guardianship. They were not as sovereign as independent foreign nations, Chief Justice John Marshall said, but they were political bodies that could govern their internal affairs and enter agreements with the U.S. government.
- In 1832, an opinion in Worcester vs. Georgia reinforced the idea of limited tribal sovereignty, called the "Worcester doctrine." The Supreme Court said the Cherokee tribe could resist infringement of Georgia state law on the tribe's reservation.

The two Cherokee tribe decisions established two important points affecting the sovereignty of Indian tribes: 1) The tribes exist under the federal government's protection, so their sovereignty is limited. They are subject to supremacy of the federal government. 2) Indian tribes are distinct political communities, and states cannot intrude on their self government unless permitted by the tribes or authorized by Congress. (Flynn 1991, pp. 59-60)

These and later cases affirmed Congress has absolute authority to regulate tribal matters or to abolish a tribe. Federal authority over Indian tribes is mentioned in the U.S. Constitution only in the Commerce Clause (Article 1, Section 8). The Supreme Court has based the idea of federal sovereignty on military conquest of Indian tribes and on the role of the government as trustee for the tribes.

The idea of tribal sovereignty continues to be disputed. Janet Flynn, in her book *Tribal Government*, defines sovereignty as "that power and quality of independence nations have which entitles them to govern themselves." (p. 60) Many Indians reject the idea of limited tribal sovereignty. Some believe they enjoy sovereignty as a natural right that cannot be granted or limited by another power. Some believe sovereignty is derived by those who are being governed.

The Supreme Court considers some tribal powers "inherent." That means they belong to the tribes naturally. They include:
- Right to form a government
- Right to determine membership
- Right to tax
- Right to maintain justice
- Right to regulate domestic relations (marriage and divorce)
- Right to regulate property use
- Right to regulate commerce and trade

In addition, the Wind River tribes are affected by a section of the Wyoming Constitution (Article 21, Section 26) that says Wyoming citizens have no claim to lands owned or held by Indians, and those lands are exempt from state taxes. The land is under absolute jurisdiction of Congress. (Flynn 1991, p. 62)

Tribal sovereignty was affirmed in 1968, with the passage by Congress of the Indian Civil Rights Act. The law, which amended Public Law 280, prohibited states from exercising jurisdiction over tribes without their express consent. It also gave federal constitutional rights to persons under the jurisdiction of tribal governments. Other federal legislation in the late 1960s and 1970s gave tribes greater authority to manage resources and programs.

Self-determination comes at a price. It promotes tribal autonomy, but it also lessens the trust relationship between federal government and tribes, and some Indians fear that discontinuing federal guardianship could threaten their survival. (Flynn 1991, p. 64)

Tribal Government Today

The Northern Arapaho and Eastern Shoshone tribes each elect a six-member Business Council. Members serve for two years and select a chairman. The councils also meet together as the Joint Business Council, chaired alternately by leaders of the Shoshone and Arapaho councils.

Absolute tribal authority is the General Council, which includes all adult members. General Councils meet as necessary to consider tribal enrollment, game and fish management, and any matter that falls outside the business councils' usual dealings. The Wind River tribes do not have constitutions that would dictate governing bodies and their responsibilities. Business council members sometimes find it useful to hold meetings of the general council to discuss important issues.

The Shoshones and Arapaho are under a system of government different from other tribes in the nation, without a constitution approved by the secretary of the Interior. They are not constrained to a system of government requiring approval of decisions by the Interior secretary. They may adopt or reject any features of a constitutional government that meet their needs. The authority of business councils is strictly limited to routine matters. Any non-customary matter must come before the full general councils. (Flynn 1991, p. 46)

The Arapaho tribe operates the Arapaho Ranch on about 300,000 acres of the land the tribes bought back. The tribes also get royalty income from production of oil, gas, and other minerals on the reservation.

When the tribes came to live on the reservation, their traditional culture and religious practices continued to shape their self-government. Native American philosophies of governing have been retained, but structure and procedure of council government on the

Wind River Reservation are heavily influenced by political forms of the American culture.

The Northern Arapaho traditionally governed by consensus and distributed goods and income fairly. The highest religious authorities for the Arapaho were ceremonial elders who achieved status in the tribe. They approved activities and were responsible for ritual objects. When the BIA pressed the tribes to elect council members by majority vote, the Arapaho let their elders select the members, and then they notified the BIA of the results. The Eagle Drum Ceremony, conducted by elders, commemorated the selections, who were reminded of their tribal obligations and subordinate role to the elders.

Shoshones had ceremonial elders, as well, but they separated the religious and political more than the Arapaho. These elders were a unifying element among the bands in pre-reservation days, and they continued to influence business council affairs. The Shoshones accepted majority rule, although they respected views expressed in the general council. Their Native American values and priorities and their desire for good relations with their creator directly influenced their manner of government.

The Arapaho and Shoshone tribes continue their own philosophies of management, budgeting, and representation. An example is passing laws. The Arapahos give their Business Council authority to enact legislation for the tribe, although they do so based on consensus of all members. The Shoshones keep legislative authority in the general council. Political representatives of each tribe must accommodate these differences and the needs of two distinct political bodies of equal voting power to resolve issues that affect both tribes. (Flynn 1991, p. 79)

At the same time, the tribes work with the Bureau of Indian Affairs in its administrative role.

The business councils benefit from growing sophistication and use of legal expertise in their dealings with the state and federal government. Recurring areas of dispute are taxation, commerce regulation, criminal jurisdiction, and reservation resources of water, land, and minerals.

Indians disagree among themselves whether the Bureau of Indian Affairs is still useful, as tribes become less dependent on the agency.

Some see continuing benefits in dealing with the BIA, because of its established bureaucracy in Washington, D.C., and on reservations. They wonder if they would fare as well as the BIA in securing federal programs they depend on. The U.S. government is still bound by treaties to help preserve the health and welfare of tribes. Defenders of the current system recall the hardships suffered during the days of termination, when tribes tried to become more self-sufficient and were left "high and dry" by the government. (Flynn 1991, p. 69)

The BIA provides basic services on the Wind River Reservation. It administers: social services; law enforcement; oversight of land ownership; transfer and leases; road construction and maintenance; distribution and management of per capita monies; facilities and grounds management; soil conservation and range management; and irrigation projects. (Flynn 1991, p. 27)

The BIA also functions as an oversight agency, ensuring tribal activities comply with federal laws. The BIA can take the role of mediator among members of a tribe, between tribes, between tribes and the federal government, or between the tribes and non-Indians on the reservation. The BIA may be a liaison and facilitator between tribes and the Wyoming state government. (Cawley et al. 1996, p. 153)

Courts on the Reservation

The Indian Reorganization Act of 1934 allowed creation of tribal courts to handle mediation and judicial functions performed previously by tribal councils. The Joint Business Council on the Wind River Reservation established the tribal court in March 1988.

Traditionally, tribes resolved conflicts by bringing matters before an elder recognized as the authority in the area of conflict. The goal was to restore harmony through negotiations, so parties in a dispute could feel satisfied. Restitution to an injured individual or family was a major part of the resolution. Guilt and punishment were not goals of the judicial process.

Subsequently, the Bureau of Indian Affairs set up the Court of Indian Offenses, known as "CFR courts" because they followed the Code of Federal Regulations. The courts were an extension of BIA powers, and reservation agents exerted great influence over the selection of judges and their decisions. The author of *Tribal Government – Wind River*

Reservation writes, "These courts were accused of being a form of cultural oppression, particularly in their formative years, since many of the cases they tried involved banning Indian religious dances, ceremonials, and other native traditions." (Flynn 1991, p.71)

CFR courts handled civil cases involving disputes between two tribal members or by a non-Indian against an Indian. In modern tribal courts, civil jurisdiction is determined by location of the incident, not the ethnic background of the parties. Tribal courts most often deal with civil disputes and minor crimes. Unless Congress says otherwise, Indians who live on reservations are subject to their tribe's criminal laws. With few exceptions, tribal criminal codes do not apply to non-Indians, and states do not have jurisdiction over Indians on reservations.

Tribal courts generally are more informal than state and federal government courts. Judges usually are not lawyers and are selected for their judgment, integrity, and esteem of others. They may be picked by business councils, general councils, or religious leaders. On the Wind River Reservation, there are four tribal court judges – one chief justice and three associate judges. They apply to the Joint Business Council for appointment. The chief justice must have a law degree and is appointed for life. Associate justices must complete a tribal legal examination and are appointed for four-year terms. They stand for retention by voters for additional terms.

Wind River tribal councils may participate in an Intertribal Supreme Court that was approved by the Montana-Wyoming Tribal Court Judges Association in 1991. It would provide an independent review of cases, but it also would put cases before judges who might not share the legal philosophy of the Wind River Reservation.

The Shoshone tribe in 2005 approved the use of Peacemaker Code as a voluntary alternative to the Law and Order Code. The Peacemaker Code is patterned after traditional models of justice that use social sanctions, mediation, and compromise to settle disputes. The courts appoint "peacemakers" to find resolutions to such things as disputes among family members, alcohol-related problems, and minor business transactions in dispute. Tribal prosecutors may offer accused persons the option of using the Peacemaker Code.

Tribal court decisions are seldom appealed. Cases and penalties usually are minor, and some reservations may have the original trial judge hear the appeal. In the Wind River tribal court, trial judges do not hear appeals from their own courts.

Tribal courts struggle with lack of legal training for judges, lack of staff, difficulty enforcing court orders, and influence on decisions by councils, religious leaders, or the BIA. Tribal court decisions are not always recognized by other courts. Some states are establishing through their Supreme Courts the idea that any territory of the United States (including that of tribes) should receive "Full Faith and Credit," meaning legal jurisdictions honor each other's decisions.

Northern Arapahoe Business Council in 2005

Left to right: Chairman Samuel J. Dresser, Co-Chairman Richard Brannon, Anthony Addison Sr., Nelson P. White Sr., Norman P. Willow Sr., and Harvey T. Spoonhunter. (Photo courtesy Northern Arapahoe Business Council)

Eastern Shoshone Business Council in 2005

Left to right: Kassel Weeks, Valeria Arkinson, Chairman Ivan Posey, Willie Noseep, Arlen Shoyo Sr., and Mike Lajeunesse. (Courtesy Eastern Shoshone Business Council)

Chapter 12

History of Wyoming Government & Politics

Government is more than an impersonal blueprint of laws and institutions, carried out with detachment . A study of Wyoming government must include the key events and political personalities that have shaped the state. Politics can be understood as the give and take of conducting the state's business, which can produce petty battles in the Legislature or can give Wyoming the nation's first female governor.

The institutions and laws of our government change in response to opportunities, problems, and demands of its citizens. However, it is interesting to note how many of the important issues are perennial: use of public lands, taxing and regulating the mineral industry, reorganizing government, and standing up to federal influence.

This chapter covers the particularly human aspect of government, the politics of making laws and running our government.

One of the first things a student of Wyoming government notices is the dominance of politics and elections by members of the Republican Party. Appendix 4 shows the party affiliation of winners in Wyoming federal, state and legislative races since statehood.

Republicans dominate party affiliations of voters in nineteen of the twenty-three counties, particularly concentrated in the northern and rural counties. The GOP claimed an overwhelming 61.5 per cent of registered voters in the state in 2005. (See the table in Chapter 13 Political Parties.) Democrats, with 27 percent of Wyoming voters in 2005, tend to claim majorities in the cities and the counties along southern Wyoming's Union Pacific Railroad.

Political activity and elections were occasions for lively discussion during territorial days. One reason the Wyoming Territory elected its congressional delegate and its Assembly members at the same time in 1882 was to "cut in half the excitement and strife which were

part of campaigning and voting." (Larson 1978, p. 220.) It seems
residents of the Wyoming Territory welcomed the diversion of political
gatherings, debates, and torchlight parades.

Early Politics

Historian T.A. Larson describes a lively political scene in Wyoming in the 1870s and 1880s: "Politicians played for keeps, packing
primary conventions, stuffing ballot boxes, lying about one another,
and buying votes with whiskey and money."

Practitioners of such activities tended to lose by the decade of the
1880s, but many reprehensible practices continued. In May of 1888,
there was an election to determine if the county seat of Converse
County should stay in Douglas. Bill Barlow's *Budget*, in Douglas,
charged that Lusk and other eastern precincts had voted children,
canary birds, and poodle dogs in their attempt to win the seat. According to the *Budget*, 200 out of the 226 votes cast in Manville (which
finished third) were fraudulent. (Larson 1978, p. 221)

Organization of new counties and determining county seats were
contentious issues. Territorial Gov. Thomas Moonlight, a Democrat,
bitterly opposed the organization of Natrona County in 1888. A bill to
appoint three commissioners for organization passed the Legislative
Assembly over his veto, but he refused to make the appointments.
After his removal from office by the president of the United States,
Republican Francis E. Warren was appointed governor, and he named
the commissioners.

In the subsequent local vote to determine the Natrona County
seat, Bessemer beat Casper by a margin of 378 votes, historian Virginia Trenholm writes in her book *Footprints on the Frontier*. "Inas-
much as Bessemer had a population of fewer than 100 and all votes
for that location were cast in its precinct, the election commissioner
declared the vote irregular and awarded the county seat to Casper."
(Trenholm 1945, p. 191)

Deliberations of the territorial Legislative Assemblies could be
just as lively, as could enforcement of laws once they were enacted. A
failed attempt to outlaw gambling was a major issue of the 1888
session. Rep. Tom Hooper of Crook County declared gambling an
"inherent attribute of the human heart." That October, the town of

Douglas reported monthly revenue of $300 from six monte games. (Larson 1945, p. 214)

Gambling also was the reason Congressman Frank Mondell carried a .45-caliber bullet near his spine most of his life. In the winter of 1889-1890 he was mayor of Newcastle, a municipality he called "the banner wide-open frontier town of all the Northwest." In the spring, he and the city council decided they needed to rid the town of gamblers and other undesirables. They gave the marshal a list of 20 men who had to be gone in 24 hours. A hotelier wanted the 20 to stay until they paid their bills, and he shot Mayor Mondell. (Larson 1978, p. 214)

Another early burning issue was location of the territorial capital. Evanston and Laramie were rivals to Cheyenne, and the question led to legislative turmoil in 1873. A bill to move the capital to Laramie had passed the House by a vote of 7-6. Cheyenne members of the Territorial Council were in a panic, and the next day, only six members showed up, denying the body a quorum. The members in attendance declared the empty seats vacant and passed the bill, although Gov. John Campbell did not approve the bill. (Larson 1978, p. 127)

The Wyoming Territory survived attempts in the 1870s in Congress to "dismember" it, so its land could be divided and assigned to Utah, Montana, Idaho, and Colorado. U.S. President Ulysses Grant remarked in 1872 that Wyoming's population was less than 10,000 and probably would not be enough for statehood (60,000) anytime soon. In fact, about half of Wyoming's population thought it might be a good idea to be part of another sovereign state. However, Colorado gained statehood in 1876 without taking in the southeastern portion of Wyoming. (Larson 1978, p. 120)

The top territorial offices were appointed by the U.S. president. The appointments were influenced by political intrigue, shameless promotion, and character assassination communicated by influential men in the territory to Washington, D.C.

Gov. Francis E. Warren accomplished much with the Republican-controlled Legislature in the 1886 session. Cheyenne and Laramie together controlled a majority of legislators that year, and they pulled together on many issues. Among their accomplishments were construction of the Capitol Building in Cheyenne, a university in Laramie, and a hospital for the mentally ill in Evanston. Two years later, Rawlins won approval of funding for a penitentiary.

However, delegates to the Constitutional Convention in 1889 decided to leave permanent location of state institutions to a vote of the people after ten years.

The question of a permanent home for the state capital was put on a statewide ballot in 1904. Cheyenne came in first with 11,781 votes. Lander was second with 8,667 votes, Casper third with 3,610, followed by Rock Springs with 429, and Sheridan with 122. Although it received the most votes, Cheyenne failed to get a majority, as required by the Constitution. Cheyenne remains the temporary capital of Wyoming. (Roberts 2001, p. 389)

Wyoming citizens also voted to locate the state's agricultural college in Lander, but nothing was ever done about it, and it remains in Laramie as part of the University of Wyoming.

Statehood Politics

Despite the Democrats' influence in early territorial assemblies, Republicans typically have dominated the Legislature and statewide offices through Wyoming's history as a territory and a state. The northern part of the state historically has been a stronghold for Republicans, while the southern part, especially along the Union Pacific line, has supported Democratic candidates.

The one exception was 1934, when Democrats won majorities in both the Wyoming House (38-18) and Senate (14-13) and won all five top elected offices, led by Gov. Leslie A. Miller. Democrat Joseph O'Mahoney was returned to the U.S. Senate, and Democrat Paul R. Greever won our seat in the U.S. House of Representatives.

As Wyoming entered statehood, Republicans enjoyed the strong leadership of Joseph Carey and Francis E. Warren, who were elected by the First Legislature as Wyoming's first U.S. senators. (U.S. senators were elected by state legislatures until the 17th Amendment to the U.S. Constitution in 1913 provided for direct election by voters.) Warren resigned his office as governor just 17 days into his term to take the Senate seat, and Secretary of State Amos W. Barber moved into the job as Wyoming's governor.

(Top elected officials since statehood are listed in Appendix 3.)

The First Wyoming Legislature had quite an agenda to accomplish tasks assigned by the Wyoming Constitution and to resolve disputes that had been debated during the constitutional convention. There was very little partisan bickering, thanks to overwhelming Republican control of the Legislature and the top elected offices.

- The Constitution required reapportionment of legislative seats among the counties, based on the 1890 census, but nothing could be passed. Indeed, reapportionment has been a painful process throughout the state's history, culminating in a federal court order in 1992 that the state had to observe the one-person-one-vote principle. In 1890, counties along the Union Pacific Railroad in southern Wyoming had three-fourths of the population, and they wanted three-fourths of the state Senate seats. Northern counties objected. They wanted one senator per county, regardless of population.
- The first legislators debated and then dropped the idea of a production tax on coal.
- The Legislature created the office of attorney general, to be appointed by the governor.
- The Legislature created the Board of Charities and Reform, composed of the state treasurer, auditor, and superintendent of public instruction.
- The Legislature set up the Board of Land Commissioners, to include the governor, secretary of state, and superintendent to manage some 4 million acres of federal land grants.
- The Legislature established a miners' hospital (sited by voters in 1892 in Rock Springs) and a Wyoming College of Agriculture, temporarily located at the University of Wyoming in Laramie.

Populists emerged as a third party in the early days of statehood and had quite an impact on politics, but they never wielded power as a political party largely because of dissension among party leaders. Also, there were few crop farmers and virtually no silver production in Wyoming, and laborers and miners were intimidated by employers. (Larson 1978, p. 285)

In 1892, Populists figured in one of the less auspicious chapters in Wyoming politics, which resulted in our state having just one U.S. senator, Joseph Carey, from 1893 to 1895.

Populists joined with Democrats to elect John Osborne of Rawlins governor in 1892, and Democrat Clarence D. Clark was elected to Congress. Republicans held the state Senate, and Democrats and Populists held the House.

U.S. senators were picked by a joint session of the Legislature, which was evenly split between Republicans on one side and Democrats and Populists on the other. The 1893 Legislature passed a state budget and 33 essential bills, but most of the session was spent on argument and intrigue and 30 ballots for U.S. senator. No one received the required 25 votes. Accusations of bribery and poisoning raged.

Governor Osborne appointed A.C. Beckwith of Evanston as senator, but the U.S. Senate refused to seat him, and he resigned.

Republicans re-established their dominance in the next election, 1894, with the election of Gov. William A. Richards. Republicans won overwhelming majorities in the state House and Senate, which then unceremoniously dumped Carey and picked Francis E. Warren and Clarence D. Clark to go to the U.S. Senate. Warren stayed in the Senate until his death in 1929, and Clark continued until 1917.

Republicans enjoyed even more dominance in Wyoming at the turn of the 20th century, led by the so-called "Warren Machine." In 1898, they gained almost complete control of the Legislature, state executive positions, and the whole congressional delegation. During the next decade, Democrats had just nine of the fifty-seven seats in the Legislature. The Warren Machine had support of several newspapers.

In 1910, Republican Joseph Carey ran for governor as an "independent" nominated by the Democrats. He won, and Democrats won state offices (two of them) for the first time since 1892. As usual, Republicans controlled both houses of the Legislature.

Carey, who was a leader of the Progressive movement in Wyoming, accomplished a great deal during his administration, and historian T.A. Larson calls him "one of the most outstanding governors in all of Wyoming history." (Larson 1978, p. 323-325)

Some reforms proposed by Governor Carey:

- **Direct primaries.** The Legislature agreed and established primary elections to select nominees for the general election.
- **Corrupt practices act.** The act would require publication of election expenses and would limit campaign expenditures. The

Legislature passed a law limiting expenses to 20 percent of one year's salary for the office.

- **Initiative, referendum, and recall.** The Legislature attempted an initiative-and-referendum constitutional amendment, which failed the popular vote. The Legislature rejected the recall. Wyoming still has no provision to recall elected officials.
- **Commission form of government for cities.** Enacted.
- **Reapportionment after the 1910 census.** The Legislature distributed 27 Senate seats and 57 House seats among 14 counties.
- **New counties.** The Legislature added 7 counties to the existing 14: Campbell, Goshen, Hot Springs, Lincoln, Niobrara, Platte, and Washakie.
- **Lobbyist registration.** No action.
- **Prohibition against legislators' competing for contract awards created by laws and appropriations they had approved.** No action.
- **Corporation law allowing cooperatives for marketing agriculture products.** No action.
- **Immigration board.** Legislature appropriated $40,000 and set up a five-member board to encourage immigration.
- **Prison reform.** Legislature setup office of warden and established a state commission on prison labor. The state set up the Wyoming Industrial Institute in Worland for young prisoners.
- **Full-time director of State Hospital for insane in Evanston.** No action.

Balance in the Legislature between Republicans and Democrats and an active third party, Teddy Roosevelt's "Bull Moose" Progressives, produced lively results in 1912 to rival those of 1892.

Republican political reporter John Charles Thompson Jr., of the *Wyoming State Tribune* in Cheyenne, reminisced later that the 1913 Legislature had been "the most disorderly" in state history. He recalled "conspiracies, counter-conspiracies, contests, cross, double-cross and super-double-cross, shouting, tumult, riot, criminal charges. For more than a fortnight, the state was agog." (Larson 1978, p. 328)

Republicans had the Senate 16-11 and seemed to have the House 30-27. Democrats, with the help of Governor Carey, convinced two Republicans to vote with them, giving Democrats a 29-28 margin.

One of the defectors, Martin Luther Pratt of Powell, was promised the House Speaker's chair for voting with Democrats. U.S. Sen. Francis Warren hurried home from Washington, D.C., to restore order in the Republican ranks. Ten days into the session, Pratt, a freshman, restored his loyalty to Republicans and but kept his speakership. (Larson 1978, p. 329). Rumors of bribery by Republicans were unproven. When the speaker pro tempore challenged him, Pratt responded by grabbing the man, throwing him to the floor, and taking the chair. A melee ensued, but the House eventually came to order to complete the session.

The 1913 Legislature approved an amendment requested by Gov. Joseph Carey to authorize a workmen's compensation act, which voters approved. The Legislature also agreed with the governor to approve a U.S. constitutional amendment providing for popular election of U.S. senators. The nation ratified the amendment that same year.

One of Carey's 16 vetoes during the 1913 session killed a measure that would have created Shoshone County out of the northeastern part of Fremont County, with Shoshoni the county seat. Carey quoted alleged threats by Republican Party leaders to divide Fremont County if it sent a Democratic delegation to the Legislature, which it did.

It was Democrat John B. Kendrick, a Sheridan County rancher, who won the northern counties in 1914, and he was elected governor. Republicans held three of five state elective positions and continued traditional control of the Legislature. (Larson 1978, pp. 387-88) Kendrick enjoyed enviable harmony with the Legislature and won some significant actions: workmen's compensation act; public utilities commission; constitutional amendment permitting farm loan legislation; extension of women's rights; game and fish laws; authority for the Board of Equalization to equalize assessments; two experimental farms; provision to remove unfaithful county officers; amendment of direct primary law; and extension of the Capitol Building.

Kendrick was Wyoming's first popularly elected U.S. senator in 1916, despite fairly blatant violation of conflict of interest and anti-corruption state laws. He had spent three times the allowed $3,000 on the campaign and had bought 9,666 acres of state lands while governor

Francis E. Warren, governor of territory and state of Wyoming and U.S. senator for 37 years until 1929.

Joseph M. Carey, Wyoming governor and U.S. senator, governed during progressive, tumultous legislative sessions, 1910-1914.

and president of the State Land Board. The land had been selected to control waters of Waddle Creek, Hanging Woman Creek, and Seventy Six Creek in Sheridan County. (Larson 1978, p. 392)

The 1918 Legislature responded to a phenomenal increase in "gasoline buggies" and created the State Highway Department under a highway commissioner. The law authorized acceptance of federal highway funds, to be matched by the state. Wyoming residents approved a $2.8 million bond issue in 1919 and another bond issue of $1.8 million in 1921. That used up the state's entire bonding capacity.

By 1918, Wyoming had 15,900 registered automobiles, ten times the number of just five years earlier.

Grand Old Men

T.A. Larson wrote in 1978 in his *History of Wyoming* that three political leaders deserved the term "Grand Old Man." They were Joseph M. Carey, Francis E. Warren, and John B. Kendrick. Carey and Warren

Democratic Gov. John B. Kendrick enjoyed a congenial working relationship with a Republican Legislature and won the first popular election of a U.S. senator from Wyoming. (Photo courtesy of Wyoming State Archives)

were Republican, Kendrick a Democrat.

During territorial days, Carey was U.S. attorney, Supreme Court justice, and delegate to Congress. He was U.S. senator 1890-1895 and governor 1911-1915. He was capable of being vindictive, according to contemporaries, but he was a great stump speaker. He died on February 5, 1924, at age 79.

Warren was territorial governor and the first state governor for a few days until he was elected to the U.S. Senate. He served in the Senate 37 years, until his death on November 24, 1929, at age 85. He was preparing to run again in 1930. He was chairman of the U.S. Senate Appropriations Committee 1921-1929 and worked hard to bring federal projects to Wyoming. The *Denver News* called him the "West's great patronage dispenser." (Larson 1978, p. 448)

Kendrick was governor 1915-1917 and defeated three prominent Republicans to win U.S. Senate elections in 1916, 1922, and 1928. He had arrived in Wyoming from his native Texas with a trail herd in 1879, a 21-year-old cowboy with a seventh grade education. When elected governor, he was a prosperous Sheridan County rancher with many friends in the Wyoming Stock Growers Association and the Republican Party. Rarely has any governor, Republican or Democrat, worked so harmoniously with a Republican Legislature. He died in office on November 3, 1933, at age 76. (Larson 1978, p. 389)

First Woman Governor

Nellie Tayloe Ross was governor 1925-26, giving Wyoming another distinction as the Equality State. She was the first woman to be governor in the United States.

Her husband, Gov. William B. Ross, was in the middle of his term when he died a month before the general election of November 4, 1924. A special election on that day would decide who would complete the term. The Democratic Party nominated Ross' widow to be on that

Wyoming Gov. Nellie Tayloe Ross, 1924-26. (Wyoming Archives photo)

ballot, and she out-polled her Republican opponent by 8,000 votes. Texans elected a woman governor on the same day, Miriam A. "Ma" Ferguson. However, Mrs. Ross is acclaimed as the first woman gover-

Nellie Tayloe Ross, on the right, at her desk as Director of the U.S. Mint, with an unidentified woman. She served in that position 1933-1953. (Wyoming State Archives photo)

nor because she was inaugurated and assumed office 20 days before Mrs. Ferguson.

Republicans had majorities in the House and Senate and held the other four top elected offices during her term. Mrs. Ross, who had not been politically active before her election, is credited with giving the state a "respectable, dignified, and economical administration," according to historian T.A. Larson.

Mrs. Ross was nominated again by Democrats for the gubernatorial election in 1926, but she lost by 1,365 votes to Republican businessman Frank Emerson.

During the campaign, women's suffrage supporters criticized her for failing to advance the cause of women. Theresa A. Jenkins, who had delivered a speech at a statehood celebration in Cheyenne in 1890, asked, "What has Mrs. Ross done to particularly deserve the votes of women? Has she ever, since coming to Wyoming, taken any interest in Woman's Suffrage?" (Larson 1978, p. 460) Her critics said she had been elected out of sympathy and was unqualified for the office. They also were critical that her public appointments included 174 men and only five women, and none of those to an office previously held by men.

Mrs. Ross never ran for another office in Wyoming. She served as director of the U.S. Mint from 1933 to 1953. She died at age 101 in Washington, D.C., on December 19, 1977.

Public Lands, Politics, Prohibition, and Taxes

The decades of the 1920s and 1930s saw regulation of federal lands for grazing, a distaste for prohibition, and approval of Wyoming's first sales tax.

In 1926, Wyoming Congressman Charles E. Winter resurrected the idea that the federal government should transfer the public lands in eleven Western states to those states. This idea was called "cession." Winter was joined in this campaign by Wyoming Senate President Perry W. Jenkins of Big Piney, who led the Legislature to unanimous approval of a "memorial" to Congress to "return" to the states "all vacant and unappropriated lands, together with all resources, including water power, power sites, forests, and minerals, now held in trust by the federal government within the border of any of the said states."

(Larson 1978, p. 426) The idea fizzled, as Winter lost a bid for the U.S. Senate and Jenkins lost in his attempt to be elected to Congress.

In 1929, the Hoover Administration proposed the idea of giving states 190 million acres of public domain grazing land to support public schools. In Wyoming, that was 17 million acres, 27 percent of the state's area. President Herbert Hoover appointed a twenty-two-member Committee on Conservation and Administration of the Public Domain, which issued a report in 1931. It recommended cession of grazing lands to states that would accept them, while the federal government would keep rights to known mineral deposits. The federal government also would keep defense areas, parks, forests, monuments, reclamation and reservoir sites, and migratory bird refuges. Home-steaders and cattlemen in Wyoming opposed cession, fearing what would happen to their individual rights and privileges. Opponents also demanded that the state take ownership of subsurface mineral rights, as well as the surface.

Supporters said the proposal was better than the alternative, which would be to keep the land in the hands of the federal govern-ment, to be leased under federal regulation with permits and fees. But that is exactly what happened, in the adoption of the federal Taylor Grazing Act of June 28, 1934. Wyoming Congressman Vincent Carter protested that the measure would give the secretary of the Interior "practically dictatorship over our livestock industry of the West and can be compared to the dictatorship of Russia." The president of the Wyoming Stock Growers Association, Dugald R. Whitaker, called it "another example of the bureaucrats in Washington trying to extend their power and their control more and more." (Larson 1978, p. 429)

Conservationists, who suspected damage to public lands by poor grazing management, favored the Taylor Grazing Act.

Under the Taylor Grazing Act, the secretary of the Interior set up five management districts on 16 million acres in Wyoming, on which 150,000 cattle, 1400 horses, and 1.5 million sheep were permitted to graze on a fee basis.

Under the Oil and Gas Leasing Act, federal lands in Wyoming were open to oil development. Wyoming collected revenue on the production (property taxes) and also received a share of royalties collected by the federal government. Wyoming wanted half the royalties but had to settle for 37.5 percent, which was divided thusly: 50 percent to schools, 41 percent for highways and roads, and 9 percent for capital improvements at the University of Wyoming. Wyoming also received a share of royalties the federal government put into a reclamation fund.

In the first year, 1921, Wyoming received $748,445. That amount grew to $4.2 million in 1924. Oil prices dropped and revenue declined, but it reached new highs after World War II.

Wyoming also collected royalties and property taxes on oil production from state lands, including the very profitable Salt Creek field on a school trust section in Natrona County.

In 1922, State Geologist G. B. Morgan stated that oil had made the mining industry more important than livestock or agriculture in the state's economy. He also raised the warning that oil reserves would be tapped out in 20 years.

This fear that the oil would soon be gone strengthened calls for a severance tax on oil, which had support from both Republicans and Democrats during the 1923 Legislature. A bill by Republican rancher John A. Stevenson of Albany County called for a 1 percent severance tax on oil. That would have required that oil companies pay the state 1 percent of the value of oil produced in return for the privilege of "severing" the mineral and taking it. The battle was furious. The oil industry would be ruined and half the population thrown out of work, the oil lobby claimed. The House killed the bill 29-20. Opponents argued that the proposed severance tax required amending the Wyoming Constitution, and they said the industry already was burdened by a property tax on oil since 1913. The 1923 Legislature approved such an amendment, but it failed a vote of the people in the 1924 election..

Prohibition

Wyoming's experience with prohibition on liquor production and sales demonstrated the ineffectiveness of laws not supported by the public. Wyoming citizens voted overwhelmingly in November 1918 for the Eighteenth Amendment to the U.S. Constitution, to prohibit importing, exporting, transporting, selling, and producing intoxicating liquor. The amendment took effect in January 1920, when the Congress passed the National Prohibition Act.

Federal, state, and local officials in Wyoming kept busy in the 1920s and 1930s trying to enforce the law.

In 1921, federal law enforcement officials announced they had made a raid in Sweetwater County that was the biggest and most successful raid of its kind west of the Mississippi. They arrested 62 people in Rock Springs, Green River, and Superior. They confiscated 1,400 boxes of raisins, 3,000 gallons of wine, and 1,000 gallons of other intoxicants. Gov. William B. Ross told the Legislature in 1923 that violation of the law was bad enough, but it was "breeding contempt for all laws." The Legislature gave him permission to remove county officers who failed to carry out their duties. Ross secured the resignation of a county sheriff and county attorney. (Larson 1978, pp. 439-441)

Disregard for prohibition was evident in the defense presented by a Rock Springs man who refused to pay for three tons of grapes and four barrels ordered from Rock Springs Commercial Co. The business sued. Claiming breach of warranty, defendant Mike Perko said the company "warranted the [grapes] to be fit and proper for making wine, and intoxicating liquor." Perko complained that the grapes were "musty, damp, and green, and that they did not make wine, but vinegar, and that said grapes when received were in a spoiled condition and unfit for use in the making of wine." He lost in District Court and on appeal in the Wyoming Supreme Court. (*Perko v. Rock Springs Commercial Co.,* 37 Wyo. 98, 259 P 250 (1927).

While public sentiment in Wyoming deemed prohibition a failure, the state Senate cast only four votes in 1927 for a memorial to Congress seeking a popular vote on the issue. In fact, the 1927 Legislature stiffened the penalties to include a three-year prison term for ownership of a still. In the House, Rep. Milward Simpson, who later served as Wyoming governor 1954-58, said his county, Big Horn, was "sopping wet and saloons run wide open." He warned that juries would be less likely to convict if it meant a jail term. (Larson 1978, p. 441)

Prohibition created opportunities for official corruption. William C. Irving, state law enforcement officer 1927-28, was convicted and sentenced in 1930 to 18 months in prison for conspiracy to violate national prohibition laws. Two people from Thermopolis and two from Kemmerer also were convicted of conspiracy. Irving was charged with collecting "protection money" while he was the head of the state law enforcement department. For example, operators of a large still paid him $1 per gallon. City officials in Thermopolis and Rock Springs were charged with using fines as a kind of licensing system to help the municipal treasuries. A jury found them innocent. Another jury cleared the mayor, police chief, and 34 other citizens of Casper who were tried for conspiracy to accept protection money in 1933.

Meanwhile, popular opinion in Wyoming had shifted against prohibition. The Legislature put the issue on the ballot in 1932, as a referendum on repeal. The vote was 62,957 for repeal of prohibition and 21,015 for retention of the law. By December of 1933, three-fourths of the states, including Wyoming, ratified the Twenty-first Amendment to the U.S. Constitution to repeal prohibition.

In 1935, a Democratic-controlled Wyoming Legislature established the Wyoming Liquor Commission to be the liquor wholesaler to retailers and consumers in the state. Republicans complained it was "socialism," but Democrats said the state needed revenue. Republican majorities in the Legislature have retained the Liquor Commission.

Government Welfare

Wyoming residents suffered greatly during the Great Depression, but they were reluctant to take help from the federal government. They agreed with President Herbert Hoover that the responsibility to help others should be shouldered by individuals and private groups. Wyoming was the only state that rejected the Reconstruction Finance Corporation's offer in 1932-33 of loans to states for emergency relief purposes. States promised to repay the loan out of future federal aid road appropriations.

Meanwhile, the taxable valuation of property in Wyoming shrank from $448 million in 1929 to just $300 million in 1935.

Gov. Leslie Miller, a Democrat who had served in both the state House and Senate, told a special session of the Wyoming Legislature in December 1933 that self-help had failed. He secured $75,000 for distribution to counties for food, clothing, fuel, and shelter. The state had already accepted $95,443 in outright grants from the federal government. At the time, one Wyoming person in five was receiving some form of relief.

The federal government spent $141 million in Wyoming between 1933 and 1939. The government bought cattle and sheep that were starving in a drought during 1933-36. In 1936, the federal Resettlement Administration paid $9 million to buy 300,000 acres of land in Goshen, Plate, Converse, Campbell, and Weston counties. Then, conservation practices were introduced to restore the land. The federal Public Works Administration put up many buildings in Wyoming: post offices, county court buildings, the student union building at the University of Wyoming, the state Supreme Court building in Cheyenne, 33 school buildings, and others. The Rural Electrification Administration increased the number of electrified farms and ranches from 527 in 1935 to 3,300 in 1939. (Larson 1978, p. 444-445)

During these hard times, Communism gained a following elsewhere in the nation. In Wyoming, Communist Party candidates for governor, congressman, and secretary of state received just 150-170 votes in 1934. The party held a convention in Cheyenne in July 1936, but it mustered only 91 votes for its presidential candidate. (Larson 1978, p. 446)

Wyoming's First Sales Tax

It was in this context of hard times that Gov. Leslie Miller won approval of Wyoming's first sales tax.

Property taxes had been the foundation of Wyoming's tax system since territorial days, and the Legislature resisted adding other taxes. The state still has no individual or corporate income tax and is considered unlikely to have one any time soon.

Some delegates to the Constitutional Convention in 1889 favored a severance tax on coal, and they managed to win initial approval of such a tax. But that decision was quickly reversed after intense lobbying by the Union Pacific Railroad, which owned mines and produced coal along its line across southern Wyoming.

Wyoming suffered an agricultural depression in the early 1920s. Democrat William Ross was elected governor in 1922. He had gained support in the Legislature to put a severance tax constitutional amendment on the ballot in November 1924, and it was the central issue of the campaign. He died a month before the election, and the amendment was overshadowed by the election of his widow, Nellie Tayloe Ross, to replace him for the last two years of his term. The amendment lost by a narrow margin. ("A History of the Wyoming Sales Tax and How Lawmakers Chose it from Among Severance Taxes, an Income Tax, Gambling and a Lottery," *Wyoming Law Review*, Vol. 4, Phil Roberts, pp. 157-243)

In the 1930s, dire financial needs of the state, cities, and towns stimulated renewed interest in the idea of adding another kind of tax to property taxes. Other states in the region had adopted an income tax, and the idea was proposed during the 1933 Wyoming Legislature. The idea was supported by agricultural interests and a few legislators representing labor interests. However, it was opposed by business interests and professionals. The income tax idea failed. A measure that would have legalized all forms of gambling passed the House and Senate but was vetoed. Meanwhile, the Wyoming Tax League formed and opposed new taxes without drastic cuts in government spending, which the 1933 Legislature did.

In 1935, Democratic Governor Miller aligned with legislators who wanted a "temporary emergency" sales tax to get the state through hard times. The Legislature approved a 2 percent tax, which helped the state treasury and also cities and counties that were struggling with welfare costs associated with a 25 percent unemployment rate. The same session approved formation of the Wyoming Liquor Commission to make the state a liquor wholesaler.

In 1937, the Legislature renewed the sales tax and made it permanent. However, Governor Miller failed to win approval for other tax proposals. He had proposed increasing the sales tax to 3 percent, exempting food from the sales tax, introducing a use tax on goods brought into the state, and amending the Wyoming Constitution to authorize a graduated income tax.

The sales tax became the primary source of revenue for the state until 1969, when the Legislature approved a severance tax on minerals.

Drastic Suggestions

It is said that drastic times call for drastic measures. However, it is hard to imagine the Wyoming Legislature would have adopted many of the recommendations made by a group hired by a legislative committee to study Wyoming's problems.

Griffenhagen and Associates of Chicago was hired for $8,750 and made its report during a special session of the Wyoming Legislature that had been called for December 4-23, 1933, to consider several depression-related issues. The firm suggested, among other things:

- More centralized state control and consolidation of the 399 school districts.
- A state police force to absorb duties of sheriffs, livestock inspectors, water commissioners, highway patrol, and other law enforcement agencies.
- Reduction of the number of counties from twenty-three to twelve or even six.
- A one-house Legislature of between nine and twelve members elected from the state at large.
- Election of the governor by the Legislature from among its members, or by the electorate directly, to serve as presiding officer of the Legislature and official head of state government but not as an administrative officer.
- A state administrator to be hired by the Legislature as general manager of state government, to be appointed without a set term and to appoint heads of all administrative offices.

The 1933 Legislature rejected all the suggestions, although subsequent Legislatures have acted on the first idea to consolidate school districts. There were 48 school districts in 2005, which operated with substantial state control over finances, construction, standards, and testing. (Larson 1978, p. 464)

Public Lands and States Rights

Wyoming residents have resented interference by the federal government in state affairs since territorial days. They tolerated expansion of federal powers in the 1930s as necessary to survive the Great Depression, but elected officials and other states rights champions protested further expansion during World War II.

Those protests became particularly shrill when President Franklin D. Roosevelt issued an executive order creating the Jackson Hole National Monument on March 16, 1943. The order set aside 221,610 acres of land on the east side of Grand Teton National Park. It included 49,117 acres of private land, including 32,117 acres that had been

Wyoming cattle drive in early 1900s, when public range was open to all. The Taylor Grazing Act of 1934 created the Bureau of Land Management to manage grazing leases on public land. (Wyoming State Archives photo)

purchased over several years by John D. Rockefeller Jr. expressly for that purpose.

Opponents complained it would take a third of taxable land in Teton County off the tax rolls, and it would threaten grazing rights, hunting and fishing privileges and control of the elk herd. It was opposed by Gov. Lester Hunt, U.S. Senators Joseph O'Mahoney and Edward V. Robertson, Congressman Frank A. Barrett, Milward Simpson, Felix Buchenroth, the Wyoming Stock Growers Association, Dude Ranchers Association, and the Wyoming Taxpayers Association. Simpson was the attorney for a group called Citizens Committee of Jackson Hole. Senator Robertson and Congressman Barrett introduced a bill to require state approval for creation of national monuments. Governor Hunt and governors of five other Western states – California, Nevada, Arizona, Colorado, and Utah – signed a resolution condemning the monument. Hunt even threatened to use his police power to remove federal officials who assumed authority in the monument area.

The Wyoming Stock Growers Association president, Charles A. Myers, said, "This is the 'Boston Tea Party,' and we will never rest until we are in fact, as well as in name, Sovereign States." He vowed the state would "retake the Monument" and reclaim the surface lands and mineral rights owned by the federal government in Wyoming.

In Washington, D.C., opposition was portrayed as a few self-interested individuals.

Finally, former Gov. Leslie Miller came out in defense of the new monument and the protection it would provide the Tetons. If opponents were successful, he said, the day would come when "Wyoming will hang her head in shame." The conservation-oriented Izaak Walton League joined Miller.

President Roosevelt vetoed the bill to abolish the monument, but Congress would not appropriate money for the Interior Department to administer the monument. Then in 1950, a compromise bill by Sens. Joseph O'Mahoney and Lester Hunt passed Congress and was signed by President Harry Truman to abolish the monument but to add most of the area to Grand Teton National Park. The measure compensated Teton County for lost property taxes and provided for rights of way for livestock, preservation of existing leases and permits, and cooperation between state and nation in managing the famous elk herd.

For generations, Wyoming and other Western states have chafed under federal government regulation of public lands, the environment, and highways. Two ideas have been at the base of the discontent. One is that federal management ignores states' desires and individual circumstances. The other is that the millions of acres of public land are rightfully the property of the state. Western states were particularly upset with what was perceived as an arrogant power grab with the 1976 Federal Land Policy and Management Act, which said public lands would be kept in trust by the federal government. Between 1976 and 1980, the administration of President Jimmy Carter put 37.8 million acres of land in parks, wilderness areas, wildlife refuges, and other designations that restricted development. Indignation in the West in the late 1970s took the form of the "Sagebrush Rebellion," when state legislatures passed laws claiming ownership of vast portions of public land. Some Westerners hoped the election of Republican President Ronald Reagan in 1980 and his appointment of James Watt of Wyoming as Interior secretary meant they would get control of public lands. However, the administration chose a policy of wise use.

The Bureau of Land Management, in the U.S. Department of Interior, was created by the Taylor Grazing Act in 1934. The BLM continues to manage 262 million surface acres and 700 million acres of subsurface mineral estate in Wyoming and 11 other Western states.

In fact, the original policy of the federal government in 1776 was to transfer all lands to private ownership, and the General Land Office was created in 1812 to dispose of public domain lands in the Midwest and West. By the 1870s, however, Congress was converted to the idea of retaining public land because it was so remote or because of great public value. Congress created Yellowstone National Park in Wyoming in 1872, and the 1891 General Land Reform Act created forest reserves. In the next four decades, just about all the federal land now in existence was reserved by Congress or by presidential order. The Taylor Grazing Act of 1934 established the idea that the federal government should manage lands with scientific conservation. After World War II, many people wanted public domain lands managed not just for grazing, but for watershed, wildlife, and recreation – known as "multiple use."

The next major development was the Federal Land Policy and Management Act of 1976. Congress' policy was that the remaining public domain land would be retained in federal ownership unless disposal of a particular parcel served the national interest, and then only at fair market value. Congress said the guiding principles for public land management would be multiple use, sustained yield, and environmental protection. (Public Law 94-579)

The Bureau of Land Management (part of the federal Department of the Interior) has ten field offices around Wyoming, where it manages about 18 million surface acres of public land and 23 million acres of federal mineral estate. There are inevitable disputes over how closely grazing operators will be monitored and regulated, how much and what kind of multiple use will be guaranteed, and what kind of mineral development is allowed. The BLM has faced criticism over its dealing with environmental impact resulting from coal bed methane wells on public land in the Powder River Basin of northeastern Wyoming. Conservationists consider the BLM too lax, while producers consider the BLM too restrictive.

The BLM has the responsibility to keep the number of wild horses and burros on agency land to manageable numbers, figured at about 3,200 animals. It reported rounding up and offering for adoption 203 wild horses and burros in 2003.

Although the issue of public lands' remaining under federal management seems settled, the issue occasionally resurfaces. In 1995, Sen. Craig Thomas of Wyoming and Rep. Jim Hansen of Utah introduced bills in Congress to turn over all public lands administered by the Bureau of Land Management to the states. Both bills were referred to committee, where they died for lack of action. (S. 1031 and H.R. 2032)

Postwar Government

Democratic Gov. Lester Hunt had a rough first administration, 1942-1946. The Republican Legislature resisted all but a handful of his initiatives. In 1945, legislators refused to confirm ten of Hunt's key appointments.

Republicans continued to dominate state government in general, and in the northern counties and small towns and rural areas in particular. However, Wyoming voters re-elected Governor Hunt and U.S. Sen. Joseph O'Mahoney, both Democrats. Republicans won the other top four state offices. Hunt and legislators worried about declining state revenues. The 1947 Legislature approved a statewide property tax of 6 mills for schools, which was submitted to voters and approved in 1948. The Legislature defeated a proposal to move the College of Agriculture from Laramie to Sheridan, saying the state could not afford two four-year schools.

Governor Hunt was elected to the U.S. Senate in 1948. Then Secretary of State Arthur Griswold Crane, a former president of the University of Wyoming, became governor. He presided over the 1949 Legislature, which came close to approving a severance tax on oil, something oilmen had feared since 1923. Revenue from the 4 percent tax would have gone into a permanent fund. It passed the House but failed the Senate.

Severance taxation was a major issue in the gubernatorial election of 1950. A severance tax on oil exported from Wyoming was supported by the Democratic candidate, John J. McIntyre of Casper, who had served one term in Congress, 1941-1943. The Republican candidate was Frank Barrett, who left Congress after two terms to run for governor. Cattlemen and woolgrowers lionized Barrett, who had been chairman of the House Subcommittee on Public Lands, and they joined the oil industry in opposing an oil severance tax.

Republicans swept every statewide contest in 1950. Barrett won by 12,000 votes and held a tight rein on an overwhelmingly Republican Legislature. He left in 1952 to run for the U.S. Senate, and Secretary of State C.J. "Doc" Rogers became acting governor. Republicans gained an even bigger majority in the Legislature in 1952, and state spending held steady.

That conservatism changed with the administration of Republican Gov. Milward Simpson, a third-generation Wyomingite and long-time president of the University of Wyoming board of trustees. He beat Democrat Scotty Jack in a congenial contest by only 1,112 votes. Simpson was ready to spend money, and the Republican Legislature appropriated $32 million in 1955, $7.5 million more than the previous budget. The trucking industry showed the strength of its influence in achieving the death of one truck tax bill in the House and the demise of two other truck tax bills by veto.

Simpson was one of Wyoming's greatest promoters and declared in his 1957 State of the State address: "There never was, and there never will be, a better state or a better system of government." He got most of what he asked for from the Republican Legislature, including creation of a Department of Revenue, authorization of voting machines, higher state worker salaries, authorization of a personnel director, a Division of Mental Health, an increase in school funding, and an underground water code.

Another accomplishment was approval of a civil rights bill, drawn up by Democrat Teno Roncalio, which said: "No person of good deportment shall be denied the right of life, liberty, pursuit of happiness, or the necessities of life because of race, color, creed, or national origin." Simpson later served in the U.S. Senate and there voted against the federal civil rights law.

The 1957 House killed a 2.5 percent severance tax measure and a proposed investigation into high gasoline prices. The proposed state budget was about the same as two years earlier and survived an attempt to impose a 10 percent cut across the board by three Republican state senators: Dick Jones, Albert Harding, and R.L. Greene.

It was a surprise to most people when Governor Simpson lost a re-election bid in 1958 to Democrat Joseph J. Hickey of Cheyenne. Democrats also won the state House and the offices of secretary of state and superintendent of public instruction. Simpson's margin of loss of 2,582 votes could be accounted for by the people he angered by shutting down gambling in Jackson and by going along with a route for Interstate 90 that went through Buffalo and then up to Sheridan.

Governor Hickey stressed economy and wanted a commission to study and recommend reorganization of state government. He had talked about eliminating most of the power of boards and commissions: limiting each department to one function, separating accounting and auditing, establishing direct lines of authority to the governor, and giving the Legislature control of Game and Fish Commission funds.

Governor Hickey and 1959 legislators took up as a states' rights issue a fight to choose their own color for painting stripes on federally-funded highways. Wyoming folks insisted yellow lines were necessary for visibility and safety in snowstorms. However, the federal highway administration insisted on federal standards and white stripes.

There was quite a shuffle of elected officials in 1960. U.S. Sen. Joseph O'Mahoney, a Democrat, decided to retire. Republican Keith Thomson, a three-term congressman, won the U.S. Senate seat. One month and one day after his election, Thomson died of a heart attack at age 41. Democratic Governor Hickey resigned his seat on January 21, 1961. Then, Secretary of State Jack Gage, as acting governor, appointed Hickey to fill the Senate vacancy.

Governor Gage presided over a 1961 legislative session whose fiercest issues were reapportionment, trading stamps, and federal aid to education. Trading stamps were a popular marketing device used by grocery stores and other retailers to keep customers returning. Customers received stamps based on the amount of money they spent, and the stamps were then redeemed for household items. All the reapportionment bills were killed. Stories are told of people in the galleries in the House and Senate chambers throwing notes down to their lawmakers during votes on whether to allow trading stamps. The ban stayed in place. The Legislature restored a prohibition against taking federal aid for education that required matching state funds. That made Wyoming the only state unable to accept such aid. Proposals for a severance tax and increased sales tax died in the House. Governor Hickey had sent a proposal to reorganize state government to the Legislature, where it died.

Notable accomplishments of the 1961 session were a rewrite of the Election Code, stronger civil rights, a model business corporation code, a school for the deaf in Casper, and sale of the Saratoga Hot Springs State Reserve.

The 1962 gubernatorial election was won by Republican third-generation Jackson Hole cattleman Clifford P. Hanson, a newcomer to politics. Jack Gage blamed at least part of his own defeat on Wyoming's distaste for the liberalism of national Democrats.

Swept out in the Republican victories of 1962 was Velma Linford, one of the most progressive, forceful, and competent superintendents of public instruction Wyoming has ever had. She lost by 737 votes to Cecil M. Shaw, a former professional basketball player who had come from Oklahoma three years earlier and had changed his party affiliation from Democrat to Republican just before he filed for office. During her two terms, 1955-1963, Linford fought for acceptance of federal education aid, equalization of educational opportunity, higher teacher standards, and consolidation of school districts. She was a native of the Star Valley and had taught in Laramie before serving as schools superintendent. She held various appointed jobs in Washington, D.C., after her defeat.

Another notable woman won political office in 1962. Thyra Thomson, widow of Senator-elect Keith Thomson, became the first elected woman secretary of state. She served until 1986, and then her son, Bill Thomson, ran for office. He was defeated by Democrat Kathy Karpan.

Yet another capable woman was elected in 1962, Republican Minnie Mitchell as state auditor. She had completed her deceased husband's unexpired term as treasurer and then was elected to that office for four years. She served three terms as auditor.

One of the most controversial proposals of the 1963 session was to make Wyoming a "right-to-work" state, so labor union membership or dues payment would not be a condition of employment. It was pushed by a statewide organization backed by agriculture, construction, truckers, automobile dealers, retailers, the mining and petroleum industry, and others. The bill passed largely on party-line votes, Republicans for and Democrats against.

The 1963 session vented frustration with federal government regulation by approving resolutions against intrusion on a range of issues including wilderness designations, legislative apportionment, and U.S. Supreme Court jurisdiction.

A major accomplishment of the 1963 session was reapportionment of the Legislature. The Constitution required it after every federal decennial census, but no Legislature since 1933 had been able to tackle the politically difficult decisions to take legislative seats from one county and give them to another. The reapportionment increased the house from 56 to 61 members and decreased the Senate from 27 to 25 members. Sheridan and Sweetwater counties were reduced from two senators to one each, and only Laramie and Natrona counties had two senators. After a fruitless special session in 1964 and a court challenge, a three-judge federal panel in October 1965 ordered the Senate seats to be increased from 25 to 30 and to be apportioned on the basis of "one man, one vote."

Governor Hansen had a different state Legislature for the 1965 session, which followed the landslide victory of Democratic President Lyndon B. Johnson. Even Wyoming went for Johnson that year. The house had a Democratic majority and nearly an even split in the Senate. After two years in office, the moderate governor assumed stronger leadership and delivered one of the most progressive gubernatorial messages in the state's history. Hansen urged a strong state government as a way to assert states' rights. His recommendations included:

- Initiative and referendum procedures
- Repeal on the ban on federal education aid
- Allowing urban renewal projects
- Raising the hourly minimum wage from 75 cents to $1
- Higher workers' compensation payments
- Reapportionment of the state Senate to conform with federal court rulings
- More generous support of the University of Wyoming
- Greater use of regional cooperative programs of the Western Interstate Commission for Higher Education

- Stricter qualifications to establish community colleges
- A fair employment practices act
- Elimination of a requirement that a natural parent appear at adoption hearings
- Repeal of a law prohibiting interracial marriages
- Higher retirement pay for state employees
- More generous state and local support for public schools
- Uniform school district legislation
- Long-range tax structure study

Democrats came close to repealing the right-to-work law. They had no trouble in the House and seemed to have the votes in the Senate, where one Republican had been won over. It came to a vote on a day when one Democratic member was absent. It failed by one vote.

To help finance some of these activities, the Legislature raised the sales tax from 2 percent to 2.5 percent and included lodging in the tax base. Municipalities and counties were allowed to levy an additional .5 percent.

The winner of the 1966 gubernatorial election was another political newcomer, young Torrington attorney Stanley K. Hathaway, a Republican, who had the privilege of presiding over a period of great economic growth. He had the benefit of Republican majorities and strong veterans in the state House and Senate to help him with his goals of economic growth, strong state government, and reorganization of some agencies. He urged spending to promote business and tourism.

Governor Hathaway has received low marks from environmentalists, but as governor he supported laws that would protect the quality of Wyoming's environment. Republican state Sen. Thomas Stroock of Casper sponsored the Wyoming Air Quality Act.

Republicans wrote a bill to create single-member legislative districts, but Democrats detected gerrymandering in the bill and they filibustered the measure.

The 1967 Legislature easily defeated a 3 percent severance tax on oil and gas but raised the sales tax to 3 percent and included services in the tax base to cover the higher state budget.

This is quite a list of accomplishments, but Governor Hathaway said the biggest accomplishment was a proposed constitutional amend-

Wyoming Gov. Stan Hathaway, 1966-1974, presided over governmental reforms, passage of severance taxes, and creation of the Permanent Wyoming Mineral Trust Fund. (Wyoming State Archives photo)

ment to allow an initiative and referendum process so citizens of Wyoming could put proposed laws on the ballot and call for a popular vote on actions by the Legislature.

In the next session, pressure for a severance tax required the 1969 Legislature to pass something. State government needed the revenue, and a 1 percent severance tax was politically less dangerous than raising sales taxes or imposing an income tax. So, finally, it was a Republican Legislature, with Republicans in the governor's office and the other top four elected positions, that approved a severance tax in Wyoming.

Legislators also approved more of Governor Hathaway's government reorganization plan. They created a Department of Economic Planning and Development, with four divisions for water, industry, minerals, and planning. They created a position for planning coordinator and created a Department of Health and Social Services to centralize authority and eliminate duplication.

Col. Theron F. Stimson of the Laramie National Guard was the hero of what could have been a major event during the Hathaway Administration. In May 1970, about 100 students at the University of Wyoming campus held a rally to protest the U.S. invasion of Cambodia. This came right after National Guardsmen shot to death four students at

Kent State University in Ohio. Wyoming students raised a flag with a peace symbol on the flagpole on Prexy's Pasture at the center of campus, above the United States flag. Governor Hathaway, a self-professed law and order advocate, ordered all Wyoming Highway Patrol officers in the area and city and campus police in Laramie to remove the peace flag. They found unarmed students standing six deep around the flagpole. National Guardsmen stood by in the armory a mile away. Colonel Stimson telephoned Hathaway and urged him to "cool it." After an all-night vigil, students and law enforcement officers drifted away. Colonel Stimson removed the flag without incident. (Larson 1978, p.564)

The next Legislature in 1971 enacted even more government reforms and reorganization. It created the Legislative Service Office, whose professional staff serves Wyoming's citizen legislators. It approved the Department of Administration and Fiscal Control, a revised Criminal Code, a new state office building, and six proposed constitutional amendments. One of the amendments established annual legislative sessions, instead of every other year, so there could be a long 40-day general session followed by a short 20-day budget session. The other amendment set up what was called the "Missouri system" for selecting state district and Supreme Court justices. Both amendments were approved by voters in November of 1971.

The Legislature's reapportionment plan, which survived a court challenge, increased House seats from 61 to 62. (Senate seats remained at 30.) New House seats went to Albany, Campbell, and Natrona counties. Losing one each was Sheridan and Washakie. During a special session in July 1971, the Legislature ratified the 26th Amendment to the U.S. Constitution, lowering the voting age from 21 to 18.

Another notable achievement of the Hathaway Administration was the creation by the 1973 Legislature of the Department of Environmental Equality to regulate air and water quality and mined-land reclamation at the beginning of a period of mineral development that proceeded at a breakneck pace.

The 1973 Legislature submitted a constitutional amendment to the voters that would make a passage of a state income tax very difficult. Voters approved it in 1974. It said "no tax shall be imposed upon income without allowing full credit against such tax liability for all sales, use, and ad valorem taxes paid in the taxable year by the same taxpayer to any taxing authority." With this provision, any income tax must allow people to deduct the amount they have paid that year in sales, use, and property taxes. The result is most people in all but the highest income brackets probably would pay little.

The 1974 budget session raised the minerals severance tax from 1 percent to 3 percent, adopted a new Election Code, and approved a pipeline to take coal slurry from Campbell County to Arkansas. The pipeline would use water pumped out of an aquifer in the Madison Formation, which was thought to be brackish. However, when the water proved of drinking quality, Wyoming residents opposed the plan.

Government reorganization can be controversial, if it results in the shifting of budgets and personnel from powerful agencies and if it is considered ineffective. That was the case for the Department of Administration and Fiscal Control, in 1973 and 1974. It centralized purchasing, mailing, accounting, computer services, statistics and research, and mailing. Some in state government complained it just added a layer of bureaucracy, and it became an issue in the gubernatorial election of 1974. Hathaway ended his eight years as governor staunchly defending government reorganization and, in particular, the centralization of services.

Hathaway was the first governor to complete two terms -- in fact, the first to serve more than six years. He left the office a popular man. However, it has taken a generation for Wyoming residents to fully appreciate one of the most far-reaching accomplishments of his administration, which was creation of the Permanent Wyoming Mineral Trust Fund, where a percentage of severance taxes are deposited automatically and are held there permanently and invested. The 1974 Legislature put a constitutional amendment creating the PWMTF on the ballot, and voters approved it in November of that year. Income from the PWMTF is used to run general operations of state government.

The PWMTF is Wyoming's hedge against the ups and downs of the mineral industry, as production and prices rise and fall. It also is a hedge against the day when the minerals are gone, and it will continue producing income for the state. The PWMTF had grown to $2 billion by 2003 and contributed $61.4 million income for the General Fund in fiscal 2003. (*Annual Report of the Treasurer of the State of Wyoming*, Fiscal 2003). During recent revenue surpluses, some legislators have viewed the PWMTF as a vehicle for enforced savings – a way to put money off-limits. An alternative discussed by legislators in 2005 would be a "rainy day account" that could be tapped only by a two-thirds legislative vote.

The issue of constitutional financing of public schools has been a dominant issue of state government for 25 years. The consolidation of school districts during Governor Hathaway's administration was an important step in bringing major inequities among the school districts to light and to court. The process of consolidating hundreds of districts into 49 was substantially completed by the statutory deadline of 1978. (Wyoming now has school 48 districts.) In that same year, a lawsuit was filed by several school districts, led by Washakie County School District Number One, to clarify the state's responsibility for ensuring fair and equal public school financing. (*Washakie County School Dist. No. One v. Herschler*, 606 P2d 310. Wyo 1980) Supreme Court mandates resulting from that case set the stage for decades of litigation and legislative efforts to remake its education funding scheme so it complies with the Wyoming Constitution's requirement that schools be funded adequately and equitably.

President Gerald Ford appointed Stan Hathaway secretary of the Interior on April 4, 1975. Many leaders in Wyoming, both Republican and Democrat, supported the nomination. But he had to battle critics of his pro-development policies to win confirmation in the U.S. Senate by a vote of 60-36. Secretary Hathaway learned his agency was staffed largely by environmentalists who would oppose his energy development goals. After six weeks, he was hospitalized for what was reported as exhaustion, depression, and a mild case of diabetes. He tendered his resignation from his hospital bed. He had served June 12 to July 25, 1975. He returned to Cheyenne to a hero's welcome and opened a successful law practice specializing in energy development issues.

Wyoming citizens elected a Democrat for their next governor, Edgar Herschler of Kemmerer, a World War II Marine sergeant with a Purple Star and Silver Star and a ten-year veteran of the Legislature himself.

Gov. Ed Herschler's style of governing was influenced by his ease in working behind the scenes with the Legislature and his personal relationships with many of the lawmakers. The other four top elected officials were Republicans. The Senate was evenly divided 15-15 between Republicans and Democrats, and Republicans had a thin edge in the House 32-29, with one Independent. Governor Herschler had campaigned on "quality of life" issues relating to helping communities deal with the impact of energy development, as well as water development and greater funding for schools.

A major law enacted during the 1975 legislative session established land-use planning, plant siting, water resources development, pay raises for state employees, and an increase in the severance tax on oil and gas by 1 percent to a total 4 percent. The Legislature increased the amount of sales tax going to local governments and funded planning for a proposed medical school at the University of Wyoming.

The 1976 session was less accommodating to Governor Herschler and, in his opinion, more accommodating to special interests. The Legislature had flexed its muscle in the balance of power among the executive, legislative, and judicial branches of government. Legislators cut the governor's budget requests for travel, technical assistance, land-use planning, and the Department of Environmental Quality. The Legislature added footnotes to the appropriations bill to control not just how much the executive agencies would spend, but also how.

In 1977, Governor Herschler found himself in the familiar position of being a Democratic governor with a Republican Legislature, although the GOP advantage was slim: 18-12 in the Senate and 32-29-1 in the House. He fought hard for a $250 million capital facilities construction account, supported by an increase in severance tax on coal, trona, and uranium. The first project was a new prison at Rawlins. By the end of the 1977 session, the Legislature had increased the severance tax on trona and uranium by 2 percent and coal by 3 percent. The rates were 10.1 percent on coal, 5.5 percent on uranium and trona, and 4 percent on oil and gas. Congress had increased Wyoming's share of federal mineral royalties from 37.5 percent to 50 percent, and the Legislature had the pleasure of dividing the extra revenue (about $12 million in 1976) between cities and towns, impacted communities, a new highway fund, and school construction. A strong effort by Governor Herschler saved eleven new positions requested by the Department of Environmental Quality, to monitor strip mining reclamation on federal and state land.

Governor Herschler's second term straddled the end of the spectacular energy boom of the late 1970s and the beginning of the bust in the early 1980s. He became the only governor to serve three terms, being re-elected in 1978 and 1982. After he left office, the Legislature enacted a two-term limit for governor.

During his first two terms, severance taxes on oil, gas, coal, uranium, and trona were increased to pay for increased government activities connected to the energy development and for water development. During Herschler's third term, as production and prices dropped and development slowed, severance tax increases that had expiration dates were allowed to expire. Tax rates were decreased as incentives for underground coal mining and uranium extraction. (See "Significant Statutory Changes Affecting State Taxation," a list compiled by the Legislative Service Office, in Appendix 17)

Meanwhile, the Legislature began taxing cigarettes, starting with a use tax of 8 cents a pack in 1981.

During Ed Herschler's second term, the Wyoming Legislature got the first unequivocal word from the Wyoming Supreme Court that the past system of supporting public education with local property taxes was unconstitutional and had to change. This was the *Washakie v. Herschler* case. (606 P2d 310. Wyo 1980) Three subsequent Supreme Court opinions have reinforced the mandate by the Wyoming Constitution that the Legislature is responsible for a public education system that is uniform, complete, and not reliant on local property wealth. (Read more about this in Chapter 17 Education. Also, find school finance-related Supreme Court opinions, legislation, and reports on Legislative Service Office's Web site, http://legisweb.state.wy.us.)

Every other year, as the Legislature heads into budget sessions, decisions on how to spend predicted revenue for the next two years are difficult enough. Before Governor Herschler's second term, wrangling over the appropriations bill was preceded by wrangling over revenue predictions themselves. The executive and legislative branches created their own independent forecasts of revenue. In 1983, the governor and Legislature agreed to create the Consensus Revenue Estimating Group, known by the acronym "CREG," to come up with a single revenue estimate. The co-chairs are the administrator of the

Rare gathering of four Wyoming governors in 1990, to sign commemorative print of Teton Mountains by Conrad Schwiering. Pictured, left to right, are Ed Herschler, Mike Sullivan and Clifford Hansen. Standing is Stan Hathaway. (Wyoming State Archives photo)

Economic Analysis Division and the budget manager from the Legislative Service Office. Members include staff from executive agencies and the University of Wyoming, and they predict the ability of Wyoming's economy to generate revenue in the upcoming biennium.

The CREG meets twice a fiscal year: in October to provide an initial forecast of revenues and in January to update the forecast before the Legislature convenes. CREG reports are non-partisan, professional estimates that the executive and legislative branches rely on to plan government spending.

By the 1980s, property appraisals were woefully out of date in some counties, resulting in an unequal property tax system for the state. During Herschler's third term, in 1984, the Legislature ordered a mass reappraisal to ensure property taxes were fair, uniform, and up to date across the state. In the next administration, the Legislature proposed a state constitutional amendment to allow different assessment rates for three classes of property: mineral, industrial, and all other real/personal property. Voters approved the amendment in 1988.

Governor Herschler was followed by Democrat Casper attorney Mike Sullivan, who capped his first run for elective office with victory as Wyoming governor in 1986. He was the beneficiary of a hard-fought Republican gubernatorial primary that split the usually cohesive party for the general election. In his first term, there was a 3-2 Democratic advantage among top elected officials, which was reversed during his second term. However, he enjoyed a smooth and congenial working relationship with the other four officials, who agreed on many non-partisan issues.

The state undertook government reorganization in earnest during the two administrations of Governor Sullivan. The only major realignment of executive branch functions to increase efficiency had been during the administration of Stan Hathaway 15 years earlier. The Legislature had consolidated several agency activities to create the Department of Administration and Fiscal Control in 1973. It re-formed the Department of Health and Social Services and created the Department of Environmental Quality to deal with energy industry impact.

In 1988, the Joint Legislative-Executive Efficiency Study analyzed Wyoming's executive branch. It found "a mish-mash of boards, commissions, councils, agencies, departments, offices and institutions." There were seventy-nine executive branch entities, but only nineteen reported directly to the governor, and nine of those required state Senate confirmation. The study made some drastic recommendations. (*A Study in State Government Efficiency*, 1989, pp.87-103)

Wyoming had enlarged state government over the years, as the population, revenue, and need for services grew. The result at the state's centennial was a confusion of boards, commissions, and councils, with few direct lines of authority anywhere. Wyoming citizens hold the governor responsible for performance of state agencies, boards, commissions, and entities, but in 1989 Sullivan had very little direct authority over sixty of the seventy-nine executive branch departments. "Many function without a clear definition of their purpose, role, or responsibility. Unfortunately, many function without an adequate understanding of the state's policy or objectives with regard to their particular program or function. Thus, coordination of activities and efforts with those of other agencies is often difficult," the report said.

The state apparently did not entrust the governor, the highest elected official of the executive branch, with full authority to manage state government as a representative of the people, the study noted. At the same time, it said, the state will "endow enormous authority to lay, frequently nonprofessional, appointees to boards and commissions for the purpose of overseeing vast programs." Most agency heads were responsible not to the governor, but to another level of authority, a board, or commission. The governor needs the authority to appoint and remove agency heads, in order to be responsible for policies and programs and to exercise the public trust for an effective government, the study said.

The study committee said better executive authority could be accomplished, while keeping important citizen input through boards, commissions, and councils.

The Legislature approved the Wyoming Government Reorganization Act of 1989, which established procedures and a process for reorganization of the executive branch of state government. The law provides that the entire executive branch be organized into no more than twelve principal departments, excluding the top five elected officials and the attorney general's office. The governor appoints the department directors, with confirmation by the Wyoming Senate, who serve at his pleasure. The directors appoint division administrators, who serve at the directors' pleasure.

The goals of reorganization are clear lines of authority and greater efficiency. The new agency configuration is expected to reduce duplication, which saves money and effort and improves service to Wyoming citizens. Reorganization is intended to make the governor's authority more rational and effective. However, reorganization does little to enhance the chief executive's power relative to the Legislature, the other top elected officials, or governors in other states.

Using the Wyoming Government Reorganization Act, the Legislature immediately created the Departments of Audit, Commerce, and Employment, which regrouped existing functions from several agencies. In 1990, the Legislature created four other departments: Health, Family Services, Administration, and Transportation.

Subsequent reports were written in 1990 and 1991 by the Joint Reorganization Council with further recommendations for reorganization. The final report was called the "Ferrari Report," because it was headed up by Dave Ferrari, state auditor 1990-1998.

The third phase of reorganization envisioned by the original study was creation and re-constituting of three departments: Education, Public Safety, and Agriculture and Natural Resources. The 1991 Legislature did not act on those proposals. The proposed Education Department would have brought together all education systems, including public schools, community colleges, and University of Wyoming. It would have been an agency answerable to the governor, not a statewide elected official, i.e., superintendent of public instruction).

In the administration of the next governor, Republican Jim Geringer, the Legislature created the Department of Workforce Services to bring into one agency employment services, job training, and vocational rehabilitation.

The current executive branch organization places directly under the governor the attorney general's office, the State Engineer, and thirteen major departments: Administration and Information, Agriculture, Audit, Corrections, Employment, Environmental Quality, Family Services, Game and Fish, Health, Revenue, Parks and Cultural Resources, Transportation, and Workforce Services. (The organization of the executive branch in 2006 is shown in the chart on page 40.)

Governor Geringer, elected in 1994 and re-elected in 1998, had been in the House and Senate for ten years and had been chairman of the House Appropriations Committee. As he finished his second term, he said the Legislature had been his "first love." (Interview in *Casper Star-Tribune* by Joan Barron, December 22, 2002)

During both terms, the Legislature had overwhelming Republican majorities, and all five top elected officials were Republican. During his first term, Geringer was at odds with three other Republicans who were among the top elected officials and who sat with the governor on the Board of Land Commissioners: Secretary of State Diana Ohman, Auditor Dave Ferrari, and Treasurer Stan Smith. The fifth top elected official was Superintendent of Public Instruction Judy Catchpole, who often allied with Geringer in disputed matters.

Geringer, a Wheatland farmer and an engineer by training, earned admiration from fellow lawmakers while in the Legislature. But as governor, disputes with the Legislature resulted in three proposed constitutional amendments that would have strengthened the legislative branch at the expense of the governor's office. One was approved by voters, to allow the Legislature to call itself into special session. The governor retains authority to call special sessions, as well. The other two amendments addressed limits on the governor's veto power. One would have limited line-item veto power to just appropriations bills, not any bill that spends money. The other would have allowed the Legislature to send proposed constitutional amendments directly to voters without submitting them for gubernatorial approval, as with other bills.

Governor Geringer presided over some of the most austere budgets in recent years, and he advocated for the creation of the Wyoming Business Council in 1998 to promote economic development in Wyoming. At meetings of the National Governors Association, he favored cooperative agreements so states could collect sales tax on items purchased tax-free over the Internet. Legislators credited Geringer with improving the budget-setting process. He also promoted the creation of a study group to examine Wyoming's tax system and to make recommendations. Recommendations by the "Tax Reform 2000" project are summarized in Appendix 18. Although the project was praised at the time, nothing much came of it. John Hines, a member of the state House at the time, said he was sure his endorsement of a state income tax would end his political career. However, Campbell County voters continued to send the Republican rancher to the Legislature, and he was named chairman of the Senate Appropriations Committee in 2005.

Geringer is credited with promoting use of technology by the executive branch. During his administration, the state set up the Wyoming Equality Network, a statewide, high-speed voice, data, and video network. It is used by public schools, community colleges, University of Wyoming, businesses, government agencies, and communities for video conferencing and distance learning.

Geringer also tried to strengthen the office of governor with a so-called "one voice" policy, which required executive agency administrators to clear policies and statements through his office.

In 2002, Democrat Dave Freudenthal, a Cheyenne attorney and native of Thermopolis, defeated veteran Republican legislator and former House Speaker Eli Bebout to win election as governor. Freudenthal had been state planning coordinator for Gov. Ed Herschler and had been U.S. attorney under the Clinton Administration. However, he had never been elected to office before the governor's race.

As usual, a Democratic governor had to work with a Legislature with an overwhelming Republican majority. Democratic membership of the House in 2004 was just fourteen of sixty members. Only three Democratic representatives had more than four years of seniority. In the Senate, Republicans held a 23-7 advantage. The first two years of Freudenthal's administration were marked by attempts by three of the other top elected officials to become more autonomous, reducing oversight by the governor. State Treasurer Cynthia Lummis, Auditor Max Maxfield, and Superintendent of Public Instruction Trent Blankenship achieved changes in state law to increase their authority to award contracts, to hire their own attorneys, and to select the state land director. Blankenship, who resigned in mid-term to take a school district superintendent's job in Barrow, Alaska, publicly complained that he was a victim of politically-motivated scrutiny and criticism. Freudenthal appointed Jim McBride from within the Department of Education to serve out the superintendent's term.

As Governor Freudenthal took office, revenue poured into the state treasury from mineral production, creating unprecedented budget surpluses of $1 billion or more a year. A challenge for his administration and the Legislature was to decide how to spend this "one-time" money, with a backlog of capital construction and infrastructure needs and the desire to put money into savings for the day when the surpluses ended.

Governor Freudenthal touted an "open door" policy with legislators, and he worked with Republican lawmakers to champion his causes in the Legislature. One notable achievement was the Wildlife Trust Fund, enacted in 2005 despite great skepticism by agriculture interests.

A survey of public approval ratings of governors in May 2005 showed Freudenthal had the highest rating for a Democratic governor in any state: 67 percent approval and 20 percent disapproval. Only the Republican governors of North Dakota and South Dakota had better ratings. (The poll was taken by market research firm Survey USA, http://www.SurveyUSA.com.)

In Wyoming, it is possible for direct appeal to overcome party loyalty by voters. However, the overwhelming majority of voters who declare themselves Republican makes it difficult for Democrats to win statewide and legislative races. (See county-by-county party registration figures in the table at the end of Chapter 13.) Overwhelming majorities in the state House and Senate mean Republicans will win every party-line vote. As discussed in Chapter 5, the majority party selects legislative leaders, who enjoy great powers over legislative processes. Those leaders may determine how much minority members will participate.

However, personality and character still can drive politics in Wyoming, where a sparse population makes it possible for candidates to meet with constituents, shake their hands, and ask personally for their support. Democratic governors can work productively with a Republican-dominated Legislature. Minority party members can have influence in the Legislature.

Chapter 13

Political Parties

Republicans Majority Party

A political party is a group of individuals, often holding similar ideas about the role of government, which organizes to win elections, operate government, and determine public policy.

The Democratic Party dominated politics when Wyoming became a territory in 1869. That did not last long. Territorial governors were appointed by the U.S. president, and when Democratic President Grover Cleveland took office in 1885, he had difficulty finding a qualified Democrat willing to accept the job. (Miller 1981, p. 25)

By statehood in 1890, Wyoming's elected and appointed offices were dominated by Republicans. Appendix 4, Elected Party Affiliation, shows the political affiliation of state and legislative elected officials from 1890 to present. Wyoming's voters have elected Democratic governors eighteen times out of thirty-three elections, more than half the time, but the gubernatorial experience is the exception. Democratic candidates have won just one race for state treasurer, three for state auditor, six for secretary of state, and six for state superintendent for public instruction.

A break from this pattern occurred in 1934, when Democrats won majorities in both the Wyoming House (38-18) and Senate (14-13) and won all five top elected offices, led by Leslie A. Miller. Democrat Joseph O'Mahoney was returned to the U.S. Senate, and Democrat Paul R. Greever won Wyoming's lone seat in the U.S. House of Representatives. This was during the Democratic administration of President Franklin D. Roosevelt (1933-1945).

In 1936, Wyoming voters re-elected Roosevelt, re-elected Democratic Congressman Greever, put Democrat Harry H. Schwartz in the other U.S. Senate seat, and again elected Democratic majorities in the state House and Senate. In that election, Roosevelt carried every

Democrats after 1936 electoral victories: (left to right) Gov. Leslie Miller, Sen. Henry H. Schwartz, Congressman Paul Greever, and Sen. Joseph O'Mahoney. This photo is inscribed December 31, 1936, in the Senate Office Building in Washington, D.C. They had plenty to smile about. The Democratic Party reached its zenith in Wyoming, winning the top five elected positions and controlling the Wyoming Legislature: 14-13 in the Senate and 38-18 in the House. (Used by permission of the Central Committee of the Wyoming Democratic Party)

Wyoming county except the staunchly Republican counties of Johnson and Crook.

The Republican Party claims an overwhelming majority of registered voters in Wyoming — 146,328 of the total registered 232,396 in 2004. A substantial 23,355 registered as "other," which would include independent voters. The table at the end of this chapter shows voter registration by county in 2004. Democrats had a majority in only Sweetwater County, and Republican majorities were large in most other counties.

In his book *State Government: Politics in Wyoming*, Tim Miller attributes the dominance of Republicans to their organization, strong leaders, ability to raise money, and policies that appeal to conservative business and agricultural interests.

Third parties have not had much of a role in Wyoming politics except in the first 20 years of statehood. Populists joined with Democrats to be a factor in the election of 1892. Theodore Roosevelt's "Bull Moose" Progressives emerged as a force in 1912 and after. They advocated for social and government reforms that addressed official corruption, child labor, women's labor, and unsafe working conditions. Progressives included people from across the political spectrum.

In Wyoming, Progressives were led by Joseph M. Carey of Cheyenne. He was a Republican but was elected governor as an "independent" in 1910, and he achieved impressive reforms in the 1911 Legislature. In the 1912 election, Progressives did not field candidates but helped the Democratic cause by criticizing U.S. Sen. Francis E. Warren and other Republicans. Progressives allied with Democrats in the state House and almost gave them a majority. (Read more about Carey's term and the tumultuous 1913 legislative session in Chapter 12.)

Party Structure

The basic unit of a political party and in the electoral process is a precinct. Each party may select at least two representatives for each precinct, called committee men and committee women. They are the local contact for a party and can take an active part in finding people to run for office, to rally support for a candidate, to organize "Get Out The Vote" efforts, to raise money, and to otherwise support the party. This level of activity, however, is rare.

The next level up is the party's county central committee, composed of precinct representatives. The committee selects a chair, organizes activities on the county level, and selects a committee man and committee woman for the state central committee, which runs the state party. The county central committee calls a convention in even-numbered years, at which party faithful get together, pass resolutions, and select delegates to the state party conventions.

The state central committee picks a chairman to conduct day-to-day business of the state party. The chair does important organizing and fund-raising, but just as important is the role of public image and spokesman for the party. Sometimes chairmen go on to seek elected office.

On the second Saturday in May of even-numbered years, delegates picked on the county level attend a state convention. During presidential election years, delegates nominate their party's candidates for the Electoral College, and they pick delegates to their party's national convention. Technically, votes cast for presidential candidates on the general election ballot are being cast for these "presidential electors," who will vote for presidential candidates in the nation's Electoral College. Each state has votes in the Electoral College equal to its seats in the U.S. House and Senate. For Wyoming, that is three. The state convention also reviews county party resolutions and puts together a state party platform, which rarely becomes a campaign issue.

All the above is laid out in Title 22 ("Elections") of Wyoming Statutes. Under Chapter 4 ("Political Parties") is Article 1 for major parties, Article 3 for minor parties, and Article 4 for provisional parties.

State law defines "major political party" as a political organization whose candidate for Congress, governor, or secretary of state received at least 10 percent of total votes cast for that office in the most recent general election. Practically speaking, that refers to the Republican and Democratic parties in Wyoming. The law defines "minor political party" as a political organization whose candidate for congress, governor, or secretary of state received at least 2 percent of total votes cast for that office in the most recent general election.

The Libertarian Party put a candidate for governor on the Wyoming ballot in 2002 and qualified to put its congressional candidate on the ballot in 2004. However, the party's candidate, Lewis Stock, received just 6,581 votes in 2004. That was less than 1 percent of the 188,028 votes cast in the most recent general election, so the Libertarians lost their status as a "minor political party."

Presidential candidate Ralph Nader and running mate Peter Miguel Camejo qualified for the 2004 general election ballot in Wyoming by collecting signatures of registered voters equal to 2 percent of the votes cast in the previous congressional election. Nader and Camejo ran as independents and received 2,741 votes out of 245,789 total ballots cast in the election.

In the 2002 general election, two parties won "provisional" status – the Natural Law Party and Wyoming Reform Party.

The law requires minor parties to have at least a state party chairman and secretary. Minor parties may nominate candidates for the general election ballot by convention only, not by primary election.

Wyoming Statutes Title 22 lays out the process for citizens to form a new political party. They must file a petition with the secretary of state by June 1 of the year the party wants to qualify for the general election ballot. Then they circulate the petition, gathering signatures of registered voters. By law, the name of the party on the petition must have no more than two words and must not use the word "independent." The name may not be the same or similar to that of any other existing qualified party. To qualify for the ballot, the petition must have signatures of voters equal to 2 percent of the number of people voting in the previous congressional election.

Republicans and Democrats hold primary elections in August to determine which candidates will win nomination and represent their parties on the general election ballot. Primary elections in Wyoming are held on the Tuesday after the third Monday in August, leaving a relatively short time for campaigning before the general election on the first Tuesday after the first Monday in November. Some municipal elections are in May.

Democratic and Republican parties nominate by primary. State law requires third parties to nominate by convention. In Wyoming, primaries are "closed." That is, people may vote only in the primary of their registered party affiliation. Democrats vote in the Democratic Primary and Republicans in the Republican Primary. Those registered as "Independent" cannot vote in either party's primary election.

Voters in Wyoming are allowed to change their affiliation at the polls on election day, so they may participate in the primary of another party and then switch back before they leave the polling place. They have been known to do this in hotly contested gubernatorial primaries, to have a voice in the selection of a nominee for the other party.

The primary election also is used to narrow down the field of candidates in nonpartisan elections, so the general election becomes a kind of "runoff."

Voter Registration by County 2005

County	Democrat	Libertarian	Other	Republican	Total
Albany	5,810	33	3,697	7,298	16,838
Big Horn	694	7	381	4,321	5,403
Campbell	1,808	21	1,553	12,22	15,603
Carbon	2,560	8	1,224	3,577	7,369
Converse	1,053	9	466	4,478	6006
Crook	454	7	255	2,790	3,506
Fremont	4,569	13	1,7865	11,093	17,540
Goshen	1,693	4	509	4,187	6,392
Hot Springs	466	3	160	1,954	2,583
Johnson	370	9	417	3,353	4,149
Laramie	13,214	120	5,324	21,745	40,403
Lincoln	1,379	7	1,106	6.173	8,665
Natrona	9,018	68	4,421	19,048	32,555
Niobrara	127	1	84	1,207	1,419
Park	1,916	29	1,383	11,396	14,714
Platte	1,348	1	428	2,954	4,731
Sheridan	3,692	31	1,835	9,701	15,259
Sublette	419	3	273	3,126	3,821
Sweetwater	8,116	8	1,553	7,162	16,839
Teton	2,827	9	3,020	6,023	11,870
Uinta	2,042	7	1,215	5,025	8,289
Washakie	739	2	264	3,318	4,323
Weston	464	3	263	2,757	3,487
Total	64,778	403	31,696	154,897	251,774

Chapter 14

Women's Suffrage

The First Legislative Assembly of the Wyoming Territory took action in 1869 to recognize rights of women to own their own property (a law borrowed from Colorado), to work as teachers for the same pay as male teachers, and to have the right to vote and hold office.

Territorial Secretary Edward M. Lee wrote in a preface to the Laws of Wyoming in 1869 that the law granting women the right to vote had placed "the youngest territory on earth in the vanguard of civilization and progress." National suffrage leader Susan B. Anthony proclaimed in 1871 in Laramie, "Wyoming is the only place on God's green earth which could consistently claim to be the land of the Free!" Wyoming also was the first state to have woman suffrage, and it immediately became known as "The Equality State." (Larson 1978, p. 78)

The suffrage act passed by the 1869 Legislative Assembly reads:

FEMALE SUFFRAGE - Chapter 31

An Act to Grant to the Women of Wyoming Territory the Right of Suffrage and to Hold Office

Be it enacted by the Council and House of Representatives of the Territory of Wyoming:

Sec. 1. That every woman of the age of twenty-one years, residing in this territory, may at every election to be holden under the laws thereof, cast her vote. And her rights to the elective franchise and to hold office shall be the same under the election laws of the territory, as those of electors.

Sec. 2. This act shall take effect and be in force from and after its passage.

Approved, December 10th, 1869

The record of action by the First Legislative Assembly to enact women's suffrage is clear, although there is some dispute about the motivation and about the influence of individuals in getting the bill proposed and approved.

A reliable account is given in *History of Wyoming* by T.A. Larson, and that is summarized here.

On November 27, 1869, William H. Bright of South Pass City, who was serving as president of the Legislative Council, introduced a bill to

William H. Bright, president of the first Territorial Legislative Council, championed a bill to extend voting rights to women. The bill was signed into law December 10, 1869.

grant women the right to vote and hold elected office. It passed the Council 6-2 three days later. In the House, another South Pass City legislator, attorney Ben Sheeks, opposed the bill. He lost an amendment to extend the right to "all colored women and squaws" but won approval of an amendment to make the voting age for women 21, instead of 18. (The voting age for males was 21.) It passed the House 7-4. Gov. John Campbell signed the bill on December 10.

The proposal was not "a bolt from the blue," Larson wrote. Women in America had enjoyed limited suffrage rights since 1776, and women had been campaigning for suffrage rights since the 1840s. In 1868, proposed women's suffrage amendments to the U.S. Constitution had been introduced in the House and Senate, and women's suffrage bills and amendments had been introduced in several states and territories. In fact, the Utah Territory adopted women's suffrage two months after Wyoming, in February 1870.

"The Wyoming legislators had the option of jumping in at the head of the parade or of watching it pass by," Larson wrote.

Some members of the 1869 Legislative Assembly reported being motivated by a desire to do the right thing. Some were hoping to gain what the *Cheyenne Leader* newspaper called the "widespread notoriety" the act would create for the state.

An editorial in the *Wyoming Tribune* newspaper October 8, 1870, suggested the proposal originated as a joke, passed by the Council with every expectation that it would be defeated by the House or at least vetoed by territorial Governor Campbell. However, William H. Bright maintained he was serious about winning women's right to vote.

Other accounts alleged ulterior motives: that the largely white female voters would counteract the largely unmarried black male vote.

Louisa Swain, credited with being the first woman to vote in a general election in Wyoming, September 6, 1870. She cast her vote in her hometown of Laramie. (Wyoming State Archives photo)

Territorial Justice E.A. Thomas wrote in an article entitled "Female Suffrage in Wyoming" (*Potter's American Monthly*, XVIII (May 1882), pp. 492-495), that the legislation was "instigated partly by a desire to make their infant territory famous, partly to annoy the young Republican governor." To the legislators' astonishment, Governor Campbell signed the bill.

Apparently, it did not hurt that suffragists Anna Dickinson and Redelia Bates were quite attractive. The Cheyenne newspapers *Leader* and the *Wyoming Tribune* made a point of complimenting their charms in reporting the women's lectures in Cheyenne in 1869. *Leader* Editor Nathan A. Baker wrote, "Won't the irrepressible 'Anne D' come out here and make her home? We'll even give her more than the right to vote – she can run for Congress!" (Larson 1978, p. 83)

Susan B. Anthony, by contrast, was described by the *Leader* in 1870 as a homely "old maid."

The *Wyoming Tribune* greeted the new law enthusiastically with the headlines: "WOMAN SUFFRAGE, Wyoming in the Van, All Honor to the Youngest Territorial Sister!"

Territorial residents wondered whether women would exercise their right to vote, run for office, and sit on juries. An estimated 1,000 women were eligible to vote. How would women's participation affect politics, government, and public morality?

In early 1870, Esther Hobart Morris and two other women were appointed justices of the peace, although she alone served in that office. Women began serving on grand and petit juries in Laramie in 1870 and in Cheyenne in 1871. Morris served as justice of the peace for eight and one-half months in South Pass City.

Female jurors had a salutary effect on law enforcement and on behavior of male jurors, according to Larson's history. No longer did male jurors interrupt deliberations with drinking and gambling, nor did they smoke and chew tobacco while on duty. Female jurors were more willing to enforce saloon closures on Sunday and were more disposed to convict and impose heavy sentences. They were less likely to accept at face value a claim of self-defense in murder cases, Larson writes.

Despite the able service of women on juries, Wyoming residents were split on the subject. Some objected to the disruption of home life and the expense of needing additional bailiffs and overnight accommodations for female jurors.

New judges in 1871 decided jury service was not part of suffrage, and they stopped using women on juries.

Most eligible women voted at the first opportunity in September 1870. Observers disagreed on whether women favored Republicans or Democrats. They apparently enhanced civility at the polls. Editors said the presence of women inhibited drunkenness and rowdyism, making the day seem more like Sunday than Election Day. (Larson 1978, p. 85)

The Wyoming territorial government gave women the right to vote on December 10, 1869. This wood engraving, made from a photograph of women voting in Cheyenne, appeared in Frank Leslie's Illustrated Newspaper *on November 24, 1888. (Library of Congress)*

Democrats were exasperated with women's support for a Republican delegate to Congress and with their support for Sunday saloon closing. Led by House Speaker Ben Sheeks, Wyoming lawmakers voted to repeal women's suffrage in 1871. Gov. John Campbell vetoed the repeal, which was upheld by a margin of only one vote. Larson writes that the only attempt by women to influence the Legislature at this crucial time was a petition from Laramie supporting suffrage.

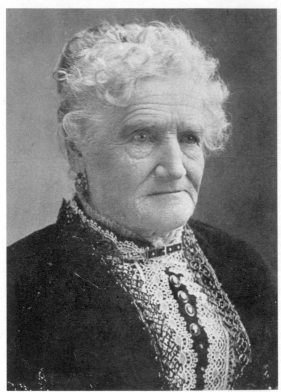

Esther Hobart Morris, first female justice of the peace in the United States. Her son, Edward Slack, helped confer on her the title of "Mother of Woman Suffrage." (Wyoming State Archives photo)

Those who expected national accolades and an influx of immigrants and investments to the territory must have been disappointed. There was little comment in national newspapers and magazines.

Women also discovered it would be a long time before they shared in political and economic affairs with men. Neither men nor women would vote for female candidates, aside from county schools superintendents, so they stopped trying to put women on the ballot. Only two women ran for the territorial Legislative Assembly in 22 years. One received eight votes, the other five – far short of the some 500 votes needed to win. (Larson 1978, p. 88)

The first woman elected to the Wyoming House of Representatives was Mary G. Bellamy of Albany County in 1910. The first woman elected to the Wyoming Senate was Dora McGrath of Hot Springs County in 1930. Both were Democrats.

Assigning credit for women's suffrage in Wyoming has prompted some debate. Wyoming historian T.A. Larson found many second-hand sources that credited Esther Hobart Morris with being the "Mother of Women Suffrage," as she was named in the *Cheyenne Sun*, published by her son. However, Larson says historical documents and accounts point to William H. Bright as the person primarily responsible for establishing women's suffrage in Wyoming.

Morris moved to the frontier mining community of South Pass City, population 460, in June 1869, with a son by a first marriage, Edward A. Slack, a second husband, John Morris, and 18-year-old twin sons Robert and Edward Morris. She was 56 years old and an imposing figure, at 180 pounds and nearly 6 feet tall. She was appointed justice of the peace on February 17, 1870, to replace a man who had resigned. She handled 26 cases in eight and one-half months. She was not nominated as a candidate in the 1870 election.

UNCLE SAM—Have been waiting for you, Miss Wyoming. Welcome to my house.
MISS WYOMING—I bring with me a constitution giving equal rights to ALL.

Editorial cartoon of nation's reception to Wyoming's request to join the Union as the 44th state. (Courtesy Wyoming State Archives)
UNCLE SAM: Have been waiting for you, Miss wyoming. Welcome to my house.
MISS WYOMING: I bring with me a constitution giving equal rights to ALL.

After domestic problems, Morris left her husband in 1871 and lived with her sons in Laramie and then Cheyenne. Laramie women nominated her and another woman to serve in the Legislature, but she withdrew her name two weeks later.

In 1890, Edward Slack began referring to his mother in his *Cheyenne Sun* as "Mother of Woman Suffrage."

In February 1919, the *Wyoming State Journal* in Lander printed a letter that put Morris squarely in the position of being the prime motivator for legislator William Bright's support for women's suffrage. H.G. Nickerson of Lander wrote a letter describing a tea party in the fall of 1869, where Morris reportedly exacted a promise from Bright and Nickerson, his opponent in the upcoming legislative election, to support a woman's suffrage bill in the First Legislative Assembly.

University of Wyoming historian Grace Raymond Hebard wrote her version of the events in a 19-page booklet, *How Woman Suffrage Came to Wyoming*, in 1920. This booklet was widely read by Wyoming school children and greatly influenced Morris' legacy in the history of women's suffrage.

Hebard attributed Bright's championing of women's suffrage to the effects of the Civil War. Bright, a native of Virginia and a former officer of the Confederate Army, came West during the years of Reconstruction and settled in the mining boom town of South Pass City. There, he met Esther Hobart Morris, she said.

Hebard described "serious talks around the fireplace" about calls in the East for women's suffrage, "Mrs. Morris usually being the brilliant leader of the conversation. ... The inspiration derived from these fireplace conferences with the master mind of Mrs. Morris gave Mr. Bright the final courage to carry into action his convictions born of after-war observations." (Hebard, 1920, pp. 9-10)

Hebard said Morris was admired for her "sterling character, for her sympathy for womankind, for her breadth of learning, her logical way of reasoning, and her work for true democracy." (Hebard 1920, p. 18)

Bright reportedly also was motivated by his wife, Julia. Newspapers reported Bright thought his wife, mother, and other women should enjoy a franchise that had been given to Negroes.

Historian T.A. Larson concludes, "On the basis of verifiable evidence, Colonel Bright must still be regarded as the leading actor in the drama, and the chief supporting actor may well have been Edward M. Lee, secretary of the territory." Lee was an outspoken supporter of women's rights, and his relatives insisted he actually had written Bright's bill. A letter written by Robert Morris also indicates Esther Hobart Morris met Bright *after* the 1869 Legislative Assembly.

Historian Phil Roberts of the University of Wyoming also concluded the South Pass City tea party did not take place.

Larson wrote:

"Although Mrs. Morris was, no doubt, in her quiet way an advocate of women suffrage, it cannot be established that she influenced Bright or anyone else. She was not the usual type of reformer, since she campaigned for no public office for herself or others, wrote nothing for publication, and made no public addresses except for very brief remarks on a few occasions. There is nothing to indicate she was in Cheyenne during the 1869 legislative session." (Larson 1978, pp. 93-94)

Morris was a natural choice for those seeking a heroine and figurehead for the cause, as the first woman judge. Morris deserves credit in a supporting role, among the suffragists in Wyoming and in

Wyoming Gov. Nellie Taloe Ross, attending a ceremony at Fort D.A. Russell during her term 1924-26. She was the first woman to serve as governor in the United States. (Wyoming State Archives photo)

the East, whose work surely contributed to the major step taken in women's rights in Wyoming in 1869.

Women's suffrage again was the subject of debate at Wyoming's Constitutional Convention in September 1889. All fifty-five delegates were men. On the fourteenth day, Cheyenne attorney A.C. Campbell proposed women's suffrage be submitted to the voters as a separate article. He personally supported women's right to vote, and he thought it would be approved by a two-thirds vote, but he believed the people of Wyoming should have a chance to vote on it. Louis J. Palmer of Sweetwater County said many voters in his county opposed women's suffrage but desired statehood and would like separate votes.

The suggestion inspired lofty speeches in defense of women's suffrage.

Delegate C.W. Holden said, "I say rather than surrender that right, we would rather remain in a territorial condition throughout the endless cycles of time."

Henry A. Coffeen of Sheridan County (U.S. House 1893-1895) declared, "I am unwilling to stand here and by vote or word or gesture disenfranchise one-half the people of our territory, and that the better half. ... Let us catch inspiration from the glorious features of nature about us, the grand valleys, the lifting mountains, the reverberating hills, the floating clouds so lovely above them."

Melville C. Brown, an attorney from Albany County, said, "I would sooner think ... of submitting to the people of Wyoming a separate and distinct proposition as to whether a male citizen of the territory shall be entitled to vote." (Larson 1978, p. 249)

Campbell's proposal lost 8-20, and the constitution submitted to voters included women's right to vote.

Chapter 15

Revenue:
Paying for Government

Governments need money to pay police and run jails, buy books for the libraries, build and repair roads, buy and maintain landfills, haul away garbage, inspect restaurants, operate schools, run courts, bring clean water to homes, and take sewage away. All governments need money to conduct business for their residents. They get it by collecting taxes and fees from residents who receive the services and from enterprises doing business there. Governments also may receive grants and loans from other governmental entities.

As of 2003, there were 461 units of government in Wyoming exercising taxing authority: the state, 23 counties, 98 municipalities, 48 school districts, seven community colleges, and 284 special districts. (Wyoming Taxpayers Association)

Wyoming is one of seven states that do not collect personal income tax from their residents. (The others are Alaska, Florida, Nevada, New Hampshire, South Dakota, Texas, and Washington.)

Wyoming also is unusual in the extent it depends on revenue generated by the minerals that are mined or pumped out of the ground. The big revenue-producers for Wyoming are coal, oil, and gas. However, other minerals that produce revenue for our state include bentonite, clay, decorative stone, feldspar, granite ballast, gypsum, leonardite, limestone, sand and gravel, shale, sodium sulphate, trona, uranium, and zeolite.

The Wyoming Taxpayers Association notes, "Mineral income and interest on mineral savings accounts easily replace personal and business taxes levied by other states." (*Wyoming Fiscal Facts,* Wyoming Taxpayers Association, 2004, p. 4) In fact, reliance of state and local governments on revenue paid by the mineral industry can be a problem when production and prices decline, and the state finds itself in the "bust" phase of the "boom and bust cycle."

Tax collections in 2004 boomed, at $1.5 billion, according to the U.S. Census Bureau. That averaged to $2,968 per resident, second only to Hawaii ($3,047.61). Nearly half the amount came from mineral production. Steve Sommers, co-chairman of the state's Consensus Revenue Estimating Group, said, "It's safe to say if we didn't have any minerals, we wouldn't have any money." (*Wyoming Tribune Eagle*, April 29, 2005)

Another indication of Wyoming residents' dependence on mineral tax income is in these figures from the Division of Economic Analysis, in the Wyoming Department of Revenue. The first list describes the typical tax burden for a Wyoming family of four with an annual income of $50,000 and a home appraised at $140,000. The second list describes the value of services the family receives from various publicly-funded entities.

Personal Taxes Paid	**Services Received**
Property tax $1,000	State services $6,360
Vehicle registration $500	K-12 education $5,850
Tobacco $120	Special districts $1,100
Gasoline $160	City or town $4,360
Retail sales tax $1,620	County $5,090
Total $3,410	**Total $25,760**

Elected representatives may be influenced by various factors when they set tax rates. They may raise some taxes to discourage behavior, as with tobacco use. They may lower taxes as an incentive, as with severance tax cuts on oil from low-volume "stripper" wells to encourage production. Or taxes may be motivated by the need to cover government expenses. The Wyoming Constitution requires governments to balance their budgets.

Title 39 of Wyoming Statutes, "Taxation and Revenue," authorizes taxes and fees and directs how the revenue must be distributed.

The State Board of Equalization is a constitutionally created board of three Wyoming citizens appointed by the governor and confirmed by the Wyoming Senate to advance a stable, equitable, and uniform tax system for state residents. The system is intended to provide a process for equalization and a forum for appeals from decisions by county boards of equalization and Department of Revenue.

In 1991, the State Board of Equalization became a separate operating agency, existing apart from the fourteen principal departments in the executive cabinet. Under the 1991 reorganization plan, the Tax Commission was eliminated and its administrative functions came under the purview of the Department of Revenue.

The Board of Equalization continued to prescribe the appraisal methods and systems for determining fair market value, as well as monitoring county assessors' work and instructing assessors about their duties. In 1995, the board's duties were again reorganized by the Legislature, so the board now clearly operates as the agency responsible for the equalization of property valuation and as the independent hearing body for appeals from county boards of equalization and the Department of Revenue.

In addition to tax collections, Wyoming receives half the Federal Mineral Royalties collected from production of federally-owned minerals in the state. The state also gets income from interest and investments of money in permanent funds. The largest of these are the Permanent Wyoming Mineral Trust Fund, $2 billion, and the Permanent School Trust Fund, $1.1 billion, in 2005.

Most revenues collected by the state go into the account for general spending, the General Fund. The Legislature has wide discretion in how to spend this money. But a great deal of revenue is "earmarked," which means state law has destined the revenue to go to certain accounts to be spent in predetermined ways. An ongoing debate in the Legislature is how much of the "revenue stream" to earmark, which puts the money out of the control of the legislators and makes it unavailable for other government needs.

Another policy issue for legislators is how much to put into savings accounts, especially revenue from taxes on minerals, which eventually will be depleted. A related question is how difficult to make the process of removing money from savings accounts. This issue became especially urgent when production of oil, gas, coal, and coal bed methane brought the state annual budget windfalls of $1 billion or more, beginning in 2003, and lawmakers wanted to make sure some of that income would be available in future lean times.

The major savings accounts are the Permanent Wyoming Mineral Trust Fund and the Budget Reserve Account. The PWMTF, established during the term of Gov. Stan Hathaway, collects 1.5 percent of severance taxes levied on coal, oil, and natural gas production. The principal cannot be spent but will generate interest and investment income for the state long after the minerals are gone. The Budget Reserve Account receives two-thirds of the severance tax income that exceeds $155 million a year and two-thirds of the Federal Mineral Royalties that exceed $200 million a year.

The Legislature also can decide to tuck an extra amount away into accounts or create new accounts when money is plentiful. The 2005 Legislature wanted to capture more of the severance tax income, so it passed a law to put an extra amount in the PWMTF equal to two-thirds of the current flow. In 2006, the Legislature voted to put a constitutional amendment before the citizens to make additional deposits to the PWMTF inviolable, as is the 1.5 percent severance tax flow.

The 2005 Legislature created the Legislative Stabilization Reserve Account to receive bonus bids offered by coal companies for federal coal leases.

An idea discussed but not enacted in 2005 was a "rainy day" account that would require two-thirds vote for withdrawals. The competing idea was to use surplus on infrastructure and other deferred needs.

State and local governments can issue bonds to raise revenue, as allowed by state law, although the Wyoming Constitution limits the debts governments can have, based on their assessed valuations. For instance, a school district can bond up to 10 percent of the assessed valuation of property in that district. General obligation bonds, which are paid off by property taxes, must be approved by voters.

What follows in this chapter on revenue is a description of some taxes levied by state and local governments in Wyoming. That is followed by a description of the budget process practiced by the state and a typical budget process for local government.

Property Taxes

A property tax is an "ad valorem" tax, that is, based on the value of property. There is an "appraised value" of property, which is the market value of that property. A property tax is applied not to the market value, but to the "assessed value" of the property. The assessed value is a percentage of the appraised value, and it is used to compute the taxes due.

Wyoming is a "fractional assessment" state, which means the assessed value may be a "fraction" of the market value. Wyoming voters amended the state Constitution in 1988 to provide for three assessment levels of ad valorem property taxes:

- Minerals and mine products are assessed at their full gross value, i.e.,100 percent of market value.
- Property used for industrial purposes, for extracting or processing minerals, or for the transformation of property into new products is assessed at 11.5 percent of market value.
- All other real and personal property, including homes, are assessed at 9.5 percent of market value.

Minerals have the higher assessment rate because they are taxed just once, when they are taken from the ground and sold. By contrast, other property is taxed every year.

Governments apply their individual tax rates to that assessed value. The rates are expressed in terms of "mills." A mill is one-tenth of 1 percent. So, a 1 mill tax on property with the assessed value of $10,000 will produce $10 of revenue.

The Legislature sets the maximum number of mills that can be collected by local governments. State law may allow local governments to set some of the mills but require popular votes for other mills. In Wyoming, county treasurers collect property taxes within the county and distribute the revenue to the state treasurer and local governments.

The table on page 242 describes the kinds of property taxes that might be levied in a typical county, and it calculates a sample county tax bill a property owner might get from the county assessor. The average tax burden to Wyoming property owners is 66 mills. (Wyoming Department of Revenue)

The personal property tax burden in Wyoming is relatively low, in part because of the substantial property taxes paid by mineral producers. Mineral production accounts for about half the entire state's assessed

Sample Property Tax Calculation

Property: Home appraised at $100,000
Assessed value of property: 9.5 percent x $100,000 = $9,500
Mill levies that are applied to this property:

K-12 Education

School District Levy	25.0
Mandatory County Levy	6.0
Foundation Fund Levy	12.0

Additional County-wide Levies

County Levy	12.0
Weed and Pest District	2.0
Hospital District	3.0
Conservation District	1.0

City or Town Levy   8.0

Special District Levies

School District Recreation	1.0
Fire	3.0
Cemetery	3.0

Total Mills Applied   76.0

Total Property Tax Bill $722.00 ($9,500 x .076)

valuation and so produces about half the property tax revenue. Minerals for 2003 were assessed at $5.6 billion, compared to the state total of $10.34 billion. Mineral producers paid 54.4 percent of the total $668.6 billion in property taxes paid that year. (*Wyoming Property Taxation 2003*, Wyoming Taxpayers Association)

Appendices at the back of this book provide information about property taxes in Wyoming. Appendix 10 summarizes where property taxes come from and where they go. Appendix 11 is a table of Wyoming's 23 counties, their assessed valuation and how much revenue the valuation generates. Appendix 12 is a table of assessed valuation of the 48 school districts. There is great variance among counties and districts in their ability to raise revenue through local property wealth, primarily because of mineral production.

State law provides for property tax exemptions and other tax relief measures that benefit agricultural producers, veterans, low-income homeowners, the elderly, and the disabled.

Excise Taxes

Another major category of taxes is excise tax. One kind of excise tax is a sales tax, which is levied as a percentage of the amount of money spent to buy goods and services. The state of Wyoming collects revenue from a 4 percent sales tax. The Legislature added the fourth penny as a temporary measure when education finance costs climbed in the 1990s. In 2000, the Legislature made it permanent. The state shares this revenue with local governments: 69 percent to the state General Fund and 31 percent to cities, towns, and counties.

Use taxes are levied on goods that are purchased outside the state, tax-free, for use in Wyoming. Use taxes remove the advantage an out-of-state merchant might have over a Wyoming business, which must charge customers sales tax. Wyoming residents who buy items tax-free from out-of-state merchants by phone, mail, or Internet orders should report the purchases to the Wyoming Department of Revenue by the end of the next month and pay 4 percent use tax.

A 4 percent sales tax is collected statewide, and revenue is shared by the state and by cities, towns, and counties: the state receives 69 percent and the cities, towns, and counties 31 percent. The counties' share is distributed based on several factors but mostly on population. The Legislature may change that distribution formula at any time.

In addition, the Legislature has authorized sales taxes that may be imposed by local governments:

- The county may impose a 1 percent sales tax to fund general operations, anything from human services to roads. The county commission must submit the so-called "fifth penny" to voters for

244 A Look at Wyoming Government

their approval for a period of four years. The county may ask voters to renew the tax every four years.

- The county may impose a "specific use" tax of up to 2 percent, which pays for a project or list of projects desired by a county's residents. The county may put projects on the ballot individually or grouped together, for approval by all voters in the county. The tax remains in place until a certain amount of money, enough to pay for the projects, is collected. Counties with a 1 percent general operations tax can add only 1 percent specific use tax, so the two together do not exceed 2 percent.
- Municipalities may impose up to 4 percent in lodging taxes. Revenues must be spent to promote the local tourism industry. This tax also must be approved by local voters.

Other excise taxes are imposed on goods by the unit of sale. Some are considered "sin" taxes, imposed on items whose use is completely discretionary. Officials do not mind if the taxes discourage use of those items. An example in Wyoming is the tax on cigarettes. In 2003, the tax was raised from 12 cents a pack to 60 cents a pack. Other tobacco products are subject to a 20 percent excise tax on the wholesale price.

Another excise tax is imposed with the idea that the revenue will benefit the people who bear most of the tax burden. So, state law might impose an excise tax on gasoline and specify that the revenue pay for highways. Wyoming collects a tax of 13 cents a gallon on sales of gasoline and diesel fuel, in addition to a 1 percent license fee.

Title 39 of Wyoming Statutes describes taxes authorized by the state, how the revenue is distributed, and sales tax exemptions granted by the Legislature. The list of goods and services exempt from sales tax is a long one. Legislative attempts to remove exemptions fill the committee rooms and galleries of the Legislature with people who defend the exemptions as good for the state and its people. Proposals to exempt groceries from the sales tax failed repeatedly until 2006, when the Legislature approved a two-year exemption.

Liquor Division Revenue

State government also collects revenue earned by the Liquor Division of the Wyoming Department of Revenue. The division is unusual in the executive branch in the fact it is 100 percent "enterprise funded," which means it operates off funds it generates and gets nothing from the state General Fund.

The division acts as a wholesaler to all liquor outlets. It showed net earnings in fiscal year 2003 of $6.5 million, which was 13 percent of sales. The division's goal is 13.6 percent. (*Department of Revenue 2003 Annual Report,* p. 77)

Total cases sold in fiscal 2003 was 666,328.

According to the Liquor Division's resale figures for 2003, Teton County outlets led the state, accounting for 18.38 percent of state resale dollars. Laramie County was second at 15.2 percent, and Natrona County was third at 13.9 percent. The lowest amount of sales was one-fourth of 1 percent, in Niobrara County. Sales in volume, measured by "cases," involved the same top three counties, but in different order. Laramie County led the state with 15.9 percent of statewide volume, followed by Natrona at 14.9 percent, and then Teton at 14.6 percent. Again, Niobrara County accounted for the least amount purchased, .22 percent of the statewide total.

License and User Fees

Governments collect revenue by charging for franchises, licenses, and use of government services. Franchise licenses are purchased by providers of local cable, telephone, gas, and electricity utilities. Counties collect vehicle registration fees and issue licenses to businesses. They charge fees for water, sewage, garbage pickup and disposal, parking, and recreation facilities.

One example is the license tax imposed on gasoline and diesel fuel. The state collects 14 cents a gallon. The revenue goes into accounts for county roads, state highways, underground storage tanks, and other purposes related to motor vehicles. (See Wyoming Statutes 39-17-104 and 39-17-204 for the tax and 39-17-111 for distribution of the revenue)

Federal Funds

Local governments get a share of federal mineral royalty payments, based on population. They use block grants from the federal government to support a range of projects, from homeless shelters to transportation. Counties also receive federal Payment in Lieu of Taxes

(PILT) money. PILT compensates counties for land owned by the federal government, which does not generate property taxes.

Severance Taxes

Severance taxes are paid by people who take, or "sever," minerals from Wyoming. They are fees, rather than an actual tax, to compensate the state for the minerals. Rates are set by the Legislature and are collected by the state. The Legislature may decrease severance tax rates by scheduling the cuts into law. In some cases, the Legislature may cut rates as an incentive for producers. For instance, the severance tax on oil is 6 percent. However, the rate for low-production "stripper oil" is 4 percent. The severance tax break kicks in differently, depending on the market price for oil, at two levels of production, ten barrels a day and fifteen barrels a day. Legislators fear the higher tax rate would make stripper wells unprofitable, and producers would just shut them in. The effectiveness of severance tax incentives is difficult to verify.

The severance tax rates of minerals in 2004 were:
- Oil and Natural Gas   6 percent
- Stripper Oil   4 percent
- Tertiary Oil   4 percent
- New Wells   2 percent
- Incremental Oil and Gas from Workovers and Recompletions   2 percent
- Coal – Surface Mines   7 percent
- Coal – Underground Mines   3.75 percent
- Trona   4 percent
- Uranium   0 percent
- Other minerals   2 percent

Some revenue is "earmarked" for state funds. Severance tax income also is destined for local governments. The formulas for applying severance taxes and distributing the revenue are complex and can be found in the statutes.

Mineral Royalties

Another source of income from mineral production is royalties. That is the money paid by the producer to the "owner" of the minerals, based on the value of the minerals removed. The United States government collects royalties on minerals produced on federal land in Wyoming and gives half back to the state. The state of Wyoming also collects royalties from production on state land. The Permanent School Trust Fund collects royalties on production from school trust land. School trust land and the minerals beneath the surface were given by the federal government to Wyoming at statehood to be managed as a trust to support public schools.

Income Tax

Wyoming has no personal or corporate income tax, and there is little interest in adopting one. The idea has been suggested time and again since statehood. It was a recommendation by a study conducted for the Legislature called "Tax Reform 2000," which evaluated all kinds of revenue-raising systems in the state. However, proposals to create an income tax for Wyoming never get far. (A summary of the Tax Reform 2000 report is in Appendix 18.)

Other Revenue Sources

The Legislature has resisted repeated proposals to raise revenue through a lottery or other gambling. In 2005, the Wyoming House considered a bill to establish a Wyoming Lottery Corporation to oversee a multi-state lottery and operate "instant ticket" games. Revenue would have gone to senior citizen services, parks and historic site capital construction, and early childhood development services. Opponents argued the proposal was impractical and undermined morality. It failed on third reading with a 29-29 tie vote.

However, the Northern Arapaho Tribe operates casino-style gambling on the Wind River Reservation, under the federal Indian Gaming Regulatory Act of 1988. (See Chapter 11, Tribal Government.)

Using the Revenue

Distribution of tax revenue can generate some heated debate when legislators are deciding how much to save, how much to put in state accounts, and how much to pass on to local governments.

Distribution formulas can get complex. An example is distribution of severance taxes in 2004: the Permanent Wyoming Mineral Trust Fund received 1.5 percent of the severance taxes collected on oil, natural gas, and coal. A small amount went in the so-called LUST account to clean up damage from leaking underground storage tanks (hence the acronym "LUST"). The next $155 million collected in a year was distributed as follows: 62.26 percent to the General Fund, 12.45 percent to Water Development I, 2.1 percent to Water Development II, 4.33 percent to the Highway Fund, 3.88 percent to counties, 2.9 percent to county roads, 9.25 percent to cities and towns, 2.83 to capital construction. Of the balance that exceeds $155 million, one-third goes to the General Fund and two-thirds to the Budget Reserve Account.

The table on page 249 shows the relative contribution of various revenue sources to the support of state and local government.

Appendix 13 shows how revenue from various of sources was deposited automatically in various accounts in 2003.

State Revenue Figures Fiscal 2003

Sales Taxes
To the General Fund - $271 million
To Local Governments - $230.3 million

Use Taxes
To the General Fund - $29.4 million
To Local Governments - $25.2 million

Ad Valorem (Property) Taxes
Total collections - $668.6 million (From minerals $363 million)

Minerals
Total ad valorem taxes collected on minerals - $352.3 million (estimate)
Total severance taxes on all minerals - $331.4 million (estimate)

Severance Taxes
Total collections - $429.1 million

Federal Mineral Royalties
Total to state - $476.3 million (includes coal bid bonus payments)

Revenue to the General Fund in fiscal 2004:

Severance Tax	$184.4 million
Sales Tax	$295.7 million
Interest PWMTF	$ 98.1 million
Interest on pooled funds	$ 28.7 million
Use Tax	$ 31.4 million
Sales and Service Charges	$ 24.3 million
Franchise Tax	$ 21.7 million
Revenue from other source	$ 5.3 million
License and Permit Fees	$ 4.1 million
Inheritance Tax	$ 6.1 million
Property/Money Use	$ 7.8 million
Penalties and Interest	$ 9.0 million
Federal Aid and Grants	$ 11.6 million
All Other	$ 16.7 million
Total	**$744.5 million**

Source: Wyoming Department of Revenue

Chapter 16

Economy

For nearly 200 years, Wyoming has drawn settlers by offering economic opportunities, provided largely by its rich natural resources. It is useful to understand the development of its economy and to trace the influence of certain sectors in state government today.

Mining & Minerals

Vegetation and marine life laid down in seas and swamps millions of years ago -- converted to coal, oil, and gas -- fuel much of Wyoming's government today. The minerals industry is the largest single contributor to Wyoming economy and to the state's treasury. Wyoming residents rely heavily on minerals and mining to pay for government services -- from schools to courts to public health nursing. The 2004 valuation of all minerals produced in Wyoming was $8.6 billion. That is 63 percent of the state's total valuation. Income from collections on all minerals in 2004 was $1.7 billion. (See Appendix 9 and Appendix 10.)

Mining and minerals were prominent features of Wyoming geology and economics in the 20th century and continue into the 21st century. Wyoming's reliance on coal, oil, and gas production means the state rides the same boom-and-bust cycle of that industry.

Coal

Captain John C. Fremont, known as The Pathfinder, made the first written account of coal in Wyoming in 1843, in an area near Kemmerer in western Wyoming. In 1852, Captain John R. Stansbury of the U.S. Army Corps of Engineers reported an outcrop of coal near Rock Springs and at Point of Rocks just east of Rock Springs. Union Pacific Railroad was a major coal producer in territorial days, using coal to fuel its trains as they traveled across southern Wyoming.

By 1908, coal mining was the leading industry in Wyoming with production of about 6 million tons a year. One-third came from the Rock Springs area. (*Wyoming 2004 Mineral and Energy Yearbook,* Energy and Transportation Division, Wyoming Business Council, p. 28)

Production declined to a low of less than 2 million tons in 1959. Later, development of low-cost strip mines and demand for Wyoming coal for electric power plants sparked increased production that continues to climb. Wyoming led the nation in coal production in 2003 with 376.8 million taxable tons.

Coal is found in eleven of the state's twenty-three counties. Wyoming had eighteen active surface coal mines in 2003. The Powder River Basin accounted for 95 percent of Wyoming coal production and boasted three of the biggest surface coal mines in the nation: Belle Ayer Mine, Jacobs Ranch Mine, and Black Thunder Mine. Coal valuation from 2003 production was $1.8 billion. (*2003 Annual Report,*

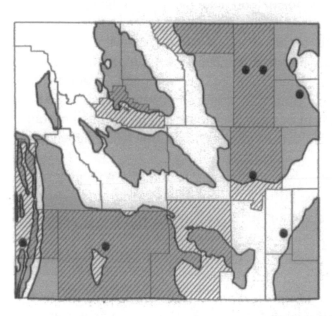

Coal-bearing area		
Coal-producing county		
• Coal-fired power plant		

0   50   100

Miles

Total Area of State:
97,914 square miles
Area Underlain by coal:
40,055 square miles

Map from Energy Information Administration, U.S. Department of Energy

Wyoming Department of Revenue. *2004 Mineral and Energy Year-book*, Wyoming Business Council.)

About 97 percent of Wyoming's coal is used to generate electricity. Nearly half of Wyoming's coal production in 2005 went to customers in Texas.

Wyoming has the nation's third largest coal reserves with an estimated 68.7 billion tons. Montana's reserves are estimated at 120 billion tons and Illinois at 78.5 billion tons. The Powder River Basin, which covers 12,000 square miles in northeastern Wyoming, covers the coal-bearing Fort Union and Wasatch formations. It is one of the world's largest deposits of coal, with 5.3 billion tons, all of which is under less than 1,000 feet of overburden. About half the coal is in beds where the coal is more than 10 feet thick, and 1.8 billion tons of coal can be recovered economically using surface mining techniques. (Wyoming Mining Association)

In addition, the Powder River Basin in northeastern Wyoming has been undergoing rapid development of coal-bed methane (CBM), a form of natural gas that is trapped in coal seams by overlying water. In 1995, Wyoming had 427 coalbed methane wells. In early 2005, the Oil and Gas Conservation Commission reported more than 21,000 wells drilled and another 30,000 approved. ("Wastewater goes unwatched," *High Country News*, March 6, 2005, p. 13)

Coal-bed gas is recovered by pumping water to the surface and, along with it, methane gas from the coal seam. A well recovers gas from a small part of the coal bed, so hundreds or thousands of wells are needed for an area.

CBM development in Wyoming dates back to the late 1970s. Ten years later, there still were fewer than 20 wells. In 2004, there were more than 13,600 producing and shut in CBM wells across the state. The most active development was in the Powder River Coal Field, where an estimated 50,000 wells were planned in the next decade. The U.S. Geological Survey said in 2004 the Powder River Basin contained an estimated 14.2 billion cubic feet of undiscovered coal-bed gas reserves, equal to half of all estimated undiscovered reserves in the region.

Coal-bed methane development contributed greatly to the $1 billion-plus surplus in annual revenue the state has enjoyed in recent

Town of Parco, six miles east of Rawlins (no date). Producers and Refiners Corporation built a refinery and this model town for 600 persons 1922-23. Crude oil was piped from the Lost Soldier and Salt Creek fields. The Sinclair Oil Co. acquired the property in 1934 and changed the name to Sinclair. (Wyoming State Archives photo)

years, but well development and disposal of the water have caused environmental problems.

Oil & Natural Gas

The first written record of Wyoming petroleum was a 1833 description of the "Great Tar Spring" on the Popo Agie River near Lander. The first oil field was Dallas Dome at the Great Tar Spring in 1884.

By statehood in 1890, the Salt Creek oil field north of Casper was producing enough crude to make it profitable to ship oil east by rail and to supply Casper's first refinery by pipeline. The Salt Creek Field was producing about one-fifth of the nation's petroleum in the 1920s, and it remains a major oil field for the United States today. Early Wyoming oil production peaked in 1923, after development of large fields, and then it declined until the demand created by World War II.

In 2002, crude oil or natural gas was produced in every Wyoming county except Platte and Teton. The largest oil producing regions in Wyoming are the Powder River Basin, Green River Basin, Big Horn

Above:
Canadian Camp at Salt
Creek Oil Fields about
1930. (Courtesy
Wyoming Tales and
Trails)

Below:
The Wyodak coal seam in the Powder River
Basin near Gillette averages 100 feet thick and
is the top coal producing bed in the United
States. (Courtesy Science and Mathematics
Teaching Center, University of Wyoming.)

Basin, Overthrust Belt, and Wind River Basin. The largest natural gas production is in Sublette County, followed by Campbell and Uinta counties. (Petroleum Association of Wyoming)

Wyoming ranks eighth in the nation in crude oil production and is seventh in reserves. However, it dominates the Rocky Mountains with 40 percent of the production in the region. Wyoming accounts for 3 percent of U.S. oil production. In 2003, Wyoming oil production was 50.1 million barrels, valued at $1.2 billion. Production continues to decline, as oil reserves are tapped, but high prices keep valuation high. Currently, petroleum is the state's third most valuable mineral product behind natural gas and coal. (*2004 Mineral and Energy Yearbook*, Wyoming Business Council, p. 29, p. 113)

Wyoming began producing natural gas in 1903, in the Wind River and Big Horn basins. Most production today is in the Overthrust Belt in southwestern Wyoming, followed by the Green River Basin, Wind River Basin, and Powder River Basin. Wyoming was seventh nationally in natural gas reserves and sixth in production in 2006.

Natural gas production in Wyoming continues to rise, along with the price per thousand cubic feet (mcf), and it leads the state in value of production. Between 2002 and 2003, the price of Wyoming gas doubled to $3.20 per mcf, and so the taxable value doubled, as well. Production in 2003 was 1.6 trillion cubic feet, valued at $5.2 billion. That is 61.1 percent of the value of all minerals that were produced in Wyoming in 2003 and taxed in 2004.

Trona & Bentonite

Wyoming is the nation's leading producer of trona, a mineral that deposited on the floor of a large freshwater lake about 50 million years ago. Trona is processed into soda ash or bicarbonate of soda. About half is used in glassmaking. Other uses include soap, paper manufacturing, and water treatment. Wyoming supplies about 90 percent of the nation's soda ash from mines in Sweetwater County. (Wyoming Mining Association)

Trona production in Wyoming in 2003 was 17.8 million tons with a taxable value of $192.5 million. (*2004 Mineral Energy Yearbook*, Wyoming Business Council, pp. 107-108) All the major raw materials required to make glass are found in Wyoming, but the state has no glass manufacturing plant. (*Wyoming: A Source Book*, Jordan and De Boer, 1996, p. 178-179)

Wyoming also led the nation in bentonite production, totaling 3.6 million tons in 2003. Taxable value was $33.4 million. Bentonite is used in oil well drilling as a sealant, in cosmetics, in soap, in paper, as a binder for iron ore in making steel, and as cat pan filler.

Uranium

Uranium production, once the object of a great prospecting rush, came to a virtual standstill by the end of the 1990s. However, demand had picked up in 2005 to more than quadruple the price of a pound of uranium.

The first production in Wyoming was in 1953, when 5,156 tons of ore was mined. Production peaked in 1978, with 5 million tons. By 2003, production had dwindled to 1.2 million pounds (5,612 tons), valued at $8 million. The unit price was about $6.60 a pound. Wyoming had two active in-situ operations in Converse County in 2004. (*2004 Mineral Energy Yearbook*, Wyoming Business Council, pp. 107-108)

However, worldwide demand for nuclear power increased during 2004 and 2005, particularly in China, India, Brazil, and Eastern Europe. The spot market price for uranium in mid-2005 was $29 a pound. Wyoming ranks second behind New Mexico in reserves and first nationally in production of uranium.

In-situ production involves drilling wells and pumping a solution into a central well to leach the uranium out of rock. The uranium-bearing solution is pumped out and milled onsite to remove uranium. The uranium ore, or "yellowcake," is shipped to an enrichment facility for use in nuclear power plants.

With the collapse of the market for uranium, the Legislature suspended the 4 percent severance tax on uranium until 2009, unless the price for ore rises to at least $14 a pound for six straight months. (Wyoming Statutes 39-14-505)

Other Minerals

Jade, Wyoming's official gemstone, is found in the Wind River Mountains. The mineral name is "nephrite." Diamonds were discovered in Wyoming in 1875, in the southern Laramie Mountains and

Cowboys load range cattle for shipment to the great livestock markets of the East, in this undated photo. Livestock and crop production is considered a bedrock of Wyoming culture, and it enjoys strong support in Wyoming state government. (Wyoming State Archives photo, undated)

along the Colorado border. A 14.2-carat gemstone was recovered in 1995. Limestone, gypsum, leonardite, clay, and construction aggregate also are produced. The last iron ore mine in Wyoming was at Atlantic City, and it closed in 1983. Production that year was 2.5 million tons.

Gold was discovered in Wyoming in 1842 in the 2.8 billion year old rock of the southern Wind River Range. The South Pass area was the most important gold region. An estimated 327,000 ounces of gold were recovered in the 1800s. Wyoming has no gold production today. (Jordan and DeBoer 1996, p. 169-177)

Agriculture

Agricultural production in Wyoming was about $1 billion in 2003. Net income from crop and livestock production was $99.6

million in 2002. (*Wyoming Agricultural Statistics 2004,* Department of Agriculture Wyoming Statistical Office, p. 26)

In 2003, 9,200 farms and ranches were operating in Wyoming with a total land area of 34.4 million acres. Wyoming ranked eighth nationally in total farm and ranch land and first in average size of operations. The average size was 3,743 acres, compared to a national average operation of 441 acres. However, about a third of those farms and ranches produced less than $10,000 worth of agricultural products a year and were considered more of a sideline or hobby than a major agricultural operation. The size of operations with $10,000 or more production annually was much larger, at 31,440 acres. (*Wyoming Agricultural Statistics 2004,* p.24)

The agricultural sector provided about 17,000 jobs in 2004, according to the Wyoming Division of Economic Analysis.

The cattle industry is by far the largest component of Wyoming agriculture, accounting for more than 70 percent of all cash receipts. Cattle also led 2003 production value at $502.9 million. All livestock production in 2003 was valued at $568.5 million, up 13 percent from the year before. Sheep and hogs were far behind, with production values of $26.2 million and $24.3 million, respectively.

The USDA's January estimates for sheep and lamb reported 3.97 million in 1932. The 2003 total was 430,000. Wool production in 1909 was 46.9 million pounds. In 2003, wool production in Wyoming was down to 3.6 million pounds, but still second highest in the nation behind Texas, with a value of $26.1 million. (*Wyoming Agricultural Statistics 2004,* compiled by USDA Wyoming Statistical Office)

USDA cattle estimates for Wyoming grew to 1.3 million in 1919, declined, then recovered to 1 million in years after World War II. A record 1.7 million cattle and calves were reported on January 1, 1975. Since then, the head count has stayed relatively steady. In 2004, the cattle estimate was 1.4 million head.

Wyoming had 150 hog operations in 2003, which produced 58.2 million pounds worth $24.3 million. During the same year, Wyoming had 39,000 colonies of bees, which produced 3.2 million pounds of honey worth $4.4 million. (USDA)

Hay is by far the leading crop in Wyoming in value of production, which drought reduced to $185.7 million in 2003. Sugarbeets are second in value, $31.8 million in 2003. Barley was third in 2003 at $24.6 million, followed by corn at $16.1 million, wheat at $13.7 million, and dry beans at $10.5 million. Hay marketed for livestock had cash receipts about equal to that of sugarbeets.

Agricultural production -- how much and what kind -- tends to vary from region to region, depending on the transportation, topography, rainfall, climate, and other environmental factors. Average annual precipitation varies from a low of 6 inches at Powell, in the Big Horn Basin, to 21.5 inches at Moran in the northwestern corner of the state. Only about 10 percent of agricultural land is cultivated. About half of that is irrigated, although 85 percent of farming in the Big Horn Basin requires irrigation.

The Laramie Basin in south-central Wyoming is mostly grassland, so cattle ranching flourished there. In the Big Horn Basin, irrigation is important along the Shoshone, Big Horn, and Greybull rivers, and farmers grow sugarbeets, beans, alfalfa, and hay.

Although agriculture is a much smaller part of the Wyoming economy than minerals, it maintains great influence in state government, where the Legislature tends to support measures to help out ranchers and farmers. The political clout of stockgrowers and farmers from the days of the Wyoming Territory is described in the 2002 book *Pushed off the Mountain, Sold Down the River*, by Sam Western. Wyoming's agricultural policy "gives more financial aid to ranchers than does any other state in the union," Western writes. (p. 11)

Tourism

The tourism and the travel industry is an important sector of the Wyoming economy, and in some areas it is the major industry.

A Wyoming Business Council report listed direct impacts:
- During 2003, travel spending by all visitors to Wyoming was about $1.9 billion, about $5.2 million a day.
- Travel spending in Wyoming increased 4.5 percent per year between 1997 and 2003. In constant dollars, adjusted for inflation, travel spending increased by 2.2 percent a year during that time.
- Visitors who stayed overnight in commercial lodging facilities spent $868 million in 2003. That is nearly half of the total spent

by visitors to the state. Visitors who stayed in public or private campgrounds in 2003 spent $399 million, about 20 percent of the total.

- During 2003, visitor spending in Wyoming directly supported 27,980 jobs, with earnings of $488 million. Most jobs were in accommodations, recreation, and food service industries.
- Local and state tax revenues generated by travel spending in 2003 were $88 million.

Tax revenue generated by the travel industry is a small fraction of the revenue from minerals, but travel and tourism are major employers in Wyoming. Coal mining employment in Wyoming in 2003, for example, was 4,788. (Wyoming Mining Association)

Economic Issues

The Wyoming Legislature occasionally enacts legislation designed to help out an industry that is particularly desirable or that needs help -- for instance, removing the severance tax on uranium or exempting the sales tax on manufacturing equipment. Legislators have taken these actions based largely on speculation they would stimulate the desired business activity and that the activity would offset revenue losses.

At the request of the Legislature, the University of Wyoming Economics and Finance Department conducted a study to determine the effects of mineral industry tax incentives. "Mineral Tax Incentives, Mineral Production and the Wyoming Economy" was released December 1, 2000. It concluded that incentives could increase oil exploration. However, severance tax reductions do not produce significant increases in mineral production and employment, the study said. Meanwhile, state and local governments lose large amounts of revenue. The econometric model used for this study is available for the Legislature to evaluate the economic impact of proposed tax incentives.

State and local governments may take action to generate and support the economy in general, as with creation of the Wyoming Business Council. Or a government may support a particular industry considered vital to its economy. The Legislature perceived in 2004 that a lack of capacity in gas pipelines was limiting access to markets for smaller Wyoming producers, and so their prices were depressed. This depressed their gas prices and also income to the state based on production value. The Legislature created the Wyoming Natural Gas Pipeline Authority to promote development of intrastate and interstate pipelines to enhance development in Wyoming and encourage export to markets around the nation. Legislators also created the Wyoming Infrastructure Authority in 2004, with the task of developing transmission capacity for electric power generated in Wyoming, with the ultimate goal of diversifying and growing the state's economy.

Some state agencies promote development of natural resources, while others regulate that production to ensure protection for the environment and communities affected by the production.

The Legislature created the Wyoming Business Council in 1998 to bring together 25 programs from seven state agencies. The WBC promotes business opportunities and tourism nationally and helps communities develop and attract businesses. WBC divisions are dedicated to:
- Agribusiness
- Business and Industry
- Manufacturing
- Investment Ready Communities
- Minerals, Energy and Transportation
- Technology/Telecommunications
- Travel and Tourism
- Film, Arts and Entertainment

Legislators are well aware of the state's dependence on the energy and mineral industry. They have acted in times of decline to provide incentives through tax cuts. At other times, they tried to diversify the economy and encourage other industries. A new aspect of economic development is concern over the outmigration of young adults and lack of opportunities to attract young families to the state. The estimated change of population between 2000 and 2004 for the state was an increase of 2.6 percent. The estimated 2004 population was 506,529. However, there were losses for school-age children and for adults 35-45 years old, while numbers of senior citizens were up dramatically. Net changes for age groups estimated by the Economic Analysis Division are shown in the table on the following page.

Net Changes in Wyoming Population For Age Groups 2000-2004

Age	Change
0-4	-0.2 percent
5-9	-12.6 percent
10-14	-11.9 percent
15-19	-6.8 percent
20-24	+21.5 percent
25-29	+3.6 percent
30-34	+1.2 percent
35-39	-16.5 percent
40-44	-8.5 percent
45-49	+6.6 percent
50-54	+21.4 percent
55-59	+29.9 percent
60-64	+24.5 percent
65-69	+10.1 percent
70-74	-0.5 percent
75-59	+3.6 percent
80 plus	+9.5 percent

(*Estimates of the Resident Population by Age and Sex for Wyoming: 2000 to 2004*, Economic Analysis Division, Wyoming Department of Administration and Information)

Schools in almost every district have lost enrollment since the early 1990s, when student numbers statewide dropped below 100,000. The estimated enrollment for school year 2005-2006 was about 83,000, according to the Wyoming Department of Education.

The American Association for Retired Persons predicts that by the year 2020 Wyoming will have the nation's highest percentage of residents between 65 and 74 years of age. This trend of the "graying of Wyoming" has important policy implications for the state. Legislators and agencies must deal with the need to attract people to replace those who are retiring from such vital jobs as teachers and health care workers. An older population also puts growing demands on public and private health services for seniors and the disabled. ("Wyoming's Graying Population Compels Rethinking the Role of Public Health," *Northwest Public Health*, Fall/Winter 2004, pp. 18-19)

Students of Wyoming's long-term concern with economic development can refer to more than 40 years worth of studies and recommendations that were summarized by the Economic Analysis Division of the Department of Administration and Information in 2005. Recurring themes are: streamlining regulations, improving infrastructure, workforce training, greater use of technology, use of the state-produced raw materials, encouraging entrepreneurial efforts, and promoting the state's strengths of clean air, low taxes, natural resources, and available workforce. The 1985 Futures Project also urged investment in cultural programs. (*Summary of Economic Development Publications and Recommendations for the State of Wyoming*, January 5, 2005)

The intersection of Wyoming economy and politics was the subject *of Pushed Off the Mountain, Sold Down the River,* published in 2002. Author Sam Western stirred controversy by positing that Wyoming has destined itself to economic stagnation because it has failed to appreciate that creative people and their ideas, not natural resources, bring long-term, stable economic wealth. "The state persistently elects leaders who feel if they build one more dam, punch another logging road in a National Forest, cut agriculture another check, or give oil and gas producers an additional tax break, then prosperity will arrive," Western wrote.

Western objects to so-called "agriculturalism," a "mindset with an intrinsic sense of superiority to all other professions and an entrenched sense of entitlement, specifically expecting financial and political protection."

Union Pacific Railroad poster advertises passenger service to Wyoming in 1923. (Union Pacific Railroad photo)

Transportation

Transportation is vital to economic development, and state and local governments may enhance rail service, highways, or air service so businesses can easily move products and personnel in and out of communities. Communities can use improved transportation to attract new businesses and tourist traffic.

In 2002, the Legislature ordered a Management Audit of the Wyoming Aeronautics Commission, created in 1937. The audit report recommended making the Wyoming Business Council the agency to promote commercial and general aviation air service for Wyoming. Under this scenario, the Business Council would be responsible for air service promotion grants. The Transportation commission would approve airport infrastructure grants. The Aeronautics Commission would be given new duties or would be disbanded, under this recommendation.

The 2003 Legislature passed the Air Services Financial Aid law, which begins with the statement that the Legislature finds an adequate and comprehensive system of air service "is vital for economic development," while "competition among air service providers within the state is virtually nonexistent." The law set up a $3 million Wyoming Air Services Enhancement Account and authorized the Wyoming Business Council to give financial aid to businesses that would improve air service to the state. In 2005, the Legislature gave granting authority to the Aeronautics Commission and said the grants could go to any economic development organization to enhance air service. (Wyoming Statutes 9-12-701-702)

Ten Wyoming cities and towns have commercial air service, with a total 369,177 emplanements counted in 2003. Jackson accounted for 217,530 of those airplane riders. Another twenty-three communities have general aviation services.

The Wyoming Legislature resolved in 2005 to investigate the possibility of widening several two-lane highways to four lanes to increase safety and economy of transportation. The Legislature put $7 million in the highway fund to be used by the Transportation Commission for engineering and construction, although the cost of four-lane highway construction is about $1 million per mile.

The Wyoming Transportation Commission identified the following nine stretches of highway for upgrading to four lanes:

- U.S. Highway 20-26 between Casper and Shoshoni, 87.5 miles.
- Wyoming Highway 220 between Casper and Muddy Gap, 61.6 miles.
- U.S. Highway 287 between Muddy Gap and Rawlins, 41.2 miles.
- Wyoming Highway 59 between Gillette and Reno Junction, 31.6 miles.

- U.S. Highway 287 between Laramie and the Colorado state line, 21.2 miles.
- U.S. Highway 16 between Thermopolis and Worland, 25.9 miles.
- U.S. Highway 16-20 between Worland and Greybull, 35.9 miles.
- U.S. Highway 30 between Kemmerer and Interstate 80, 44.2 miles.
- U.S. Highway 30 between Kemmerer and Border Junction, 52.5 miles.

The Union Pacific Railroad line hauls freight east-west across southern Wyoming. The Burlington Northern Santa Fe Railroad line runs north-south in eastern Wyoming and serves the coal-rich Powder River Basin. The Chicago & North Western Railway, which merged with Union Pacific in 1995, also hauls Powder River Basin coal.

Wyoming has no passenger rail service. The National Railroad Passenger Corporation, known as Amtrak, was created by Congress in 1970, and it used Union Pacific's line across Wyoming. Amtrak ceased passenger rail service to Wyoming in 1996, citing a 50 percent drop in ridership from 1994 to 1995.

Wild horses during a roundup by the U.S. Bureau of Land Management in Wyoming. The BLM manages wild horses and burros on public rangelands under a policy of "multiple use." This policy accommodates wildlife, vegetation and people who use federal land for livestock grazing and recreation. All of these elements are important to the tourism and agriculture elements of Wyoming's economy. The BLM also approves permits for mineral exploration. (BLM Photo. Photographer unknown)

Chapter 17

Education

Government has a role to fund public education and to set standards for the schools' facilities and teachers. Both duties traditionally have been performed by local school districts in Wyoming. However, court mandates and statewide standards have resulted in greater assumption of responsibility and control on the state level.

During the 2004-2005 school year, about 83,800 students attended 362 public schools in 48 school districts. Those districts employed 6,567 full time staff. The 362 schools included 210 elementary, 65 middle and junior highs, 78 high schools and 3 comprehensive kindergarten-through-12th grade schools.

The graduation rate of Wyoming public schools has increased in the past decade. The rate in 1995-1996 was 75.6 percent. The rate in 2004-2005 was 81.5 percent. (Wyoming Department of Education news release February 11, 2006)

School districts in Wyoming vary greatly in size and property wealth (assessed valuation). It is difficult to define anything like a "typical" school district, because they are so distinct in so many ways, and this makes devising an equitable, constitutional school financing model extremely difficult.

Attendance in 2004-2005 ranged from a high of 12,900 in Laramie County District One in Cheyenne down to 105 students in Sheridan County District Three (Clearmont) and 95 students in Washakie County District Two (Ten Sleep). Most districts, 27 of the 48 total, had fewer than 1,000 students in 2003-2004.

Assessed valuation in all 48 school districts totaled $13.7 billion in 2004, ranging from mineral-rich $3.2 billion in Campbell County District One (Gillette) down to $2.2 million in Fremont County District 38 (Arapahoe). Assessed valuation per pupil ranged from an astounding high of $2.4 million in Sublette County District One (Pinedale) down to $7,931 in Arapahoe. Pinedale's valuation, which more than doubled from 2003, derived from natural gas production in the district. (See Appendix 12 for valuation and enrollment, converted to "average daily membership," for all districts.)

State expenditures per student averaged an estimated $10,229 during 2005-2006. Actual amounts ranged from about $9,200 per student in populous Laramie One (Cheyenne) and Natrona One (Casper) up to about $26,500 per student in tiny Sheridan Three (Clearmont). (Enrollment and property valuation for all school districts are in Appendix 12.)

The 2006 Legislature recalibrated the school funding formula and added money for staff, utilities, and academic programs. The action increased state education spending to about $1.1 billion a year. The result was estimated spending for 2006-2007 school year of about $12,000 per student, which was expected to put Wyoming near the top of national rankings. (Legislative Service Office estimates)

Paying for Schools

Public education is supported by property taxes, a sales tax, income from school trust lands, and coal lease "bonus bid" income.

The Wyoming Constitution contains two provisions dealing with education that have far-reaching implications for the duty owed by state government to provide an education for its citizens.

Article 1: Declaration of Rights
Section 23: Education. The right for the citizens to opportunities for education should have practical recognition. The Legislature shall suitably encourage means and agencies calculated to advance the sciences and liberal arts.

Article 7: Education; State Institutions; Promotion of Health and Morals; Public Buildings
Section 1: Legislature to provide for public schools. The Legislature shall provide for the establishment and maintenance of a complete and uniform system of public instruction, embracing free elementary schools of every needed kind and grade, a university with such technical and professional departments as the public good may require and the means of the state allow, and such other institutions as may be necessary.

Hudson School 1909. (Courtesy Wyoming Tales and Trails)

The Wyoming Constitution elevates public education to a fundamental right for Wyoming citizens, and it states the Legislature must provide a "complete and uniform" system of education. Other rights guaranteed in Article 1 include speech, due process, voting, and religious freedom.

The two constitutional provisions on education written by the Constitutional Convention in 1889 are the basis of litigation by school districts and the Wyoming Education Association to reform the state's school financing system. "Complete" applies to the quality of education, and "uniform" applies to the equity of funding available to school children in all parts of the state.

From the beginning of statehood, school districts have relied on local property taxes to support schools. Tax revenue supported operations and paid off bonds that were issued to pay for school construction. The Wyoming Constitution limits the bonded indebtedness that a district may incur to 10 percent of the assessed valuation of property in that district.

The weakness of this system is the vast disparity in local property wealth and, therefore, the vast disparity in the amount of money a district could raise with property taxes, as described at the beginning of this chapter and in Appendix 12.

The decades-long struggle to find a funding system that passes constitutional tests entered the courts in the 1970s. Hundreds of school districts in Wyoming were being organized and unified under the Wyoming School District Organization Law of 1969. A dispute over who would get to claim the oil-rich town of Bairoil, with the Lost Soldier oil field, sent Carbon and Sweetwater counties to court. Carbon County won and so got the prize of collecting ad valorem taxes (property taxes) on the oil production. (*Sweetwater County Planning Committee of Organization of School Districts v. Hinkle*, 491 P.2d. Wyo. 1971)

The opinion written by the Wyoming Supreme Court in that dispute sounded the warnings that have become familiar in subsequent rulings in 1980, 1995, 2001, and 2004.

"If ad valorem taxes for school purposes were equalized throughout the state, as required by Article 1, Section 28, Wyoming Constitution, and by the equal protection clause of the Fourteenth Amendment to the United States Constitution, cases such as the one being dealt with would not arise," the opinion said.

The School District Organization Law set a deadline of 1978 for counties to get their organization plans approved. That same year, as 49 school districts emerged from the process, Washakie County School District Number One filed suit in state court to challenge the constitutionality of a school funding system that relied on local property taxes and created great inequities.

The Wyoming Supreme Court ruled in 1980 in *Washakie County School District No. One v. Herschler* (606 P.2d) that public education was a fundamental right, and the court struck down the school finance system in effect at the time, under the equal protection provision of the Wyoming Constitution. The high court ordered the Legislature to come up with a formula that would be equitable. The court said the formula would have to be complex, to account for different costs of achieving "quality education" in districts with different transportation costs, building maintenance costs, construction costs, logistical considerations, number of pupils with special problems, and so on. "However, it is not a problem that cannot be solved, challenging though it might be," wrote Chief Justice C. John Raper. (*Washakie v. Herschler,* 606 P.2d at 315)

The Supreme Court's determination that education was a fundamental right, guaranteed to all students by the equal protection clause, is important. The state must meet the high judicial standard called "strict scrutiny" to show its school funding plan is constitutional. Under that standard, the state must show there is a "compelling state interest" to use a formula that results in funding inequalities. The state must demonstrate that funding differences are based on actual costs.

The Legislature responded in 1981 by adapting an existing funding system based on classroom units: education costs varied among schools and districts by using different "divisors." Under this system, the Legislature would pass a law specifying the funding per classroom unit (CRU), which rose to more than $90,000 by the time the system was abandoned. However, the number of students that equaled a "classroom" could be manipulated. One district might get $90,000 for every 25 students, while a rural, isolated district might get $90,000 for every 15 students, which would be the Legislature's estimate of average class size in that district. The larger the divisor (i.e., the larger the classroom size) the less per student. However these classroom unit numbers were little more than guesswork. The Legislature stated this system was temporary, until a thorough study of actual costs could set the funding levels more scientifically.

In the meantime, districts still relied on local property taxes. However, the state used an elaborate formula to subsidize local funding if it fell below statewide averages of property value per pupil, to help districts with low property values. The new system depended on a 12-mill property tax levied and collected by the state to supplement districts, along with 6 optional mills that could be imposed by a school board and local voters.

The system still produced vast inequities in spending per pupil between rural and urban, large and small, rich and poor districts.

That resulted in yet another lawsuit in 1994 by several school districts, led by Campbell County School District Number One, and by the Wyoming Education Association. They claimed the new system was still unconstitutional. The Supreme Court agreed and issued a landmark ruling in 1995 that gave the Legislature specific orders to fix the funding system for both operations and construction. (*Campbell County School District Number One v. Herschler*, 907 P.2d Wyo

1995) This opinion is sometimes referred to as "Campbell 1."

The unanimous opinion, written by Chief Justice William Golden, said the Legislature:

> "must first design the best educational system by identifying the 'proper' educational package each Wyoming student is entitled to have whether she lives in Laramie or in Sundance. The cost of that educational package must then be determined and the legislature must then take the necessary action to fund that package. Because education is one of the state's most important functions, lack of financial resources will not be an acceptable reason for failure to provide the best educational system. All other financial considerations must yield until education is funded.

> "The state financed basket of quality educational goods and services available to all school-age youth must be nearly identical from district to district. If a local district then wants to enhance the content of that basket, the legislature can provide a mechanism by which it can be done. But first, before all else, the constitutional basket must be filled."

The Supreme Court said requirements for equity and state financial responsibility applied to facilities, as well as programs and staff. The court set July 1, 1997, as a deadline for a new constitutional funding system.The state's progress would be reviewed then.

Many legislators reacted to this mandate from the Supreme Court with outrage at what they considered a breach of the "separation of powers" between the legislative and judicial branches of government.

Nevertheless, legislators hired consultants to study the condition of school buildings and to devise a cost-based school financing system. The Legislature described in law the kind of education that would be provided to every student, the so-called guaranteed "basket" of educational goods and services. The State Board of Education began working on statewide proficiency standards for the contents in the "basket."

The Legislature met in special session in the summer of 1997 to put this system into law and to make plans for school maintenance, renovation, and construction.

Some major features of the financing system are:

- A mandatory 25-mill property tax levied by each school district.

Revenue collected above the funding guarantee for that district is put into the foundation account and is available for distribution to other districts.

- School districts get block grants of funding that are based on enrollment and other factors, including an adjustment to compensate for having small schools and a certain amount of at-risk children. Transportation and special education costs are fully reimbursed.
- The state pays for maintenance, renovation, and construction of school facilities. The Legislature and the School Facilities Commission make final decisions on location, capacity, and design of facilities. The commission decides how much the state will pay to maintain new and existing facilities. The commission has seven members: four appointed by the governor, the superintendent of public instruction, and two others named by the superintendent.

A young Cheyenne student works diligently on a class assignment. Her district, Laramie County School District One, was among the plaintiffs that sued the state over its funding formula. (Wyoming Department of Education file photo)

In 2000, the state appealed a ruling in state district court, by District Judge Nicholas Kalokathis in Cheyenne, which reviewed compliance with the *Campbell I* opinion and found the state funding plan flawed. The state wanted the Supreme Court to declare its new funding scheme constitutional. So there was another Supreme Court opinion in 2001 – known informally as *"Campbell II"* — that concluded the Legislature was dragging its feet and had fallen short of the 1995 mandates. (*State v. Campbell County School District* 19 P.3d Wyoming 2001)

Justice Marilyn Kite wrote in *Campbell II*:

"As long ago as *Hinkle*, this court reluctantly made suggestions to the Legislature of ways in which the constitutional problems could be addressed by a statewide financing system. Almost ten years passed without improvement. By 1980, the situation was actually worse, and this court declared the entire school finance system unconstitutional in *Washakie County School District Number One v. Herschler*, 606 P.2d 310 (Wyo. 1980). That decision concurred with *Hinkle* in holding that disparities were dramatic and a system based principally upon local property taxes, whereby property poor districts have less total revenue per student than property rich districts, fails to afford equal protection in violation of the state constitution. *Washakie* further determined that education was a fundamental right under the Wyoming Constitution and wealth based classifications with regard to this right were subject to the strict scrutiny test, which placed the burden on the state to prove a compelling state interest is served by the classification that cannot be satisfied by any other convenient legal structure. The court expressly held, 'whatever system is adopted by the legislature, it must not create a level of spending which is a function of wealth other than the wealth of the state as a whole'." *Washakie*, 606 P.2d at 336.

The state sought a rehearing to clarify directions on capital construction and to challenge the court's perceived intrusion into legislative and executive powers. The Supreme Court agreed to the rehearing and then issued *State v. Campbell County School District* 90 P.2d (Wyo 2001) Chief Justice Larry Lehman wrote this ruling, unofficially called

"*Campbell III*," which clarified constitutional requirements for a school construction plan. On the question of separation of powers, Justice Lehman wrote, "We continue to recognize that it is our duty to declare void all legislation that is unconstitutional."

A judge who was newly appointed to the bench, Justice Barton Voigt, wrote a dissenting opinion that he thought the whole question of school financing was a political matter for the Legislature and the voters who picked their lawmakers, not for the courts.

The state made the next move by asking the Wyoming Supreme Court in 2005 to finally declare all the school funding work by the Legislature had met constitutional requirements. The court sent the question back to Judge Kalokathis in First District Court, who heard many of the old challenges and some new ones from several school districts, the Wyoming Education Association, the Wyoming School Boards Association, and a Small Districts Coalition. They contended funding for teachers, maintenance, and construction was inadequate to cover the mandated standards. Judge Kalokathis issued his ruling on January 31, 2006. He ruled the state was substantially in compliance with the Constitution, with some exceptions. The challengers filed a

State Rep. Liz Byrd, D-Cheyenne, second from left in back, is pictured with second- and fifth -graders in Cheyenne who lobbied the 1983 Legislature to make the bison the official state mammal. Gov. Ed Herschler, seated, is signing the act into law. Byrd, a teacher, used the project to teach the legislative process. (Wyoming State Archives photo)

notice of appeal with the Supreme Court.

The courts will continue to track the success of the Legislature in devising a financing scheme that complies with the Constitution and previous opinions. Meanwhile, the Legislature must decide its commitment to cover the high cost of small, rural schools. Total spending on operations and maintenance was about $1.1 billion for school year 2006-2007.

(Read the *Campbell* rulings on the Legislative Service Office Web site, http://legisweb.state.wy.us.)

As funding has become more centralized, so have standards and accountability. Years before the federal No Child Left Behind Act required statewide achievement testing, Wyoming began testing all students in fourth, eighth, and eleventh grades on reading, writing, and mathematics to determine how well schools were covering the standards. This was called the Wyoming Comprehensive Assessment System, known by the acronym "WyCAS." The Department of Education revamped the test in 2005 and renamed it Proficiency Assessment for Wyoming Students, or "PAWS." It covers the subject areas of reading, writing, mathematics, and science. While WyCAS was intended to evaluate the effectiveness of school programs, PAWS is designed to measure individual student proficiency on state standards.

No Child Left Behind requires states to ensure their public school students make yearly progress toward the goal of proficiency for all students. In Wyoming, the State Board of Education defines standards, approves the statewide assessment, and determines cut-scores for the performance levels: advanced, proficient, partially proficient, and novice. While some states have set their test score cut-offs low enough to ensure high rates of proficiency, Wyoming test cutoffs remain high. Many states that bragged of high test scores in 2005 were faced with the discrepancy of low scores on the National Assessment of Educational Progress, which is taken by students around the nation. Wyoming was one of four states whose state test results tracked closely with those of the rigorous national test. The other states were South Carolina, Missouri, and Maine. (*New York Times*, 26 November 2005.)

Education funding is the biggest single expenditure in the state budget, an estimated $1.1 billion in block grants to districts during school year 2006-2007. Wyoming is unusual in its decision to fund transportation and special education by reimbursing actual expenses. The rural, isolated nature of many schools and the small enrollments create problems in working out funding formulas that work for all sizes of schools and districts, and these characteristics also result in high per-pupil funding numbers.

The Legislature recalibrated the school funding model and in 2006 approved a version that responded to concerns of the courts and school districts. Notable features included:

- Addition of "instructional facilitators" to improve teaching
- Providing $4,000 annual payments to teachers who earn National Board Certification
- Increased staffing, especially for "specialist" teachers and very small districts
- Maintaining class sizes of 16 for elementary students and 21 for secondary students
- Increased funding for activities and utilities
- A regional cost adjustment that came closer to real costs of living
- Added professional development for teachers
- Greater funding for summer school for both remediation and enrichment

Legislators and educators praised the recalibrated model for being much more "transparent" and understandable than earlier versions.

A source of school funding since statehood has been income from school trust lands, which were granted to Wyoming in its Act of Admission in 1890. Lands were granted to schools in every state under the General Land Ordinance of 1785, which established a uniform public survey system. The federal land survey system created townships of thirty-six square miles, each square mile being one section. Initially schools received section 16, in the middle of the township. States entering the union after 1845, including Wyoming, were granted two sections numbered 16 and 32. Arizona, New Mexico, and Utah received four sections numbered 2, 16, 32 and 36. The states act as trustees and manage the land for the beneficiaries, the schools.

In Wyoming, income from the school land that is nonrenewable, including land sales and mineral royalties, goes into the Permanent School Fund. Income that is renewable, including surface leases and investment and interest income on the permanent fund, goes to a spending account for schools. The state Board of Land Commissioners acts as trustee and manages the trust estate, including land and the permanent fund, for the beneficiaries, which are Wyoming school children.

In 2005, the school trust estate included 3.2 million surface acres, 4.2 million acres of subsurface minerals, and $1.1 billion in the Permanent School Fund. School trust lands earned $92.9 million in 2004, mostly from mineral leases and royalties ($84.8 million). Wyoming's permanent school trust fund was the third largest in the nation, behind Texas at $20.7 billion and New Mexico at $5.6 billion. (*Office of State Lands and Investments Annual Report 2004.*)

History & Organization

The first school in Wyoming was begun by the Army Chaplain the Rev. William Vaux at Fort Laramie in 1856.

The first publicly-supported free school in Wyoming opened its doors in Cheyenne on January 6, 1868, in response to complaints of children running unsupervised in the street. The school opened with a standing-room-only crowd of 125 children in a building on 18th Street, on the site of the current County Government Complex. (*Wyoming's Wealth, A History of Wyoming*, Bill Bragg, 1976, p. 221) (Roberts 2001, p. 432)

The first school in Laramie opened a year later, February 15, 1869. The first school in Evanston opened on July 8, 1871, above a saloon on Front Street, with eight students.

In Casper, Mrs. Adah E. Allen opened a private school on March 5, 1889, and Ama Weber taught the first classes in the first public school established July 6, 1889. The first schoolhouse opened in January 1891 with 50 students. (Roberts 2001, p. 433)

The First Legislative Assembly of the Wyoming Territory met in 1869 and enacted a public education law. It made the auditor *ex officio* superintendent of public instruction. ("Ex officio," Latin for "by virtue of one's office," typically gives a person membership without having the right to vote.) County superintendents were elected to divide settled areas into districts, distribute the county school tax and other funds, examine and certify teachers, and generally supervise schools. Elected school boards set taxes, hired teachers, and ran their districts.

Wyoming School Districts

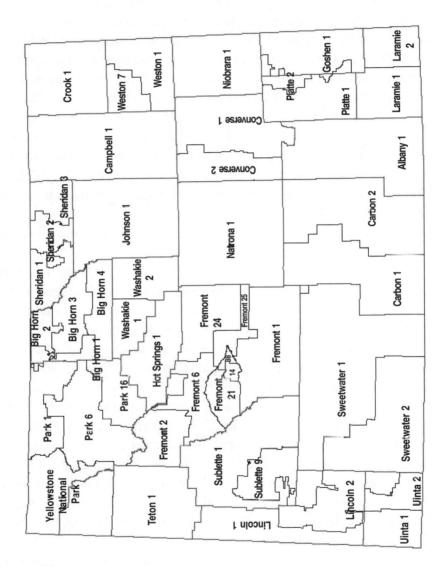

Source: Wyoming Department of Education

The 1873 Legislative Assembly directed that children between ages 6 and 18 should attend school at least three months a year. High schools were rare, and the requirements were not enforced. In the same year, lawmakers created a dual office of Superintendent of Public Instruction and State Librarian. The only woman to hold a significant territorial government post was Minnie Slaughter, who was named to the Superintendent-Librarian office to replace her ailing father. She served from March 14, 1890, to October 11, 1890. (Bragg 1976, p. 221)

By state law, public schools must provide 175 school days a year and must provide kindergarten, although compulsory school attendance starts with first grade. (Wyoming Statutes, Title 21, Article 4) The Legislature provides extra funding for school districts that offer full-day kindergarten.

The University of Wyoming opened in 1887 at Laramie with a faculty of seven and student body of forty-two.

In the early days of statehood in 1895, there were just five high schools in Wyoming: Buffalo, Cheyenne, Evanston, Rawlins, and Sundance. One pupil in forty-four was enrolled in a high school program, and the average school year was ninety days long.

Wyoming residents preferred to have a multitude of small school districts, many of which were single schools, and they resisted suggestions that districts consolidate for better efficiency. There were more than 400 districts in 1920, and an efficiency consultant for the state counted 399 districts in 1933. In 1959, Superintendent of Public Instruction Velma Linford reported 230 districts, only 64 of them unified with children in kindergarten through twelfth grade. The Legislature had passed a law in 1947 allowing counties to consolidate districts. Linford managed to negotiate the number down to fewer than 200 when she left office in 1963. Five years later, the number was 165. (Larson 1978, pp. 588-589)

In 1969, the Legislature passed the School District Organization Act, which required counties to submit efficient district organization plans to a state committee, whose members were the state superintendent and the State Board of Education. The number of districts reduced to forty-two in 1973. When some counties protested the mandatory consolidation plans, the organization committee relented and let them keep more than the one or two districts that most counties have. Fremont County has eight districts, Big Horn County has four, and Sheridan and Uinta counties have three each.

There are 48 school districts in Wyoming educating about 83,000 children. Each district has a board of trustees elected by voters within the district. The board hires a superintendent and other staff, sets policy, and approves an annual budget.

Wyoming public schools lost more than 15,000 students over the previous decade, as young families with school-age children left the state. The most drastic losses were in counties that boomed with energy development in the 1970s and then "busted" in the 1980s. Jeffrey City in Fremont County boomed with the local uranium industry and was on the verge of having enough students in its high school to field a football team in the early 1980s. Before the team could play its first game, the bottom dropped out of the uranium market, the uranium mining industry collapsed, and the families left. In 1993, Jeffrey City High School graduated two students from a school of nine. In 1995, the city's school kindergarten through twelfth grade had just 33 students. The school closed in May 1997 for lack of students.

School districts have responded to declining enrollment and tight budgets imposed by the state's financing formula by closing and consolidating schools. The Legislature has the authority to consolidate school districts, although lawmakers have been reluctant to take that controversial action. Wyoming's rural communities identify strongly with their schools and with the autonomy of their school districts. Closure of schools could spell the death of some towns.

The Legislature has provided a process to set up charter schools in Title 22 of Wyoming Statutes, the Education Code, Article 3, Section 3. Charter schools are public schools established by teachers, parents, students, and community members. They receive state funds and must meet state standards for teachers and curriculum, but they operate independently from the school district structure. Advocates for charter schools say they increase learning opportunities by allowing teachers to use innovative teaching methods and giving parents more input into school operations. However, state law prohibits the creation of charter schools just to avoid closures and consolidations by the school district trustees. In 2004-2005, there was just one charter school in Wyoming, the Snowy Range Academy in Laramie.

Consolidation during 1969-1978 ended the office of "county superintendent of education." The superintendent, usually a woman, was elected to manage all districts in the county. Consolidation also closed most one-room school houses, which numbered 1,226 in 1926.

At the same time, the law eliminated the position of state "commissioner of education." The commissioner was appointed annually by the State Board of Education, with approval by the governor, to carry out the professional administration and supervisory duties of the Department of Education. The commissioner was required to have a college degree in education and be an experienced educator. A textbook written in 1953 opined, "Since this is the case, the superintendent is left with no professional duties that cannot be better performed by the commissioner." (*The Government and Administration of Wyoming*, Herman H. Trachsel and Ralph M. Wade, 1953, p. 176)

The Wyoming Constitution provides for the election of superintendent of public instruction as one of five top executive officers of the state, along with the governor, auditor, treasurer, and secretary of state. (Wyoming is one of fourteen states that elect chief school officers.) By state law, "The general supervision of the public schools shall be entrusted to the state superintendent who shall be the administrative head and chief executive officer of the department of education." The Legislature describes administrative duties of superintendent, which are extensive, in Wyoming Statutes, Title 21, Chapter 2, Article 2.

Neither the Constitution nor statutes require any particular experience or academic credentials for the office. Superintendents have had a wide range of educational backgrounds. They rely on professional staff to administer special areas, including transportation, testing, special education, student data, and nutrition services. Superintendents vary widely in the extent they get involved with day-to-day operations or with advocating for changes in laws affecting schools.

Teacher certification in Wyoming is administered by the Professional Teachers Standards Board, within the Department of Education.

The State Board of Education sets education policy and standards. The Legislature also has given the board a lead role in developing statewide tests, with the help of Department of Education staff. The governor appoints board members from seven districts around the state, in addition to one teacher, one certified administrator, and two at-large business persons. The 2006 Legislature made the state superintendent of public instruction a voting member of the board. Board duties are set out in Title 21 of Wyoming Statutes, in Chapter 2, Article 3.

A reorganization study conducted for the state in 1990 recommended putting the Department of Education on the same footing as a dozen other major agencies in the executive branch. One aim of reorganization was to put similar programs and functions in one agency, to increase efficiency and reduce duplication, without regard to political influence. The proposed new Education Department would answer to the governor and would be merged with other education systems in the Boards of Cooperative Educational Services. No action has been taken with that recommendation, which could be expected to face stiff political opposition. (*Centennial Challenge: Accountability and Efficiency in State Government*, Joint Reorganization Council, 1990)

The University of Wyoming, in Laramie, is the only institution of higher learning in Wyoming that offers four-year college degrees and graduate degrees. It had about 2,000 students in 1940. Over the next several years, the state created seven two-year community colleges: Casper College (1945), Northwest College in Powell (1946), Northern Wyoming College at Sheridan (1948), Eastern Wyoming College in Torrington (1948), Western Wyoming College at Rock Springs (1959), Central Wyoming College at Riverton (1966), and Laramie County Community College in Cheyenne (1968). Limited four-year degrees are available at some campuses. Natrona County's legislative delegation usually is strong, and it advocated in 1971, 1973, and 1975 to turn Casper College into a four-year school. There has been little serious debate on the issue since. Today, students at Casper College can take some University of Wyoming courses at the Casper campus to complete a bachelor's degree.

Enrollment at UW was about 12,000 in 2004. Combined enrollment at the community colleges was about twice that amount.

In 2004, the Legislature tightened the law on the ability of non-accredited institutions with religious exemptions to grant college degrees in anything but religious subject areas. Previously, schools could get their religious exemptions from the state Department of Education and then offer post-secondary degrees via the Internet in any subject with minimal work. A study by the federal General Accounting Office found one of these so-called "diploma mills" required only an application, tuition, a one-day ethics course, and a 2,000-word paper.

In 2004 and 2005, Wyoming lawmakers debated the idea of imposing accreditation requirements on secular institutions that offered college and graduate degrees. Representatives of these schools appeared before legislative committees to defend the quality of their degrees, to question the value of accreditation, and to protest the expense. Twelve post-secondary institutions were licensed through the state in 2004, and only one was accredited. With few exceptions, they provided degree coursework over the Internet. The 2006 Legislature acted to require accreditation.

The 2005 Legislature put future mineral income into higher education in a way lawmakers said was "visionary" and would "change the face of Wyoming." The law diverts federal mineral royalties from the School Foundation Account, once that account reached $100 million, into two funds:

- $105 million to support endowed chairs at the University of Wyoming and to hire faculty at the community colleges.
- $400 million for a fund whose interest will provide scholarships for Wyoming students to attend the University of Wyoming or community colleges. Eligibility would require taking rigorous high school courses, getting at least average grades, and staying out of trouble. The Legislature named it the Hathaway Student Scholarship Endowment Account, to recognize contributions to education by former Gov. Stan Hathway and his wife, Bobby, who worked to establish the Fine Arts Center and the Art Museum at the university.

The 2006 Legislature deposited $13.5 million into the Hathaway Student Scholarship fund, so it could provide scholarships immediately to 2006 high school graduates. Predicted income to the account would otherwise have started producing scholarships in 2010.

Appendices

Appendix 1
Wyoming Territorial Officials

Territorial Governors	Date Appointed	Oath of Office	Term Expired
John A. Campbell (R)	April 3, 1869	April 15, 1869	March 1, 1875 (Res.)
John M. Thayer (R)	Feb. 10, 1873	March 1, 1875	May 29, 1878
John W. Hoyt (R)	April 10, 1878	May 29, 1878	Aug. 22, 1882
William Hale (R)	Aug. 3, 1862	Aug. 22, 1882	Jan. 13, 1885 (Died)
E.S.N. Morgan (R)	(Acting)	Jan. 13, 1885	Feb. 28, 1885
Francis E. Warren (R)	Feb. 27, 1885	Feb. 28, 1885	Nov. 11, 1886
George W. Baxter (R)	Nov. 5, 1886	Nov. 11, 1886	Dec. 20, 1886
E.S.N. Morgan (R)	(Acting)	Dec. 20, 1996	Jan. 24, 1887
Thomas Moonlight (D)	Jan. 5, 1887	Jan. 24, 1887	April 9, 1889
Francis E. Warren (R)	March 27, 1889	April 9, 1889	Oct. 11, 1890

Secretaries of Territory	Date Appointed	Oath of Office	Term Expired
Edward M. Lee (R)	April 7,1869	April 14, 1869	May 25, 1870
Herman Glafcke (R)	March 2, 1870	May 25, 1870	May 1, 1873
Jason B. Brown (D)	March 26, 1873	May 1, 1873	March 17,1875
George W. French (R)	Feb. 24, 1875	March 17, 1875	Feb. 25, 1879
A. Worth Spates (R)	Jan. 7, 1879	Feb. 25, 1879	April 1, 1880
Elliott S.N. Morgan (R)	March 15, 1880	April 1, 1880	April 8, 1884
Elliott S.N. Morgan (R)	March 31, 1884	April 8, 1884	April 25, 1887
Samuel D. Shannon (D)	April 9, 1887	April 25, 1887	Jan. 31, 1888
Samuel D. Shannon (D)	Jan. 24, 1888	Jan. 31, 1888	July 1, 1889
John W. Meldrum (R)	May 20, 2889	July 1, 1889	Jan. 20, 1890
John W. Meldrum (R)	Jan. 9, 1890	Jan. 20, 1890	Nov. 8, 1890

Territorial Officials, cont.

Auditors of Territory	Oath of Office	Term Expired
Benjamin Gallagher (D)	Dec. 11, 1869	June 4, 1870
James H. Hayford (R)	June 4, 1870	Feb. 21, 1872
James H. Hayford (R)	Feb. 21, 1872	Dec. 10, 1875
Orlando North (R)	Dec. 10, 1875	Dec. 17, 1877
Stephen W. Downey (R)	Dec. 17, 1877	Dec. 29, 1879
J.S. Nason (R)	Dec. 29, 1879	March 31, 1882
Jesse Knight (R)	March 31, 1882	March 31, 1884
Perry L. Smith (R)	March 31, 1884	April 2, 1886
Mortimer N. Grant (R)	April 2, 1886	Nov. 8, 1890

Treasurers of Territory	Oath of Office	Term Expired
John W. Donnellan (D)	Dec. 21, 1869	Oct. 26, 1872
Stephen W. Downey(R)	Oct. 26, 1872	Dec. 11, 1875
Amasa R. Converse (R)	Dec. 11, 1875	Sept. 30, 1876
Francis E. Warren (R)	Sept. 30, 1876	Dec. 15, 1877
Amasa R. Converse (R)	Dec. 15, 1877	Dec. 10, 1879
Francis E. Warren (R)	Dec. 10, 1879	March 2, 1885 (Resigned)
William P. Gannett (R)	March 2, 1885	March 31, 1888
Luke Voorhees (R)	March 31, 888	Nov. 7, 1890

Ex-Officio Superintendent of Public Instruction	Oath of Office	Term Expired
Benjamin Gallagher (D)	Dec. 11, 1869	June 4, 1870
James H. Hayford (R)	June 4, 1870	Dec. 12, 1873
John Slaughter (R)	Dec. 12, 1873	March 14, 1890
Minnie Slaughter(R)	March 14, 1890	Oct. 11, 1890

Source: *Wyoming History Blue Book, Vol. I*

Appendix 2
Counties As Created and Organized
by Dakota and Wyoming Laws 1867-1923

County	Date Created	Date Organized
Albany	Dec. 16, 1868	January 1869 (Dakota Territory)
Big Horn	March 12, 1890	Jan. 4, 1897
Campbell	Feb. 13, 1911	Jan. 6, 1913
Carbon	Dec. 16, 1868	January 1869 (Dakota Territory)
Converse	March 9, 1888	May 21, 1888
Crook	Dec. 8, 1875	Jan. 22, 1885
Fremont	March 5, 1884	May 6, 1884
Goshen	Feb. 9, 1911	Jan. 6, 1913
Hot Springs	Feb. 9, 1911	Jan 6, 1913
Johnson	Dec. 8, 1875	May 10, 1881 (Orig. Pease County)
Laramie	Jan. 9, 1867	January 1867 (Dakota Territory)
Lincoln	Feb. 20, 1911	Jan. 6, 1913
Natrona	March 9, 1888	April 12, 1890
Niobrara	Feb. 14, 1911	Jan. 8, 1913
Park	Feb. 15, 1909	Jan. 3, 1911
Platte	Feb. 9, 1911	Jan. 6, 1913
Sheridan	March 9, 1888	May 11, 1888
Sublette	Feb. 15, 1921	Jan. 2, 1923
Sweetwater	Dec. 27, 1867	Early 1868 (Dakota Territory, orig. Carter County)
Teton	Feb. 15, 1921	Dec. 2, 1922
Uinta	Dec. 1, 1869	April 7, 1870
Washakie	Feb. 9, 1911	Jan. 6, 1913
Weston	March 12, 1890	May 16, 1890

Source: *Wyoming History Blue Book, Vol. II*

Appendix 3
Roster of Top Wyoming Officers

Year	Name	Office	City
2005	James McBride (R)*	Supt.Pub.Inst.	Cheyenne

(Appointed on resignation of Trent Blankenship Aug. 18, 2005)

Year	Name	Office	City
2003	Dave Freudenthal (D)	Governor	Cheyenne
	Joseph B. Meyer (R)	Secretary of State	Laramie
	Max Maxfield (R)	Auditor	Cheyenne
	Cynthia M. Lummis (R)	Treasurer	Cheyenne
	Trent Blankenship(R)	Supt.Pub.Inst.	Pavillion
1999	Jim Geringer (R)	Governor	Wheatland
	Joseph B. Meyer (R)	Secretary of State	Laramie
	Max Maxfield (R)	Auditor	Cheyenne
	Cynthia M. Lummis (R)	Treasurer	Cheyenne
	Judy Catchpole (R)	Supt.Pub.Inst.	Casper
1995	Jim Geringer (R)	Governor	Wheatland
	Diana J. Ohman (R)	Secretary of State	Gillette
	Dave Ferrari (R)	Auditor	Cheyenne
	Stan Smith (R)	Treasurer	Thermopolis
	Judy Catchpole (R)	Supt.Pub. Inst.	Casper
1991	Mike Sullivan (D)	Governor	Casper
	Kathy Karpan (D)	Secretary of State	Cheyenne
	Dave Ferrari (R)	Auditor	Cheyenne
	Stan Smith (R)	Treasurer	Thermopolis
	Diana J. Ohman (R)	Supt.Pub.Inst.	Gillette
1987	Mike Sullivan (D)	Governor	Casper
	Kathy Karpan (D)	Secretary of State	Cheyenne
	Jack Sidi (R)	Auditor	Casper
	Stan Smith (R)	Treasurer	Thermopolis
	Lynn Simons (D)	Supt.Pub.Inst.	Casper
1983	Ed Herschler (D)	Governor	Kemmerer
	Thyra Thomson (R)	Secretary of State	Cheyenne
	James B. Griffith (R)	Auditor	Lusk
	Stan Smith (R)	Treasurer	Thermopolis
	Lynn Simons (D)	Supt.Pub.Inst.	Casper

Officers Roster, cont.

Year	Name	Office	City
1979	Ed Herschler (D)	Governor	Kemmerer
	Thyra Thomson (R)	Secretary of State	Cheyenne
	James B. Griffith (R)	Auditor	Lusk
	Shirley Wittler (R)	Treasurer	Cheyenne
	Lynn Simons (D)	Supt.Pub.Inst.	Casper
1975	Ed Herschler (D)	Governor	Kemmerer
	Thyra Thomson (R)	Secretary of State	Cheyenne
	James B. Griffith (R)	Auditor	Lusk
	Edwin J. Witzenburger (R)	Treasurer	Cheyenne
	Robert G. Schrader (R)	Supt.PubInst.	Cheyenne
1973	Edwin J. Witzenburger (R)*	Auditor	Cheyenne

(*Appointed on resignation of E.T. Copenhaver on June 30, 1973)

Year	Name	Office	City
1971	Stanley K. Hathaway (R)	Governor	Torrington
	Thyra Thomson (R)	Secretary of State	Cheyenne
	Everett T. Copenhaver (R)	Auditor	Cheyenne
	James B. Griffith (R)	Treasurer	Lusk
	Robert G. Schrader (R)	Supt.Pub.Inst.	Cheyenne
1967	Stanley K. Hathaway (R)	Governor	Torrington
	Thyra Thomson (R)	Secretary of State	Cheyenne
	Everett T. Copenhaver (R)	Auditor	Cheyenne
	Minnie A. Mitchell (R)	Treasurer	Casper
	Harry Roberts (R)	Supt.Pub.Inst.	Kaycee
1963	Clifford P. Hansen (R)	Governor	Jackson
	Thyra Thomson (R)	Secretary of State	Cheyenne
	Minnie A. Mitchell (R)	Auditor	Casper
	Everett T. Copenhaver (R)	Treasurer	Cheyenne
	Dr. Cecil M. Shaw (R)	Supt.Pub.Inst.	Casper

1962: Richard J. Luman, Deputy State Treasurer, assumed duties of Treasurer upon the death of C.J. "Doc" Rogers in May 1962.

1961   Jack R. Gage (D)* Secretary of State Sheridan
(*and Acting Governor on resignation of Governor Hickey)

Year	Name	Office	City
1959	J.J. "Joe" Hickey (D)	Governor	Cheyenne
	Jack R. Gage (D)	Secretary of State	Sheridan
	Minnie A. Mitchell (R)	Auditor	Casper
	C.J. "Doc" Rogers (R)	Treasurer	Cheyenne
	Velma Linford (D)	Supt.Pub.Inst.	Laramie

Officers Roster, cont.

Year	Name	Office	City
1955	Milward L. Simpson (R)	Governor	Cody
	Everett T. Copenhaver (R)	Secretary of State	Douglas
	Minnie A. Mitchell (R)	Auditor	Casper
	Charles B. Morgan (R)	Treasurer	Cheyenne
	Velma Linford (D)	Supt.Pub.Inst.	Laramie
1953	C.J. "Doc" Rogers (R)*	Secretary of State	Cheyenne

(*and Acting Governor on resignation of Governor Barrett)

| 1952 | Minnie A. Mitchell (R)* | Treasurer | Casper |

(*appointed at the death of J.R. Mitchell May 1952. Elected Treasurer November. 1952)

1951	Frank A. Barrett (R)	Governor	Lusk
	C.J. "Doc" Rogers (R)	Secretary of State	Cheyenne
	Everett T. Copenhaver (R)	Auditor	Douglas
	J.R. Mitchell (R)	Treasurer	Casper
	Edna B. Stolt (R)	Supt.Pub.Inst.	Sheridan
1949	A.G. Crane (R)* Secretary of State Cheyenne

(and Acting Governor upon resignation of Governor Hunt)

1947	Lester C. Hunt	Governor	Lusk
	A.G. Crane (R)	Secretary of State	Cheyenne
	Everett T. Copenhaver (R)	Auditor	Douglas
	C.J. "Doc" Rogers (R)	Treasurer	Cheyenne
	Edna B. Stolt (R)	Supt.Pub.Inst.	Sheridan
1944	William "Scotty" Jack (D)*	Secretary of State	Casper
	John J. McIntyre (D)	Auditor (appointed)	Douglas
	Carl Robinson (D)**	Auditor	Afton

(*appointed upon the death of Mart T. Christensen)
(**appointed for 11 months)

1943	Lester C. Hunt (D)	Governor	Lander
	Mart T. Christensen (R)	Secretary of State	Baggs
	William "Scotty" Jack (D)	Auditor	Casper
	Earl Wright (R)	Treasurer	Farson
	Esther L. Anderson (R)	Supt.Pub.Inst.	Casper
1939	Nels H. Smith (R)	Governor	Horton
	Lester C. Hunt (D)	Secretary of State	Lander
	William "Scotty" Jack (D)	Auditor	Casper
	Mart T. Christensen (R)	Treasurer	Baggs
	Esther L. Anderson (R)	Supt.Pub.Inst.	Casper

Officers Roster, cont.

Year	Name	Office	City
1935	Leslie A. Miller (D)	Governor	Cheyenne
	Lester C. Hunt (D)	Secretary of State	Lander
	William "Scotty" Jack (D)	Auditor	Casper
	J. Kirk Baldwin (D)	Treasurer	Casper
	Jack R. Gage (D)	Supt.Pub.Inst.	Sheridan
1933	Leslie A. Miller (D)	Governor	Cheyenne
1931	Frank C. Emerson (R)	Governor	Cheyenne
	Alonzo M. Clark (R)*	Secretary of State	Gillette
	Roscoe Alcorn (R)	Auditor	Rawlins
	Harry R. Weston (R)	Treasurer	Jackson
	Katherine A. Morton (R)	Supt.Pub.Inst.	Cheyenne

(*and Acting Governor upon the death of Governor Emerson)

Year	Name	Office	City
1929	Roscoe Alcorn (R)	Auditor	Rawlins
1927	Frank C. Emerson (R)	Governor	Cheyenne
	Alonzo M. Clark (R)	Secretary of State	Gillette
	Vincent Carter (R)	Auditor	Kemmerer
	William H. Edelman (R)	Treasurer	Sheridan
	Katherine A. Morton (R)	Supt.Pub.Inst.	Cheyenne
1925	Nellie Tayloe Ross (D)	Governor	Cheyenne
1924	Frank F. Lucas (R)*	Secretary of State	Buffalo

(*and Acting Governor upon the death of Governor Ross)

Year	Name	Office	City
1923	William B. Ross (D)	Governor	Cheyenne
	Frank E. Lucas (R)	Secretary of State	Buffalo
	Vincent Carter (R)	Auditor	Kemmerer
	John M. Snyder (R)	Treasurer	Lovell
	Katherine A. Morton (R)	Supt.Pub.Inst.	Cheyenne
1919	Robert D. Carey (R)	Governor	Careyhurst
	W.E. Chaplin (R)	Secretary of State	Laramie
	I.C. Jefferis (R)	Auditor	Kemmerer
	Katherine A. Morton (R)	Supt.Pub.Inst.	Cheyenne

1917   Frank L. Houx (D)* Secretary of State   Cody
(*and Acting Governor upon the resignation of Governor Kendrick)

Officers Roster, cont.

Year	Name	Office	City
1915	John B. Kendrick (D)	Governor	Sheridan
	Frank L. Houx (D)	Secretary of State	Cody
	Robert B. Forsyth (R)	Auditor	Rock Springs
	Herman B. Gates (R)	Treasurer	Worland
	Edith K.O. Clark (R)	Supt.Pub.Inst.	Sheridan
1911	Joseph M. Carey (D)	Governor	Cheyenne
	Frank L. Houx (D)	Secretary of State	Cody
	Robert B. Forsyth (R)	Auditor	Rock Springs
	John L. Baird (R)	Treasurer	Newcastle
	Rose A. Bird Maley (R)	Supe.Pub.Inst.	Newcastle
907	Bryant B. Brooks (R)	Governor	Casper
	William A. Schnitger (R)	Secretary of State	Cheyenne
	LeRoy Grant (R)	Auditor	Laramie
	Edward Gillette (R)	Treasurer	Sheridan
	Archibald D. Cook (R)	Supt.Pub.Inst.	Douglas
1905	Bryant B. Brooks (R)	Governor	Casper
	William C. Irvine (R)	Treasurer	Douglas
1903	DeForest Richards (R)	Governor	Douglas
	Fenimore Chatterton (R)*	Secretary of State	Sheridan
	LeRoy Grant (R)	Auditor	Laramie
	Henry G. Hay (R)	Auditor (9 months)	Cheyenne
	William C. Irvine (R)	Treasurer	Douglas
	Thomas T. Tynan (R)	Supe.Pub.Inst.	Sheridan

(* and Acting Governor upon the death of Governor Richards)

Year	Name	Office	City
1899	DeForest Richards (R)	Governor	Douglas
	Fenimore Chatterton (R)	Secretary of State	Sheridan
	LeRoy Grant (R)	Auditor	Laramie
	George E. Abbott (R)	Treasurer	Cheyenne
	Thomas T. Tynan (R)	Supe.Pub. Inst.	Sheridan
1898	C.H. Parmelee (D)* Superintendent of Public Instruction		Buffalo

(*appointed upon the resignation of Estelle Reel)

Year	Name	Office	City
1895	William A. Richards (R)	Governor	Red Bank
	C.W. Burdick (R)	Secretary of State	Saratoga
	William O. Owen (R)	Auditor	Laramie
	Henry G. Hay (R)	Treasurer	Cheyenne
	Estelle Reel (R)	Supt.Pub.Inst.	Cheyenne

Officers Roster, cont.

Year	Name	Office	City
1893	John E. Osborne (D)	Governor	Cheyenne
1890	Francis E. Warren (R)	Governor	Cheyenne
	Amos W. Barber (R)*	Secretary of State	Cheyenne
	C.W. Burdick (R)	Auditor	Saratoga
	Otto Gramm (R)	Treasurer	Laramie
	Stephen H. Farwell (R)	Supt.Pub.Inst.	Buffalo

(*and Acting Governor upon the resignation of Governor Warren)

Source for data: *Wyoming History Blue Book,* Vols. I-IV

Appendix 4 - Elected Party Affiliation

Party Affiliation
National, State, Legislative Elected Officials 1890-2004

Year Elected	Pres	U.S. Senate	U.S. House	Gov.	Sec. State	Treas.	Aud.	Supt Pub Instruc	Wyoming Senate Dem	Wyoming Senate Rep	Wyoming House Dem	Wyoming House Rep	Other
1890	R	R	R	R	R	R	R	R	3	13	7	26	
1892	D		D	D					5	11	16	12	5
1894	R	R	R	R	R	R	R	R	4	14	2	34	1
1896	D		D						4	14*	11	23	4
1898	R	R	R	R	R	R	R	R	6	13*	3	35	4
1900	R	R	R						2	16	2	34	
1902	R			R	R	R	R	R	2	21	4	46	
1904	R	R	R	R			R		3	20	3	47	
1906		R	R	R	R	R	R	R	2	21	5	45	
1908	R		R						3	24	7	49	
1910	D	R	R	D	D	R	R	D	6	21	25	31	
1912	D	R	R						8	19	28	29	
1914	D		R	D	D	R	R	R	9	18	15	42	
1916	D	D	R						11	16	25	32	
1918	R	R	R	R	R	R	R	R	10	17	11	43	

*In 1896 and 1900, there was one third-party member in the Wyoming Senate.

Elected Party Affiliation, cont.

Year Elected	Pres	U.S. Senate	U.S. House	Gov.	Sec. State	Treas.	Aud.	Supt Pub Instruc	Wyoming Senate		Wyoming House		
									Dem	Rep	Dem	Rep	Other
1920	R		R						3	22	1	53	
1922		D	R	D	R	R	R	R	5	20	23	37	
1924	R	R	R	D			R		11	16	23	39	
1926			R	R	R	R	R	R	12	15	17	45	
1928	R	D	R						10	17	11	51	
1930		R	R	R	R	R	R	R	6	21	26	36	
1932	D		R	D					12	15	42	20	
1934		D	D	D	D	D	D	D	14	13	38	18	
1936	D	D	D						16	11	38	18	
1938			R	R	D	D	R	R	11	16	19	37	
1940	D	D	D		R	D	R	R	11	16	28	28	
1942		R	R	D	R	D	R	R	10	17	17	39	
1944	R		R						6	21	20	36	
1946		D	R	D	R	R	R	R	8	19	12	44	
1948	D	D	R						9	18	28	28	
1950			R	R	R	R	R	R	10	17	17	39	
1952	R	R	R				R		6	21	11	45	
1954		D	R	R	R	R	R	D	8	19	24	32	
1956	R		R						11	16	26	30	

Elected Party Affiliation, cont.

Year Elected	Pres	U.S. Senate	U.S. House	Gov.	Sec. State	Treas.	Aud.	Supt Pub Instruc	Wyoming Senate		Wyoming House		
									Dem	Rep	Dem	Rep	Other
1958		D	R	D	D	R	R	D	11	16	30	26	
1960	R	R	R						10	17	21	35	
1962		R	R	R	R	R	R	R	11	16	19	37	
1964	D	D	D						12	13	34	27	
1966		R	R	R	R	R	R	R	12	18	27	37	
1968	R		R						12	18	16	45	1
1970		D	D	R	R	R	R	R	11	19	20	40	1
1972	R	R	D						13	17	17	44	1
1974			D	D	R	R	R	R	15	15	29	32	1
1976	R	R	D						12	18	29	32	
1978		R	R	D	R	R	R	D	11	19	20	42	
1980	R		R						11	19	23	39	
1982		R	R	D	R	R	R	D	11	19	25	38	1
1984	R	R	R						11	19	18	46	
1986			R	D	D	R	R	D	11	19	20	44	
1988	R	R	R						11	19	20	44	
1990		R	R	D	D	R	R	R	10	20	22	42	
1992	D		R						10	20	19	41	

Elected Party Affiliation, cont.

Year Elected	Pres	U.S. Senate	U.S. House	Gov.	Sec. State	Treas.	Aud.	Supt Pub Instruc	Wyoming Senate		Wyoming House		
									Dem	Rep	Dem	Rep	Other
1994		R	R	R	R	R	R	R	10	20	13	47	
1996	D	R	R						9	21	17	43	
1998			R	R	R	R	R	R	9	21	17	43	
2000	R	R	R						10	20	14	46	
2002		R	R	D	R	R	R	R	10	20	15	45	
2004	R		R						7	23	13	47	

Appendix 5
Population by County

County	2000*	1990	1980	1970
Albany	29,060	30,797	29,062	26,431
Big Horn	11,214	10,525	11,896	10,202
Campbell	32,727	29,370	24,367	12,957
Carbon	15,437	16,659	21,896	13,354
Converse	12,396	11,128	14,069	5,938
Crook	5,778	5,294	5,308	4,535
Fremont	36,191	33,662	38,992	28,352
Goshen	12,651	12,373	12,040	10,885
Hot Springs	4,475	4,809	5,710	4,952
Johnson	6,858	6,145	6,700	5,587
Laramie	78,877	73,142	68,649	56,360
Lincoln	13,998	12,625	12,177	8,640
Natrona	63,157	61,226	71,856	51,264
Niobrara	2,684	2,499	2,924	2,924
Park	25,500	23,178	21,639	17,752
Platte	8,612	8,145	11,975	6,486
Sheridan	25,090	23,562	25,048	17,852
Sublette	5,811	4,843	4,548	3,755
Sweetwater	39,322	38,823	41,723	18,391
Teton	14,532	11,172	9,355	4,823
Uinta	20,288	18,705	13,021	7,100
Washakie	8,541	8,388	9,496	7,569
Weston	6,403	6,518	7,106	6,307

* - "Estimates of Population for Counties: 1999" as provided by the Population Estimates Branch, U.S. Census Bureau
Source: U.S. Department of Commerce, Census Bureau

Appendix 6
Decennial State Population

Year	Total	Urban	Rural
2000	493,785	Data not available	Data not available
1990	453,588	Data not available	Data not available
1980	469,557	Data not available	Data not available
1970	332,416	201,111	131,305
1960	330,066	187,551	142,515
1950	290,529	144,618	145,911
1940	250,742	93,577	157,165
1930	225,565	70,097	155,468
1920	194,402	57,095	137,307
1910	145,965	43,221	102,744
1900	92,531	26,657	65,874
1890	62,555	21,484	41,071
1880	20,789	6,152	14,637
1870	9,118	Data not available	9,118

Source: U.S. Department of Commerce, Bureau of the Census

Appendix 7 - Wyoming Voter Profile

Year	Voting Age Population	Primary Elections			General Elections		
		Registered Voters	Turnout of Registered	Turnout of Eligible	Registered Voters	Turnout Registered	Turnout Eligible
1978	290,000	181,042 62%	122,252 68%	42.2%	200,951 69%	142,299 71%	49.1%
1980	315,000	188,395 60%	122,511 65%	38.9%	219,423 70%	181,027 83%	57.3%
1982	340,000	207,838 61%	140,107 67%	41.2%	230,074 68%	162,065 75%	50.6%
1984	355,000	205,421 58%	133,077 65%	37.5%	139,974 68%	196,153 82%	55.3%
1986	349,000	216,769 62%	146,612 68%	42.0%	235,292 67%	168,651 72%	48.3%
1988	328,500	201,828 61%	126,307 63%	38.4%	226,189 69%	186,417 82%	56.7%
1990	318,100	207,393 65%	133,658 64%	42.0%	222,331 70%	164,309 74%	51.7%
1992	233,000	208,806 65%	126,620 61%	41.5%	234,260 73%	203,602 87%	63.2%
1994	343,000	221,298 65%	142,431 64%	37.9%	237,836 69%	204,023 86%	59.5%
1996	343,300	228,554 67%	126,928 56%	36.1%	240,711 70%	215,844 90%	62.9%
1998	354,000	230,360 65%	127,872 56%	36.1%	239,539 68%	178,401 74%	50.4%
2000	358,000	206,105 58%	108,238 53%	30.2%	220,012 61%	221,685 101%	61.9%

Source: Wyoming Secretary of State's Office

Appendix 8
Women in Wyoming Legislature

Name	County/District	City	Year Elected
Deborah Alden (R)	HD3	Wheatland	2002
Susan Anderson (R)	Natrona	Casper	1980, 1982, 1984, 1986, 1988, 1990
Wende Barker (D)	HD45	Laramie	1992, 1994 and 1996
Mary Behrens (R)	Natrona	Casper	1986
Mary G. Bellamy (D)	Albany	Not known	1910
Rosie Berger (R)	HD57	Big Horn	2002
Nancy Berry (D)	HD59	Casper	1996 and 1998
Lynn Birleffi (D)	Laramie	Cheyenne	1984 and 1986
Janice Bodine (R)	Uinta	Evanston	1990
Mrs. Fred D. Boice (R)	Laramie	Cheyenne	1950, 1952 and 1954
June Boyle (D)	Albany	Laramie	1962, 1964, 1966, 1968, 1970
Margaret Brown (R)	Carbon	Rawlins	1982 and 1984
R.M. Johnnie Burton (R)	Natrona	Casper	1982, 1984 and 1986
Harriet Elizabeth Byrd (D)	Laramie	Cheyenne	1980, 1982, 1984 and 1986
Mrs. Lettie D. Campbell (R)	Lincoln	Afton	1930
Virginia L. Casady (D)	HD49	Riverton	1932
Ellen Crowley (R)	Laramie	Cheyenne	1972, 1976, 1978, 1980, 1984, 1986
Barbara Cubin (R)	Natrona	Casper	1986, 1988 and 1990
Irene Devin (R)	HD14	Laramie	1992 and 1994
Lynn Dickey (D)	Sheridan	Big Horn	1982, 1984, 1986 and 1988
Barbara Dobos (D)	Natrona	Casper	1982 and 1984
Ruth Nelson Edelman (R)	Sheridan	Sheridan	1938
Madge Enterline (R)	Natrona	Casper	1948 and 1950

Women Legislators, cont.

Name	County/District	City	Year Elected
Esther Eskens (R)	Big Horn (74-76) Natrona (80)	Lovell	1974, 1976, 1978 and 1980
Mrs. Thomas M. Fagan (D)	Niobrara	Lusk	1932
Deborah Fleming (D)	HD 36	Casper	1998
Sylvia S. Gams (R)	Big Horn, HD26	Cowley	1988, 1990, 1992 and 1994
Edith V. Garcia (D)	Laramie	Cheyenne	1990
Liz Gentile (D)	HD36	Casper	2002
Mary Meyer Gilmore (D)	HD 59	Casper	2002
Matilda Hansen (D)	Albany, HD13	Laramie	1974, 1976, 1978, 1980, 1982, 1984, 1986, 1988, 1990, 1992
Elaine D. Harvey (R)	HD 26	Lovell	2002
LaVerna "Pinkie" Hendricks (D)	Converse	Glenrock	1982
Della Herbst (D)	Sheridan	Sheridan	1982 and 1984
Shirley J. Humphrey (D)	Laramie	Cheyenne	1982, 1984, 1986, 1988, 1990
Verda I. James (R)	Natrona	Casper	1954, 1956, 1958, 1960, 1962, 1964, 1966 and 1968
Lorna Johnson (D)	HD 45	Laramie	1998, 2000 and 2002
April Brimmer Kunz (R)	Laramie	Cheyenne	1984 and 1990
Clarene Law (R)	Teton,HD23	Jackson	1990, 1992, 1994, 1996, 1998, 2000 and 2002
Cynthia M. Lummis (R)	Laramie	Cheyenne	1978, 1980, 1984, 1986, 1988, 1990
Patti MacMillan (R)	Albany, HD46	Laramie	1978, 1980, 1982, 1984, 1986, 1988, 1990, 1992 and 1994

Women Legislators, cont.

Name	County/District	City	Year Elected
Mable Mathews (R)	Crook	Sundance	1928
Nimi McConigley (R)	HD59	Casper	1994
Saundra Meyer (D)	HD49	Evanston	2000 and 2002
Mrs. A.B. Miller (D)	Albany	Not known	1912
E. Jayne Mockler (D)	HD44	Cheyenne	1992 and 1994
Nyla A. Murphy (R)	Natrona	Casper	1978, 1980, 1982, 1984, 1986, 1988
Patricia Nagel (R)	HD56	Casper	1992, 1994, 1996, 1998, 2000
Mary Odde (R)	Fremont	Shoshoni	1980, 1982, 1984, 1986, 1988
Catherine M. Parks (R)	Campbell	Weston	1972, 1974 and 1976
Carolyn Paseneaux (R)	HD38	Casper	1992, 1994, 1996, 1998, 2000
Dorothy Perkins (R)	Natrona , HD35	Casper	1982, 1984, 1986, 1988, 1990, 1992, 1994 and 1996
Nancy F. Peternal (D)	Lincoln	Kemmerer	1970 and 1974
Elizabeth B. Phelan (D)	Laramie	Cheyenne	1968, 1972, 1976, 1978, 1980 and 1982
Ann Robinson (D)	HD58	Casper	1996, 1998, 2000 and 2002
Mrs. Albert Rochelle (D)	Niobrara	Lusk	1926 and 1932
Peggy Rounds (D)	HD19	Evanston	1998
Louise Ryckman (D)	Sweetwater, HD 60	Green River	1984, 1986, 1988, 1990, 1992, 1994, 1996 and 1998
Mary K. Schwope (D)	Laramie	Cheyenne	1974, 1978, 1980, 1982, 1984, 1986, 1988 and 1990
Kathryn L. Sessions (D)	HD43	Cheyenne	1992, 1994 and 1996

Women Legislators, cont.

Name	County/District	City	Year Elected
Kathryn Sessions (D)	SD7	Cheyenne	2002
Peg Shreve (R)	Park, HD24	Cody	1978, 1980, 1982, 1984, 1986, 1988, 1990, 1992, 1994 and 1996
Marlene Simons (R)	Crook, HD1	Beulah	1978, 1980, 1982, 1984, 1986, 1988, 1990, 1992, 1994, 1996, 1998 and 2000
Alice Spielman (R)	Campbell	Gillette	1952 and 1954
Glenda Stark (R)	HD58	Casper	1992 and 1994
Ann Strand (D)	Sweetwater	Rock Springs	1978, 1980, 1982 and 1984
Pamela Taylor-Horton (D)	HD11	Cheyenne	1994
Nettie Truax (D)	Crook-Campbell	Not known	1912
Pat Tugman (R)	Laramie	Cheyenne	1978
Carol Jo Vlastos (R)	Natrona	Casper	1988 and 1990
Nancy G. Wallace (R)	Uinta	Evanston	1968 and 1970
Jane Warren (D)	HD13	Laramie	2000 and 2002
Carol Watson (D)	Laramie	Cheyenne	1988 and 1990
Edness Kimball Wilkins (D)	Natrona	Casper	1954, 1956, 1958, 1960, 1962, 1964, 1972, 1974, 1976 and 1978
Morna A. Wood (D)	Crook-Campbell	Not known	1914
Sherri Wooldridge (D)	HD12	Cheyenne	1992 and 1994
N. Jane Wostenberg (R)	HD27	Worland	1998, 2000 and 2002
Virginia L. Wright (R)	Sheridan, HD51	Sheridan	1988, 1990 and 1992
Kenilynn S. Zanetti (D)	HD61	Rock Springs	1994, 1996 and 1998

Source: Wyoming Blue Book, Volumes I-IV

Appendix 9
Wyoming Minerals
2003 Production & 2004 Valuation

Mineral	2003 Production	2004 Valuation (millions of dollars)
Oil	50.1 million barrels	$1,244.2
Gas	1,646 MCF	5,265.1
Coal	376 million tons	1,846.9
Uranium	1.2 million pounds	8.0
Bentonite	3.6million tons	33.4
Trona	17.8 million tons	195.2
Misc.		50.5
Total		**$8,6160.0**

2004 Income to Wyoming, All Minerals

Collection	Income (millions of dollars)
Ad Valorem Tax	$533.5
Severance Tax	509.4
Sales and Use Tax	56.2
U.S. Rent & Royalty	554.4
State Rent	5.0
State Royalties	78.5
Gen Fund Income (filing fees, etc.)	1.4
Total	1,738.5

Source: 2004 Mineral and Energy Yearbook, Energy Section of Minerals, Energy and Transportation Division, Wyoming Business Council.

Appendix 10
Wyoming Property Taxes 2004

Where they came from:

	Assessed Valuation (millions)	Percent All Property Tax
Mineral Production	$8,616.0	63.0
Residential Property	2,484.4	18.2
Industrial Locally-Assessed	870.4	6.4
Industrial State-Assessed	796.3	5.8
Commercial Property	731.5	5.3
Agricultural Lands	181.0	1.3
Total	**$13,679.5**	

Where they went:

	Taxes Levied (millions)	Percent Property Tax Spent
Public Schools	$609.0	69.7
County Governments	190.6	21.8
Special Districts	36.4	4.2
Commuinity Colleges	24.1	2.8
Cities and Towns	13.1	1.5
Total	**$873.2**	

Source: Wyoming Taxpayers Association

Appendix 11
County Assessed Valuation &
Property Taxes 2004

County	Valuation (millions)	Tax Levy (millions)	Total Mills
Albany	$232.5	$16.2	62.750
Big Horn	147.9	11.9	57.000 - 61.412
Campbell	3,258.7	193.1	57.918
Carbon	559.8	35.5	58.126 - 58.500
Converse	417.3	24.7	55.678
Crook	98.2	6.0	60.500
Fremont	656.8	50.2	65.425 - 69.414
Goshen	93.8	6.5	62.500 - 68.195
Hot Springs	108.9	8.2	70.700
Johnson	155.2	10.9	65.952
Laramie	590.6	41.3	62.000 - 65.190
Lincoln	597.5	37.7	56.796 - 58.353
Natrona	585.5	40.9	63.250
Niobrara	43.7	3.0	64.500
Park	445.2	32.7	60.862 - 65.274
Platte	121.6	8.8	59.818 - 65.013
Sheridan	384.6	25.8	62.500 - 65.200
Sublette	2,039.1	120.5	57.525 - 59.311
Sweetwater	1,563.4	103.4	60.927 - 66.527
Teton	773.0	46.5	58.692
Uinta	588.3	36.4	56.291 -58.191
Washakie	92.8	6.7	63.419 - 64.419
Weston	85.9	6.0	64.762 - 65.311
Total	**$13,679.5**	**$873.2**	

**Note: Mills represent range among school districts in the
county, if more than one.**

Source: Wyoming Taxpayers Association

Appendix 12
Wyoming School Districts
2004 Property Valuations, Average Daily Membership (Enrollment)

District	Assessed Valuation	Avg Daily Mbrship	Valuation per ADM
Albany 1 (Laramie)	$ 232,571,920	3,612	$ 64,382
Big Horn 1 (Cowley)	40,143,955	697	57,550
Big Horn 2 (Lovell)	33,032,819	660	50,023
Big Horn 3 (Greybull)	57,311,988	510	112,348
Big Horn 4 (Basin)	57,311,988	357	100,646
Campbell 1 (Gillette)	3,258,728,320	7,154	455,449
Carbon 1 (Rawlins)	549,273,641	1,693	324,409
Carbon 2 (Saratoga)	72,481,631	682	106,274
Converse 1 (Douglas)	271,672,064	1,586	171,204
Converse 2 (Glenrock)	145,615,683	739	196,998
Crook 1 (Sundance)	98,154,583	1,088	90,213
Fremont 1 (Lander	115,017,070	1,835	62,649
Fremont 2 (Dubois)	37,906,681	234	161,557
Fremont 6 (Pavillion)	92,220,721	351	262,379
Fremont 14 (Ethete)	5,179,464	590	8,773
Fremont 21 (Ft Washakie)	7,841,522	297	26,335
Fremont 24 (Shoshoni)	339,936,423	300	1,132,782
Fremont 25 (Riverton)	85,499,302	2,396	35,673
Fremont 38 (Arapahoe)	2,204,594	277	7,931
Goshen 1 (Torrington)	92,834,411	1,882	49,315
Hot Springs 1 (Thermopolis)	108,946,451	693	157,079
Johnson 1 (Buffalo)	155,186,606	1,233	125,791
Laramie 1 (Cheyenne)	547,178,850	12,871	42,512

District	Assessed Valuation	Avg Daily Mbrship	Valuation per ADM
Laramie 2 (Pine Bluffs)	$ 43,459,943	855	$ 50,801
Lincoln 1 (Diamondville)	357,367,764	666	535,983
LIncoln 2 (Afton)	135,888,881	2,423	56,082
Natrona 1 (Casper)	585,496,267	11,419	51,271
Niobrara 1 (Lusk)	44,242,873	400	110,430
Park 1 (Powell)	136,003,610	1,574	86,359
Park 6 (Cody)	225,152,123	2,239	100,543
Park 16 (Meeteetse	75,238,456	126	595,580
Platte 1 (Wheatland)	106,057,496	1,214	87,338
Platte 2 (Guernsey)	16,039,200	262	61,200
Sheridan 1 (Ranchester)	48,267,406	868	55,565
Sheridan 2 (Sheridan)	291,298,930	3,010	96,751
Sheridan 3 (Clearmont)	45,059,498	105	426
Sublette 1 (Pinedale)	1,655,510,817	677	2,443,382
Sublette 9 (Big Piney)	487,860,020	557	874,964
Sweetwater 1 (Rock Spgs)	933,041,506	4,139	232,667
Sweetwater 2 (Green River)	538,439,612	2,625	205,054
Teton 1 (Jackson)	773,060,170	2,281	338,791
Uinta 1 (Evanston)	441,814,181	2,884	153,191
Uinta 4 (Mountain View)	41,066,337	656	62,509
Uinta 6 (Lyman)	105,421,476	677	155,536
Washakie 1 (Worland)	77,183,052	1,304	59,155
Washakie 2 (Ten Sleep)	15,656,724	95	164,589
Weston 1 (Newcstle)	70,749,161	798	88,596
Weston 7 (Upton)	15,229,202	256	59444
Wyoming (Total)	**$13,679,536,318**	**83,871**	**$163,102**

Source: Wyoming Department of Education

Appendix 13
Revenue Distribution to Accounts

	State Investment Income	State Mineral Royalties	Federal Mineral Royalties	Severance Taxes	Property Taxes	Fuel Tax	State Sales/Use Tax	Local Sales/Use Tax	Tobacco Tax
General Fund	X		X	X			X		X
Budget Reserve Acct.			X	X					
Permanent Land Funds	X	X							
K-12 Foundation Program	X		X		X				
K-12 Capital Construction		X	X						
University of Wyoming			X						
Community Colleges			X		X				
Cities and Towns			X	X	X	X	X	X	X
Counties			X	X	X	X	X	X	X
Special Districts			X		X				
State Loan and Investment Board			X	X					
Permanent Wyoming Mineral Trust Fund				X					
Highways	X		X	X		X			
Water Accounts	X			X					
Leaking Underground Storage Tanks				X					

Compiled by Wyoming Taxpayers Association in 2003 to show flow of mineral income to state and local accounts. Source of information: Wyoming Legislative Service Office.

Appendix 14
Wyoming Agricultural Income

Farms and Ranches Wyoming 2003

Value of Production	Number of Operations	Number of Acres	Average Size All Farms
$1,000-$9,999	3,700	3,360	
$10,000 & Over	5,500	31,080,000	
Total	9,200	34,440,000	3,743 acres

Value of Crop and Livestock Production 2003

	Value	Cash Receipts	Net Farm Income 2002
All Commodities	$852.8 million	$869.7 million	$99.6 million
Livestock & Products	568.5 million	723.7 million	
Crops	284.2 million	146.0 million	

Net farm income is: Ag Sector Production $ 918.8 million
plus net govt transaction $ 9.6 million
minus purchased inputs $ 548.4 million
equals gross value added $ 380.0 million
minus capital consumption $ 114.6 million
equals Net Value Added $ 265.4 million
minus pay to stakeholders $ 165.8 million
equals **Net Farm Income**   **$ 99.6 million**

Source: *Wyoming Agricultural Statistics 2004*, U.S. Department of Agriculture Wyoming Statistical Office

Appendix 15
Wyoming Agricultural Production

2003 Livestock Summary

Species	Date	Number of Head	National Rank	Value
All Cattle and Calves	Jan. 1, 2003 Jan. 1, 2004	1,320,000 1,400,000	24	$1.17 billion
All Sheep and Lambs	Jan 1, 2003 Jan 1, 2004	450,000 430,000	3	$48.2 million
All Hogs and Pigs	Dec. 1, 2002 Dec. 1, 2003	115,000 124,000	29	$9.8 million

Crop Production Summary 2002 & 2003

Crop	2002	2003	Percent change
	(1,000)		
Corn - grain	4,165 bu	6,450 bu	155 %
All Wheat	2,471 bu	4,065 bu	165 %
Oats	750 bu	1,058 bu	141 %
Barley	4,680 bu	7,125 bu	152 %
Sugabeets	659 tons	752 tons	114 %
Dry Beans	624 cwt	645cwt	103 %
Alfalfa Hay	1150 tons	1,560 tons	135 %
All Hay	1,600 tons	2,330 tons	146 %

bu = bushels
cwt = hundred weight

Source: Wyoming Agricultural Statistics 2004, U.S. Department of Agriculture Wyoming Statistical Division

Appendix 16
Wyoming Facts from 2000 Census

Population (2003 estimate)	501,242
Population change April 1, 2000-July 1, 2003	1.5 %
Population 2000	493,782
Population change 1900-2000	8.9%
Percentages reported, 2000:	
Under 5 years old	6.3%
Under 18 years old	26.1%
65 and older	11.7%
Female	49.7%
White	92.1%
African American	0.8%
American Indian, Alaska Native	2.3%
Asian	0.6%
Other race	2.5%
Two or more races	1.8 %
Hispanic or Latino origin	6.4%
White, not Hispanic/Latino	88.9%
Foreign born persons	2.3%
High school graduates, over age 25	87.9%
Bachelor's degree or higher, over age 25	21.9%
Persons with a disability, over age 5	77,143
Mean travel time to work	17.8 minutes
Housing units, 2002	227,941
Home ownership rate	70%
Median value of owner-occupied units	$96,600
Households, 2000	193,608
Persons per household 2000	2.48
Median household income, 1999	$37,892
Per capita money income, 1999	$19,134
Persons below poverty, 1999	11.4 %
Business Facts	
Private non-farm establishments, paid employees 2001	18,453
Private non-farm employment, 2001	178,299

Continued

Wyoming Facts, cont.

Retail sales, 1997	$4.5 billion
Retail sales per capita, 1997	$9,438
Minority-owned firms (% of total, 1997)	4.3%
Women-owned firms (% of total, 1997)	22.6%
Housing units authorized by building permits,2002	2,045
Federal funds and grants, 2002	$3.7 billion
Geography Facts	
Land area	97,100 square miles
Persons per square mile, 2000	5.1

Appendix 17
Significant Statutory Tax Changes
1977 through 2004

1977

• Increased severance tax on coal by 1.6% for 1977 & 2% for 19Y78 until $160M collected. ($160M capital facilities tax expired 1/1/87)

• Increased severance tax on coal by 1.5% for Water Development Account;increased severance tax on coal by 1% for highway fund;

• Increased severance tax on coal by .5% to Permanent Wyoming Mineral Trust Fund (PWMTF); effective 1/1/78 (total 10.1%);

• Increased severance tax on trona by 1.5% (total 5.5%); increased severance tax on uranium by 3.5% (total 5.5%)

1981

• Increased severance tax on oil/gas by 2% (6% total); distributed to state (highway fund, PWMTF & water development account) & cities & counties

1982

• State inheritance tax imposed

1983

• Decreased severance tax on underground coal from 10.5% to 7.25%

• School foundation program - imposed a 12 mill state levy & 6 mill county levy

1984

• Mass property tax reappraisal system passed - $5M appropriated

1985

• Imposed $.08/gallon on special fuels & repealed compensatory fees on special fuels

• Decreased severance tax on collection wells from 6% to 1.5% & exempted from property tax through 1989

1986

• 1/4 of proceeds from severance taxes (except underground coal) diverted to worker's compensation fund

• Imposed 2.5% premium tax on insurers

1987

• Coal EquityTax Act of 1987 - limited severance tax to $.80/ton on high-cost coal

• Severance taxes paid on CO_2 injected in oil production allowed as a credit againstoil severance tax

• 4% severance tax exemption for wildcat wells for 4 years (total 2%)

Tax Changes, cont.

1988
• Allowed deduction for return on investment for mineral production on certain capital investments for transportation facilities or processing plants
• Amended constitution to provide for 3 tier system for fair market value of taxation (minerals, industrial, & all other)
• Implemented 3 tier system for fair market value in assessing property for property tax (minerals, industrial, & all other)
• Diversion of severance taxes from PWMTF to budget reserve account begun

1989
• Increased cigarette taxes by $.002 to .006 per cigarette ($.12 per pack)
• Extended Coal Tax Equity Act to 1991 (3/31/91)
• Exempted coal used on processing from property & severance taxes
• Exemption for tertiary oil production from projects certified by Oil & Gas Commission.; granted severance tax exemption up to 1/2 of wages paid to resident workers or total amount of 2% severance tax
• Continued $.04/gallon tax on gasohol 7/1/89 through 7/1/93
• Created municipal rainy day account funded with excess oil & gas severance tax & federal mineral royalties
• Repealed deduction allowed for return on investment for mineral production (on transportation facilities & processing plants)
• Continued budget reserve acct diversion of severance taxes through 6/30/91
• Decreased severance tax on uranium from 4% to 2%
• Imposed a $.01/gallon tax for L.U.S.T. (Leaking Underground Storage Tanks)

1990
• Extended 1.5% severance tax on collection wells to 1/1/95 (in lieu of 6% rate)
• Eliminated ton/mile tax and implemented commercial vehicle fees
• Budget reserve account diversion extended through 6/30/92

1991
• Coal Tax Equity Act extended through 3/31/95
• Reduced insurance premium tax rate from 2.5% to .75% (retaliatory provision for other states remained in effect)
• Extension of 2% severance tax exemption on tertiary production to 12/31/94 (4% total)
• Exempted specified underground mining equipment from property tax
• Exempted uranium from 4% severance tax as long as price under $17/pound
• Extended 4% severance tax exemption on wildcat wells to 12/31/94 (2% total)

Tax Changes, cont.

1992

• Reallocated 30% of revenues from 1.5% severance tax on coal & trona to public school foundation program account

• Extended gasohol tax reduction $.08/gallon to $.04/gallon to 2000

1993

• Exempted oil & gas from 4% severance tax if well drilled (new production) between 93 to 96 (cap on oil $25/bbl; gas $2.75/mcf); same reduction for workover or completion for 24 months but no cap on price (2% total)

• Modified computation of school local property taxes/local resources (comparing resources before 7/1/91 & basing foundation program amount on before/after amounts)

• Added $.01 sales/use tax & changed tax distribution from 2/3 to 72% to general fund

1994

• Gas tax distribution 13.5% to counties; 14% to state-county road account in

1995

• Granted 50% credit against natural gas severance tax (2%) for research projects to enhance natural gas production (2% total)

• Coal Tax Equity Act extended through 3/15/99

• Exempted oil produced from previously shut-in wells from all but 1.5% severance tax for PWMTF

• Diversion of severance taxes from PWMTF to budget reserve account extended to 6/30/2000

• Extended uranium severance tax exemption through 1/1/99; lowered spot price for qualifying uranium from $17 to $14/pound

• Extended 4th cent sales/use tax through 6/30/98

• Extended 1.5% severance tax for collection wells through 1/1/99 (in lieu of 6% rate)

• Extended reduced severance tax on oil/gas wells drilled (new prod.) through 3/31/98

1997

• Extended 4% severance tax exemption for oil/gas produced from workovers & recompletions to 2001 (2% total)

• Extended tertiary production 2% exemption to March, 2001 (4% total)

1997 Special Session

• Local option 6 mills for schools to expire as of 1998 (affects amount of state funding needed for schools)

• Extended 4th cent sales/use tax through 6/30/2002

Tax Changes, cont.

1998
• Specified collection well property tax exemption applied to 1994 production
• Increased fuel tax to $.13/gallon on gas & diesel
• Extended reduced severance tax rate on oil/gas wells drilled (new production) through 3/31/2003 (2% total)
• Extended uranium tax severance tax exemption through 3/31/2003

1999
• Extended ethanol tax credit program from 7/1/2000 to 7/1/2003
• Coal Equity Tax Act extended through 12/31/2003; lowered maximum severance tax per ton from $.80 to $.60
• Imposed a limitation on sales/use tax on transportable home to be based on 70% of the sales price of the home
• Imposed sales/use tax on price of cigarettes (removed exemption)
• Imposed sales/use tax on price of tobacco products (cigars, snuff & other products)
• Oil Producers Recovery Act - reduced severance tax on oil from 6% to 4% (if oil price exceeds $20/barrel the tax returns to 6%); granted sales tax exemption for sales of power to person engaged in oil extraction
• Diversion of severance taxes from PWMTF to BRA extended to 6/30/2004

2000
• Repeal of Oil Producers Recovery Act (returned severance tax on oil from 4% to 6%; repealed sales tax exemption for sales of power to person engaged iin oil extraction
• Rail Mile Tax – imposed a 7-cent/mile tax on trains; imposed $100/year for each public grade crossing on the line of a railroad (repealed in 2004)
•Annual corporate license tax minimum raised $25 to $50 and stair step amounts changed to 2/10 of a mill on the dollar
• Made 4th cent for sales and use tax permanent (due to expire 6/30/2002)
• Extended 2-cent fuel tax on gas & diesel. No exemptions through 6/30/2000.
• Removed 4% severance tax break for new production of gas wells from natural gas produced from "shallow" wells (less than 2,000 feet deep—mainly affects coalbed methane)
• Coal Transport Tax - Imposes a one-mill (.0001) per ton of coal tax on the commercial transportation of coal transported per mile or portion thereof; minimum tax is 50 cents per truck, trailer or railcar used to transport coal (repealed in 2004)

2001
• Placed a statute of limitation on actions filed before the state board of

Tax Changes, cont.

equalization to 5 years (any action not based on fraud)
2002
• Clarified taxable services at oil/ gas well site (exempts all activities prior to the setting and cementing of production casing)
• Changed period in which audits of mineral taxes are to be commenced from within 5 years of production to within 3 years of production.
• Amended and clarified clarifiee mineral lien statutes
• Increased distribution sales/use tax to local governments (from 27% to 30%)
• Amendments to sales/use tax statutes including clarifying exemption for business personal property when business is sold; exemption for motor vehicles used in interstate commerce; increases penalty for vendor who collects tax but fails to remit to state
• Changed diversion of severance taxes (above the 1.5%) from the budget reserve account to the severance tax distribution account; repeals distribution of severance tax on shallow gas wells (coalbed methane wells) to the PWMTF and deposits in severance tax distribution account
2003
• Allowed counties to impose up to 2% optional sales/use tax for specific purpose. Total specific purpose and general revenue optional tax (1%) cannot exceed 2%
• Required all special districts to file geographical boundary information with the dept. of revenue, county assessor and county clerk
• Increased cigarette taxes from 12 cents/pack to 60 cents/pack
• Amended and clarifies property tax liens on mineral production (changes made to follow severance tax liens)
• Authorized formation of resort districts (can impose optional sales/use tax)
• Granted sales/use tax exemption for equipment used to generate electricity from renewable resources (expires June 30, 2008)
2004
• Repealed the coal transport tax enacted in 2000
• Repealed the rail mile tax on railroads enacted in 2000
• Property tax relief program amendments: Dept. of Revenue to fund property tax refunds to qualified applicants (repealed 1/1/2008)

Note: "PWMTF" is Permanent Wyoming Mineral Trust Fund. "BRA" is Budget Reserve Account

Source: Legislative Service Office

Appendix 18

Tax Reform 2000
Findings and Recommendations

• Tax collections in Wyoming are less stable than in other states. Future revenue streams may not be adequate for services provided by state and local governments. The feasibility of new revenue sources should be analyzed.

• Wyoming residents say they are concerned about state and local governmental spending. The governor and Legislature should form a separate committee to examine state and local spending.

• Wyoming residents and non-residents who use tax-supported facilities and services are not the primary taxpayers. Infrastructure and services would be much smaller if the users had to bear the full cost.

•Wyoming's current tax structure may contribute to lack of economic growth.

• More mineral tax revenue should be diverted to trust funds to secure public sevices funding for future generations. Permanent trust funds should be managed to maximize income.

• Reporting and collection of mineral taxes in Wyoming are confusing and time-consuming. A committee should be formed to simplify reporting and collection.

• Wyoming's sales tax behaves in a regressive manner. The Legislature should consider removing some exclusions and exemptions, including, perhaps, exemptions for charitable and non-profit entities.

•The state should have better compliance with use tax statutes, which are difficult to enforce. They require payment of the equivalent of sales taxes on items that are purchased tax-free out of state and brought to Wyoming.

• Market values of real estate have risen significantly in some areas of the state, creating a hardship for people on low and fixed incomes to pay property taxes. One approach to this problem is more consistent assessment of property among counties for similar properties with comparable market and production values. Property tax exemptions should be examined for applicability and ease of adminstration. In certain areas, market value of agricultural land far exceeds production

Tax Reform 200, Cont.

value, which is used to compute taxes.
• The Legislature should implement a real estate transfer tax.
• Local governments are not funded equally in Wyoming. Financial reporting by local governments is not consistent.
• Wyoming's excise tax rates on cigarettes, alcoholic beverages and motor fuels are the lowest among surrounding states. These exise taxes should be examined for possible increases.
• Tax administrative authority is not clearly defined. Assessment practices of county assessors vary from county to county. the distinction between tangible and real property is not always clear in sales tax law.
• Wyoming should consider imposition of an income tax.

Works Cited

Bragg, Bill. *Wyoming's Wealth. A History of Wyoming*. Basin: Big Horn Publishers. 1976

Erwin, Marie. *Wyoming Historical Blue Book,* Vols. I and II. Edited by Virginia Cole Trenholm. Reprinted 1974. Cheyenne: Wyoming State Archives and Historical Department.

Flynn, Janet. *Tribal Government: Wind River Reservation.* Lander: Mortimer Publishing. 1991.

Fowler, Loretta. *Arapahoe Politics, 1851-1978.* Lincoln: University of Nebraska Press. 1982.

Hansen, Matilda. *Clear Use of Power. A Slice of Wyoming Political History 1864-2000.* Laramie: Commentary Press of Wyoming. 2002.

Hebard, Grace Raymond. *The History and Government of Wyoming. The History, Constitution and Administration of Affairs.* San Francisco: C.F. Weber & Co. Eleventh edition. 1926.

_____. *How Woman Suffrage Came to Wyoming (1869).* Monograph. Originally published in Laramie in 1920. Reprinted by New York: W.D. Embree. 1940.

Hubell, Larry, ed. With Greg Cawley, Michael Horan, James King, David Marcum, Maggi Murdock and Oliver Walter. *The Equality State. Government and Politics in Wyoming.* Dubuque: Eddie Bowers Publishing Inc. Third edition, 1996.

Jordan, Roy A. and S. Brett DeBoer. *Wyoming. A Source Book.* Niwot: University Press of Colorado. 1996.

Larson, T.A. *History of Wyoming.* Lincoln: University of Nebraska Press. Second edition, revised. 1978.

League of Women Voters of Wyoming. *A Look at Wyoming Government.* Sixth edition.

Miller, Tim R. *State Government. Politics in Wyoming.* Dubuque: Kendall/Hunt Publishing Co. 1981.

Roberts, Phil, David L. Roberts and Steven L. Roberts. *Wyoming Almanac.* Laramie: Skyline West Press. 2001 edition.

Trachsel, Herman H. and Ralph M. Wade. *The Government and Administration of Wyoming.* American Commonwealth Series. New York: Thomas Y. Crowell Co.

Trenholm, Virginia Cole. *Footprints on the Frontier. Saga of the La Ramie Region of Wyoming.* Published by author. Printed by Douglas Enterprise Co. 1945.

Trenholm. *The Arapahoes, Our People.* Norman: University of Oklahoma Press, 1970.

Trenholm, editor. *Wyoming Historical Blue Book,* Vol. III. Cheyenne: Wyoming State Archives and Historical Department. 1974.

Shakespeare, Tom. *The Sky People.* New York: Vantage Press. 1971.

Stamm, Henrey E. IV. *People of the Wind River. Eastern Shoshones 1825-1900.* Norman: University of Oklahoma Press. 1999.

Western, Samuel. *Pushed Off the Mountain. Sold Down the River. Wyoming's Search for its Soul.* Moose: Homestead Publishing. 2002.

Articles

Children's Land Alliance Supporting Schools. "A Brief Primer on School Land Grant Practices." Kevin Carter, Director of the Utah School and Institutional Trust Lands Administration (http://childrenslandalliance.com)

Harper's New Monthly Magazine. "Among the Arapahoes." Vol. 60, Issue 358. March 1880, pp. 494-501.

High Country News. 1997. "Wyoming is 'Open for Business.'" July 7.

The Wyoming LAP Book. "Wyoming Legislative Redistricting." Equality State Policy Center, 2003-2004 Biennium. (http://ww.equalitystate.org)

U.S. Bureau of Land Management. "The Federal Land Policy and
    Management Act of 1976: How the Stage Was Set for BLM's
    'Organic Act.'" (http://www.blm.gov)
U.S. News and World Report. 1980. "The Sagebrush Rebellion."
    December 1.

Wyoming Law Review. 2004 Phil Roberts. "A History of the Wyoming
    Sales Tax and How Lawmakers Chose it from among Sever-
    ance Taxes, an Income Tax, Gambling, and a Lottery." Vol. 4:
    157-243.

Newsletters, Monographs and Reports

League of Women Voters. *Helping America Vote: Safeguarding the
    Vote.* Monograph. July 2004.

_____. *Helping America Vote: A Guide to Implement-
    ing the New Federal Provisional Ballot Requirement.* Mono-
    graph. August 2003.

Wyoming Taxpayers Association. Fiscal Reporter. Wyoming State and
    Local Finance. February 3, 2003.

_____ Wyoming Fiscal Facts. June 2004.

_____ Wyoming Tax Summary 2003.

_____ Wyoming Property Taxation. November 2003.

_____ Wyoming Property Taxation. November 2004.

Chief Washakie Foundation. Commentaries by Henry Stamm IV. First
    Treaty of Fort Bridger 1863, Second Treaty of Fort Bridger
    1868. Brunot Land Cession of 1874, McLaughlin Land Cession
    of 1896. McLaughlin Land Cession of 1904.
    (http://www.windriverhistory.org)
Eastern Shoshone Tribal Culture Center. Eastern Shoshone Tribal
    Culture. http://www.easternshoshone.net

Government Documents

State of Wyoming Department of Revenue 2003 Annual Report: July
    1, 2002, through June 30, 2003

_____, Ad Valorem Division. 2005 Agricultural Land Valuation Study. October 27, 2004.

University of Wyoming. "Mineral Tax Incentives, Mineral Production and the Wyoming Economy." By Shelby Gerking, William Morgan, Mitch Kunce and Joe Kerkvlier. December 1, 2000.

Wyoming State Auditor. "Comprehensive Annual Financial Report for Fiscal Year Ended June 30, 2003." State Auditor Max Maxfield

Wyoming State Constitution of 1890. Wyoming Blue Book, Vol. I. Marie Erwin, 1974 Reprint, pp. 504-540.

Wyoming State Treasurer. Annual Report of the Treasurer of the State of Wyoming For the Period July 1, 2003 through June 30, 2004. Treasurer Cynthia Lummis.

_____ Annual Report of the Treasurer of the State of Wyoming for the Period July 1, 2002 through June 30, 2003. Treasurer Cynthia Lummis.

_____ Investment Performance. March 31, 2005.

Wyoming Act of Admission. 26 Statutes at Large 222. Wyoming Blue Book, Vol. 1. Marie Erwin, 1974 Reprint pp.

United States Geological Survey. National Assessment of Oil and Gas Fact Sheet: Coal-Bed Gas Resources of the Rocky Mountain Region. Fact Sheet FS-110-01. November 2001

Reorganization Reports

A Study in State Government Efficiency. Joint Legislative-Executive Efficiency Study Committee. Robert L. Pettigrew Jr., Chairman. 1989.

Centennial Challenge: Accountability and Efficiency in State Government. Joint Reorganization Council. Robert L. Pettigrew Jr., Chairman. 1990.

The Final Report on Acountability and Efficiency in State Government. Joint Reorganization Council. David G. Ferrari and Janet Washburn. 1991.

School District Organization and Operation in Wyoming. Research
Bulletin I. State Department of Education. State Superintendent
of Public Instruction Velma Linford. April 13, 1959.

Wyoming Economic Analysis Division, Department of Administration and Information (http://eadiv.state.wy.us)

Equality State Almanac 2002. Economic Analysis Division of Wyoming Department of Administration and Information.

General Demographic Characteristics and Trends in Wyoming. June 3, 2004

CREG Monthly Report: Revenues through October 2004. (Consensus Revenue Estimating Group). Nov. 24, 2004.

Wyoming Judiciary (http://courts.state.wy.us)

Wyoming Court Overview: Supreme Court, District Courts, Circuit Courts, Municipal Court, The Business of the Courts

Supreme Court: Slip Opinions, Per-curiam Opinions, Oral Argument Schedule

Court Directory

Judicial Boards and Commissions

The Changing Face of Frontier Justice, Law Related Education. By Ronda K. Munger

Court Rules: Effective July 1, 2003

Wyoming Legislative Service Office (http://legisweb.state.wy.us)

Wyoming State Constitution

Wyoming Statutes

Significant Statutory Changes Affecting State Taxation 1977 through 2004

Legislative Information

> Administrative Rule Reviews
> Guidelines for Attending Legislative Committee Meetings
> Citizen's Guide to the Wyoming Legislature
> Current Legislators: House and Senate
> Glossary of Legislative Words and Terms
> Leadership and Committee Lists
> Legislative History of Wyoming Laws
> Legislative Policies, Procedures & Handbooks – Agency Rule
> Review Handbook, Ethics Brochure for Legislators, Management
> Council Policies, Manual of Legislative Procedures, Travel Regu-
> lations
> Legislative Service Office – Structure and function
> Rules of the Legislature

Wyoming Secretary of State (http://soswy.state.wy.us)
2004 Wyoming State Directory

State Agencies Rules and Regulations

Election Administration

> Information about issues and candidates in general elections
> 1998-2006, primary and general election returns, voter registra-
> tion data

> Constitutional Amendments appearing on Wyoming's General
> Election ballots

> Results in 1996, 1998, 2000 and 2002 primary and general
> elections

> Wyoming's Government Ethics

> Facts and Historical Data –

>> Rosters of past officers of the State of Wyoming
>> Census figures 1890-2000
>> Composition of Wyoming State Legislatures 1890-2004
>> Past officers of Wyoming State Legislatures
>> Popular vote for U.S. presidents in Wyoming

Wyoming governors and state officers
U.S. senators and representatives in Congress
Women in the Wyoming Legislature

Help America Vote Act (HAVA) of 2002 – Wyoming's State Plan, as required by Public Law 107-252.

Wyoming Election Connection. October 10, 2003

_____ June 29, 2004

History of initiatives and referendums in Wyoming and information about the initiative and referendum process

Information about Wyoming Lobbyist Registration and Disclosure

Information about political action committees and forms for filings

Political Party Information, including major, minor and provisional parties

Redistricting - Information about the State of Wyoming's redistricting project.

Voter registration statistics, information on how to register to vote

Wyoming County Election Officials

Wyoming Supreme Court Cases

Director of the Office of State Lands and Investments, Board of Land Commissioners v. Merbanco Inc., 2003 WY 73, 70 P.3d 241 (Wyo. 2003)

Sweetwater County Planning Committee for Organization of School Districts v. Hinkle, 491 P.2d 1234, 1237 (Wyo. 1971)

Washakie County School District No. One v. Herschler, 606 P.2d 310 (Wyo. 1980)

Campbell County School District v. State, 907 P.2d 1238, 1247 (Wyo. 1995)

Cathcart v. Meyer, 2004 WY 49, 88 P.3d 1050 (Wyo. 2004)

State v. Campbell County School District, 2001 WY 19, 19 P.3d 518 (Wyo. 2001)

State v. Campbell County School District, 2001 WY 90, 32 P.3d 325 (Wyo. 2001)

Perko v. Rock Springs Commercial Co., 37 Wyo. 98, 259 P 250 (1927).

Riedel v. Anderson, 2003 WY 70, 70 P.3d 223 (Wyo. 2003)

Witzenburger v. State ex rel. Wyoming Community Dev. Authority, 575 P.2d 1100, 113 (Wyo. 1978)

Index

A

B

C

D

Dakota Territory
  Creation of North Dakota and South Dakota 20
  Creation of Wyoming Territory 4, 11
Dawes Act. *See* General Allotment Act of 1887
Democratic Party
  1934 Sweep 221–222
Department of Administration and Fiscal Control 208
Department of Administration and Information
  Economic Analysis Division 264
Department of Economic Planning and Development 207
Department of Environmental Quality 208, 212
Department of Revenue 202
Douglas 181

E

Education
  Charter schools 283
  Classroom unit funding 273
  Commissioner of education abolished 284
  Consolidation
    School District Organization Act 282
    School District Organization Law 272
  Consolidation of school districts 210
  County superintendent abolished 284
  Federal aid rejected 1961 204
  First schools 280
  Hathaway Student Scholarship 286
  Permanent School Fund 23, 280
  Professional Teachers Standards Board 284
  School districts map 281
  School districts valuations, enrollment (Appensix 310
  School finance 212
  School funding 278–279
  School trust lands 22, 279–280
  State Board of Education 284
  State enrollment 283
  Superintendent of Public Instruction 284
  University and colleges 285
  Wyoming Constitution, provisions 270
  Wyoming Supreme Court 272–276
  Wyoming testing 278
Electoral College 224
Evanston 181, 182

CONSTITUTION
of
The State of Wyoming
September 30, 1889

PREAMBLE

We, the People of the State of Wyoming, grateful to God for our civil, political and religious liberties, and desiring to secure them to ourselves and perpetuate them to our posterity, do ordain and establish this Constitution.

ARTICLE NO. I
DECLARATION OF RIGHTS

SECTION 1. All power is inherent in the people, and all free governments are founded on their authority, and instituted for their peace, safety and happiness; for the advancement of these ends they have at all times an inalienable and indefeasible right to alter, reform or abolish the government in such manner as they may think proper.

SECTION 2. In their inherent right to life, liberty, and the pursuit of happiness, all members of the human race are equal.

SECTION 3. Since equality in the enjoyment of natural and civil rights is made sure only through political equality, the laws of this State affecting the political rights and privileges of its citizens shall be without distinction of race, color, sex, or any circumstance or condition whatsoever other than individual incompetency, or unworthiness duly ascertained by a court of competent jurisdiction.

SECTION 4. The right of the people to be secure in their persons, houses, papers, and effects against unreasonable searches and seizures shall not be violated, and no warrant shall issue but upon probable cause, supported by affidavit, particularly describing the place to be searched or the person or thing to be seized.

SECTION 5. No person shall be imprisoned for debt except in cases of fraud.

SECTION 6. No person shall be deprived of life, liberty or property without due process of law.

SECTION 7. Absolute, arbitrary power over the lives, liberty and property of freemen exists nowhere in a republic, not even in the largest majority.

SECTION 8. All courts shall be open and every person for an injury done to person, reputation or property shall have justice administered without sale, denial, or delay. Suits may be brought against the State in such manner and in such courts as the legislature may by law direct.

SECTION 9. The right of trial by jury shall remain inviolate in criminal cases, but a jury in civil cases in all courts, or in criminal cases in courts not of record, may consist of less than twelve men, as may be prescribed by law. Hereafter a grand jury may consist of twelve men, any nine of whom concurring may find an indictment, but the legislature may change, regulate or abolish the grand jury system.

SECTION 10. In all criminal prosecutions the accused shall have the right to defend in person and by counsel, to demand the nature and cause of the accusation, to have a copy thereof, to be confronted with the witnesses against him, to have compulsory process served for obtaining witnesses, and to a speedy trial by an impartial jury of the county or district in which the offense is alleged to have been committed.

SECTION 11. No person shall be compelled to testify against himself in any criminal case, or shall any person be twice put in jeopardy for the same offense. If the jury disagree, or if the judgment be arrested after a verdict, or if the judgment be reversed for error in law, the accused shall not be deemed to have been in jeopardy.

SECTION 12. No person shall be detained as a witness in any criminal prosecution longer than may be necessary to take his testimony or deposition, nor be confined in any room where criminals are imprisoned.

SECTION 13. Until otherwise provided by law, no person shall, for a felony, be proceeded against criminally, otherwise than by indictment, except in cases arising in the land or naval forces, or in the militia when in actual service in time of war or public danger.

SECTION 14. All persons shall be bailable by sufficient sureties, except for capital offences when the proof is evident or the presumption great. Excessive bail shall not be required, nor excessive fines imposed, nor shall cruel or unusual punishment be inflicted.

SECTION 15. The penal code shall be framed on the humane principles of reformation and prevention.

SECTION 16. No person arrested and confined in jail shall be treated with unnecessary rigor. The erection of safe and comfortable prisons, and inspection of prisons, and the humane treatment of prisoners shall be provided for.

SECTION 17. The privilege of the writ of habeas corpus shall not be suspended unless, when in case of rebellion or invasion, the public safety may require it.

SECTION 18. The free exercise and enjoyment of religious profession and worship without discrimination or preference shall be forever guaranteed in this State, and no person shall be rendered incompetent to hold any office of trust of profit, or to serve as a witness or juror, because of his opinion on any matter of religious belief whatever; but the liberty of conscience hereby secured shall not be so construed as to excuse acts of licentiousness or justify practices inconsistent with the peace or safety of the State.

SECTION 19. No money of the State shall ever be given or appropriated to any sectarian or religious society or institution.

SECTION 20. Every person may freely speak, write, and publish on all subjects, being responsible for the abuse of that right; and in all trials for libel, both civil and criminal, the truth, when published with good intent and for justifiable ends, shall be a sufficient defense, and jury having the right to determine the facts and the law, under direction of the court.

SECTION 21. The right of petition, and of the people peaceably to assemble to consult for the common good, and to make known their opinions, shall never be denied or abridged.

SECTION 22. The rights of labor shall have just protection through laws calculated to secure to the laborer proper rewards for his service and to promote the industrial welfare of the State.

SECTION 23. The right of citizens to opportunities for education should have practical recognition. The Legislature shall suitably encourage means and agencies calculated to advance the sciences and liberal arts.

SECTION 24. The right of citizens to bear arms in defense of themselves and of the State shall not be denied.

SECTION 25. The military shall ever be in strict subordination to the civil power. No soldier in time of peace shall be quartered in any house without consent of the owner, nor in time of war except in the manner prescribed by law.

SECTION 26. Treason against the State shall consist only in levying war against it, or in adhering to its enemies or in giving them aid and comfort. No persons shall be convicted of treason unless on the testimony of two witnesses to the same overt act, or on confession in open court; nor shall any person be attainted of treason by the legislature.

SECTION 27. Elections shall be open, free and equal, and no power, civil or military, shall at any time interfere to prevent an untrammeled exercise of the right of suffrage.

SECTION 28. No tax shall be imposed without the consent of the people or their authorized representatives. All taxation shall be equal and uniform.

SECTION 29. No distinction shall ever be made by law between resident aliens and citizens as to the possession, taxation, enjoyment and descent of property.

SECTION 30. Perpetuities and monopolies are contrary to the genius of a free state and shall not be allowed. Corporations being creatures of the state, endowed for the public good with a portion of its sovereign powers, must be subject to its control.

SECTION 31. Water being essential to industrial prosperity, of limited amount, and easy of diversion from its natural channels, its control must be in the State, which, in providing for its use, shall equally guard all the various interests involved.

SECTION 32. Private property shall not be taken for private use unless by consent of the owner, except for private ways of necessity, and for reservoirs, drains, flumes, or ditches on or across the lands of others for agricultural, mining, milling, domestic, or sanitary purposes, nor in any case without due compensation.

SECTION 33. Private property shall not be taken or damaged for public or private use without just compensation.

SECTION 34. All laws of a general nature shall have a uniform operation.

SECTION 35. No ex post facto law, nor any law impairing the obligation of contracts, shall ever be made.

SECTION 36. The enumeration in this Constitution of certain rights shall not be construed to deny, impair, or disparage others retained by the people.